Understanding Karl Rahner
Volume 3

A Pattern of Christian Doctrines

Part I

Understanding Karl Rahner
Volume 3

A Pattern of Christian Doctrines

Part I: God and Christ

George Vass

Sheed & Ward
London

ISBN 0–7220–9352–7

© George Vass 1996

Published in Great Britain by
Sheed & Ward Limited
14 Coopers Row
London EC3N 2BH

Edited, designed, typeset by Bill Ireson

Printed Great Britain by Biddles Limited, Guildford and Kings Lynn

Contents

Table of Abbreviations

Rahner's articles and other publications frequently quoted or referred to in the text take the form of single key words: for example, 'Theos', *Investigations*, 'Scheme', and so on. In what follows there is a list of these key words for the whole volume. In the Notes (see pp. 175–204), the page number in brackets refers to the corresponding German original: for example, 'Consciousness', p. 199 (= p. 225). For references to other works by Rahner himself or works in collaboration with other authors I have adopted standard acronymic abbreviations: for example, DS, *SM*, etc., where usually no corresponding German is indicated. In the Notes, too, periodicals and secondary literature are quoted in full. The Bibliography gives full details of these.

	the World' in *Investigations* V, pp. 157–92 (= *Schriften* V, pp. 183–221).
'Exegesis'	'The Position of Christology in the Church between Exegesis and Dogmatics' in *Investigations* XI, pp. 185–214 (= *Schriften* IX, pp. 197–226).
Foundations	*Foundations of Christian Faith*, London (1978). ET of *Grundkurs*, by W. V. Dych.
Grundkurs	*Grundkurs des Glaubens: Einfuhrüng in den Begriff des Christentums*, Freiburg-im-Breisgau (1976).
Handbuch	*Handbuch theologischer Grundbegriffe*, I–II, (ed.) H. Fries, Munich (1962).
Hearers	*Hearers of the Word*, London and New York, NY. (1969).
'Heresy'	'On Heresy' in *Quaestiones Disputatae* 11, London (1969). ET of 'Was ist Häresie?' in *Häresien der Zeit*, Freiburg-im-Breisgau (1964).
'History'	'Yesterday's History of Dogma and Theology for Tomorrow' in *Investigations* XVIII, pp. 3–34 (= *Schriften* XIII, pp. 11–47).
Hominisation	*Hominisation: the Evolutionary Origin of Man as a Theological Problem*, with Paul Overhage, London and New York, NY. (1966). ET of 'Das Problem der Hominisation' in *Quaestiones Disputatae* 12/13, Freiburg-im-Breisgau (1961).
'I Believe'	'Ich glaube an Jesus Christus' in *Theologische Meditationen* 21, Einsiedeln (1968).
'Incarnation'	'On the Theology of the Incarnation' in *Investigations* IV, pp. 105–20 (= *Schriften* IV, pp. 137–56). (No ET.)
Investigations	*Theological Investigations*, 23 volumes, London (1961–92). ET of *Schriften*.
LTK	*Lexikon für Theologie und Kirche*, 10 volumes, (eds) J. Hofer and K. Rahner, Freiburg-im-Breisgau[2] (1957).
MS	*Mysterium Salutis*, 5 volumes, (eds) J. Feiner and M. Löhrer *et al.*, Einsiedeln (1974–76).
'Observations'	'Observations on the Doctrine of God in

	Catholic Dogmatics' in *Investigations* IX, pp. 127–44 (= *Schriften* VIII, pp. 165–86).
Revelation	*Revelation and Tradition*, with J. Ratzinger, London and New York, NY. (1966). ET of 'Offenbarung und Überlieferung' in *Quaestiones Disputatae* 17, Freiburg-im-Breisgau (1965).
'Scheme'	'Scheme for a Treatise of Dogmatic Theology' in *Investigations* I, pp. 19–37 (=*Schriften* I, pp. 29–47).
Schriften	*Schriften für Theologie*, 16 volumes (various editions 1960–84). ET of *Investigations*.
SM	*Sacramentum Mundi*, (eds) C. Ernst, K. Smyth and K. Rahner, 6 volumes, London and New York (1968–70).
Spirit	*Spirit in the World*, London and New York, NY. (1968).
ST	*Summa Theologiae*, St Thomas Aquinas.
'Symbol'	'The Theology of the Symbol' in *Investigations* IV, pp. 221–25 (= *Schriften* IV, pp. 175–312).
Tanner	*Decrees of the Ecumenical Councils*, (ed.) N. P. Tanner, London and Georgetown, Washington, DC (1990).
'Theos'	'Theos in the New Testament' in *Investigations* I, pp. 79–148 (= *Schriften* I, pp. 91–168).
Trinity	*The Trinity*, New York, NY. (1974). ET by J. Donceel of *MS* II, pp. 317–97.
'Witness'	'Observation on the Concept of "Witness" ' in *Investigations* XIII, pp. 152–62 (= *Schriften* X, pp. 164–81).
ZKT	*Zeitschrift für katholische Theologie*

Preface

Nine years is a long time. Not only do the world and people in it age, but even more does a manuscript which was meant to continue my analysis of and dialogue with Karl Rahner's theology. The first two volumes of *Understanding Karl Rahner* were published by Sheed & Ward in 1985, but the manuscript of the third volume, ready since the summer of 1986 has, for unforeseen circumstances, been held back from publication. No one, only the swift passing of years, is to be blamed for this.

During these nine years I was asked to engage in other forms of academic activity: lecturing, administering the daily life of a large theological faculty, publishing of theological material in different languages. I had to undergo major surgery on three occasions, in the last two years having to struggle against a cumbersome kidney disease. My home country was opened to freedom, including the renewal of theological scholarship after forty-five years of comparative stagnation. In these years, theological literature assessing and criticizing the life-work of Karl Rahner has been steadily on the increase. Rahner died twelve years ago but, in one way and another, these years have kept him alive on the theological scene.

When I, having been asked again to prepare the third, fourth and fifth volumes on Rahner for publication, read over my own writing, it was as if it were the fruit of an alien product; I realized that it needed to be reviewed, my critical remarks criticized, and my theological counter-position partly superseded by new insights. To revise the manuscript in the light of my own development and of the new Rahner literature would have meant my re-writing it completely. I renounced this task and look forward now to seeing this third volume in print: just another book in the welter of theological literature with which to agree or to disagree. However, its publication is meant to foster further discussion aiming at a theological renewal in our day. This renewal was initiated by, amongst others, Karl Rahner – and he, were he alive, would welcome any attempts to develop its main tenets. The present volume is perhaps such an attempt.

In this and the subsequent volumes of my analysis of Karl Rahner's work I have tried to go beyond the mere presentation of his theology; and, in my alternative viewpoints and apparent 'counter-positions', I have suggested an approach extending or correcting Rahner's thought. In doing so I wish to submit my own theology not only to the criticism of my fellow theologians but especially to my former teacher, the Reverend Professor Dr Bruno Brinkman, Emeritus Professor of Heythrop College, University of London. It was Dr Brinkman who some thirty-five years ago introduced me to Rahner's *Schriften* and encouraged my *Auseinandersetzung* with Rahner's thought from the point of view of Anglo-Saxon theology.

I here express my gratitude as a former student and colleague of Heythrop College in dedicating this volume to Dr Brinkman. It will cement our friendship until we are both confronted face-to-face with the Truth of our common search.

George Vass
Innsbruck
1 February 1996

Introduction

The motive of a project intending to give a critical survey of Karl Rahner's theological work has been *Understanding Karl Rahner*. The first two volumes, published by Sheed & Ward in 1985 (and reprinted in 1989) concentrated on the preliminaries to Rahner's teaching and dealt with the philosophical sub-soil of his theology as well as with that intermediate sector between philosophy and theology proper, known as fundamental theology. The third and fourth volumes will deal with 'theology proper', that is, with some doctrinal or dogmatic tenets peculiar to Christian faith alone. They will discuss a 'pattern of doctrines' implied in Rahner's systematic theology.

Now the reader of the second volume may have observed that for Rahner those things that vaguely pertain to the doctrine of man, his origin and his destiny (cf. Volume 2, Chapter II), his supernatural destination (cf. Chapter III), God's grace (cf. Chapter IV) as appropriated through the gift of faith (cf. Chapter V) are not strictly speaking tenets of specific Christian faith. They are, in a way, common to all self-reflecting beings as they live out the mystery of human life. In dealing with these topics, Rahner did anticipate a number of subjects, like the Triunity of the Christian God, the mystery of Jesus the Christ, his atonement, etc., which in themselves should have been treated among those doctrines which are peculiar to Christian faith. They indeed feature in Rahner's short formulations of Christian faith (cf. Volume 1, Chapter I). Nonetheless, Rahner in his fundamental theology seems to have presupposed them in the human constitution or in the existential situation of man as a condition of possibility in coming to explicit faith.

Yet, at the same time, almost all of these topics have been established in definite and doctrinal form throughout the history of the Church. Some of them have become distinctive dogmas of Christian belief obligatory for the confession of faith. They belong to the objective content of our creed, articles of *fides quae credendum est.* In anticipating these tenets in fundamental theology it was not intended to establish them. Their use was anthropological in pointing out *how* to believe. Thus, for instance, the reference to the triune God or to the God-manhood of Jesus the Christ as used in explaining man's destiny or his coming-to-grace does not state anything directly about the Christian concept of God, one and three, or about the incarnate Logos, but rather suggests the way in which, how, we should approach these subjects. Directly, they speak of man and his relationship to God. This was the compass of Rahner's fundamental theology.

True enough, as we shall see, Rahner in his attempts to delve into purely doctrinal theology will often remain on the level of this kind of fundamental theology. Nonetheless, he cannot avoid facing up to the contents of an objective faith proposed by Christian tradition. Failure to envisage these dogmatic or doctrinal aspects, which he had to face, would impair our understanding of his whole theology. This is why I have chosen, in this and subsequent volumes, to discuss the pattern of those specifically Christian doctrines which are mentioned in his brief formulation of the creed for modern man.

My analysis and critique of Rahner's theology in these two subsequent volumes will be slightly different from the method of the previous ones. In discussing his tenets I strive at coherent alternative positions which, in one way or another, are inspired by Rahner and have the ambition of developing his thought. The result is submitted to the judgement of the reader. My own contribution will, therefore, be more substantial in tenor than my summary presentation of Rahner's writings. This is why my own positions will be summed up in separate chapters corresponding to the presentation of my partner in dialogue, Karl Rahner. The reader may, at his or her own discretion, skip these comments and questions, and is, of course, free to agree or disagree with what they have to say.

This slightly altered approach to the project has led to the change of the title: in the present volume we are going to see Rahner's concept of the Christian God, one and three, and in using a selected survey of his critiques with due caution an alternative view will be introduced. The same will be done concerning Rahner's doctrine of Jesus the Christ. In subsequent volumes the doctrine of the atonement in the experience of Christian life, the Church and her sacraments will feature as subjects of a dialogue with Rahner's thought.

With this the *genus literarium* of this volume is indicated. My own writing lets itself be inspired by Rahner's thought, it takes up a challenge in reconsidering a number of positions which traditional theology held and Rahner has re-shaped. If I disagree or go beyond his views, I do so with the same intention which was Rahner's own: to keep up a dialogue between Christian faith and a world of unbelief. The Christian has no option but to throw in his or her lot with an unbelieving mankind, sharing its desires and aims, its failures and misery; it is incumbent upon the Christian to know the mentality of the modern world. In this respect Rahner's theology did a pioneer's work. To take it up, even in a corrected version, to continue his own project in a dialogue with his own positions, does not detract from Rahner's achievement. The result will be a step forward in the understanding of those mysteries which, in their depth, will always remain hidden for our searching mind.

Chapter 1

Objective Faith

Christianity is not a subjective affair; it is grounded on the novelty of God's word in self-revelation which is the premise of its objective contents. My first questions to Rahner will be concerned with the new vista which he opens up in its understanding. In what follows I shall restrict his possible answer to four main points, concluding with some remarks of my own.

1.1 The First Level of Theological Reflection

To Rahner's way of thinking this objective content of the Christian message should correspond to the second level of theological reflection. Its counterpart, the first level, in its explicit form is a relative latecomer to his thought. It was crystallized in the 'theology of decision' of *Foundations* as a means of whetting the student's appetite for a more serious study of the faith.

As to what is the subject matter, the objective content of the second level, Rahner fails to give a clear-cut answer. Of course, the two main schemes which he has given us for the presentation of the whole of theology could be taken as a guideline. The first can be found at the very beginning of his *Investigations*, and the second appeared in the wake of Vatican II's suggested reform of theological studies.[1] It appears from these schemes that the second level of reflection in theology has something to do with the detailed historical and dogmatic presentation of Christian doctrine. In other words, the task to be performed by the second level of reflection is proper to experts who apparently can allow themselves the leisure to get down to scholarly details. Or, to use Rahner's rather critical classification, *Fachidiotie*, in this realm the theologian can function as an expert moving on a narrowed-down field.[2]

Now the early Rahner did indeed produce some profoundly scholarly essays which qualify for the above-mentioned expertise. I would refer the reader, especially, to Rahner's studies on the history of penance, collected in Volume XI of his *Schriften*.[3] In these, by means of analysing the ancient writers, he traces the coming-to-be of the penitential practice in the early Church. Whilst, in his later reminiscences, Rahner modestly refers to these studies as the only scholarly works he ever produced,[4] one cannot help feeling that behind this research of his there already lay a hidden systematic purpose. He intends to show that the sacrament of penance refers to the reconciliation of the sinner with the Church, and was not regarded even by these ancient authors as a magic parole transmitting divine forgiveness without any mediation of the believing community.[5]

In other words, the subject matter of a second level of theological reflection cannot be located exclusively in the *Fachidiotie* of the expert. The systematician works hand-in-hand with the researcher: he has to organize his findings. In 'Scheme' the data are organized around the anthropology of a supernaturally raised mankind,[6] whereas in Rahner's later project on the reform of theological studies the organizing factor is history in general and the history of dogma in particular.[7] The first is obviously conceived under the influence of the supernatural existential as introduced by Rahner in the 1950s, and the second is governed by his growing interest in historicity.[8] This latter is in contradistinction to the method of the then planned *Foundations,* which, as a work on the first level of theological reflection, would not be historically organized. Yet, in both schemes, the data of the researcher, on the second level of reflection, are directed to a further purpose. It serves either as subject matter to be developed by means of a philosophical theology, or as a critique of present theological views or ecclesiastical practices from the point of view of past history.[9]

In a sentence, the advanced stage of studies on this second level of theological reflection is subservient to systematics – in whatever way this latter is conceived.

Though I do not intend here to deal with Rahner's early studies on the history of penance,[10] a perusal of these essays could give a hint about his approach to doctrinal questions. They are not only presentations of the *praxis* of penance in its doctrinal and historical setting, but they are also preparing the way for present and future theological developments in accordance with modern mentality. By the more or less correct interpretation of history, Rahner gave his fellow theologians the liberating experience for the critique of present penitential *praxis* and doctrines in order to prepare their future shape. And this was exactly the programme which he announced in his two schemes for the study of dogmatic theology.

It is, therefore, not easy to keep apart in Rahner's writings the two levels of theological reflection and to see their relationship. An apparently doctrinal presentation, which his essays on penance are meant to be, already contain hints for contemporary developments. If, on the other hand, one takes his *Foundations* as exemplifying the first level of theological reflection, it will be easily seen that it is by no means a work *ad usum delphini*, introducing the student to the idea of Christianity. Rather, it is the result of a lifetime of dealing with Christian doctrines and dogmas from a systematic point of view. In other words, the second level of theological reflection, the knowledge and understanding of doctrines, is presupposed before its *communication*[11] for modern students can be attempted. The decision which Rahner expects from the readers of his *Foundations* is for the objective content of the Christian message and not for the way it is presented to 'beginners'. It is dogmatics 'in advance'.

1.2 What is a Dogmatic Statement?

We can take, secondly, the objective content of the Christian message in Rahner's theological work as being man's faithful but critical acceptance of the Church's dogmatic statements. This would be the place to discuss in detail Rahner's view of dogma in general and in particular, as well as his own concept of the possible development of Christian doctrines.[12]

However, in order to avoid unnecessary repetitions, it will be enough here to restrict ourselves to Rahner's question, 'What is a Dogmatic Statement?', a comparatively early essay from 1961.

Rahner's five theses answering this question are not meant to be a thoroughgoing historical study of the origins of what a dogma means in Christianity,[13] nor of the way in which dogma and dogmatization have been used or misused by the Catholic Church. Yet, in spite of their fragmentary character, these five theses do give us an idea of Rahner's approach to the doctrines of the Church. For his essay has a clear objective to establish: although dogmas are not identical with kerygmatic statements of the Bible, they owe their existence and validity to being rooted in the once-for-all event of divine revelation as contained and witnessed to in Holy Writ. Rahner builds up his essay in a dialectical way: dogmatic statements are human insofar as they express faith in everyday language – yet their appeal is to a free acceptance in faith, necessary for salvation (first two theses).[14] Furthermore, dogmas are by necessity decisions of an ecclesial community in facing a subject matter which, however, must ultimately be relinquished in the unutterable Mystery that is God (third and fourth theses). Note that the first half of these statements emphasizes contingent and particular facts, whereas the second half reaffirms them in their necessary and universal validity. The two-dimensional character of dogmatic statements is then brought to its original unity by reducing them to the ultimate and insuperable *norma normans* of the revelation-event as contained in Scripture (fifth thesis). With this approach Rahner remains faithful to the alleged dogmatism of the Roman Church and, at the same time, he comes nearer to the *sola scriptura* of the Reformation.

Of course, in this brief rendering of Rahner's position, there lurks the danger of a *traduttore-traditore*, his concept of dogmatic statements could be understood in both (Roman and Protestant) ways. Nonetheless, he makes it clear that, in dealing with these, however human their wording may be, we have to account for the objective side of our faith: they are about objective contents, about the *fides quae credenda est*. Unlike other statements of human speech whose function, as a rule, is to objectify a subjective state or experience of the speaker, dogma follows an inverse direction:

> It does not ultimately wish to objectify the subjectivity of the speaker, but to bring the objectivity of the matter referred to nearer the listener and thus to subjectify it in this sense.[15]

As statements expressed in terms of human speech, the objective contents of dogmas are open to public discussion or, at least, can be taken as topics of human inquiry in dialogue. They are subject to hermeneutics – however, with a proviso. Their objectivity is of a particular kind, which Rahner is going to characterize as 'exhibitive' or 'sacramental'. Hence, dogma is not merely a statement 'about' something, but one in which

> what it states actually occurs and is posited by its existence . . . In the proclamation and the hearing of dogma in faith, therefore, what is affirmed is itself present.[16]

1.3 Dogma as Fides Quae *as well as* Fides Qua

In view of this 'exhibitive' (or perhaps one should rather say 'performative') sacramental objectivity of a dogmatic statement, we can take, thirdly, the objective content of the Christian message in Rahner's theological work as the *fides quae* aspect of man's total commitment in faith. It is here, however, that a more careful exegesis of his thought is required. For what he wants to stress regarding this public objectivity of a dogmatic statement, is its obligatory and universal character.[17] This characteristic cannot be deduced from the terms it uses, unless the objective content of these statements, the *fides quae* aspect, is organically connected with its subjective counterpart: the *fides qua* aspect of human assent.

> A dogmatic statement, whenever it is genuine and lives up to its true being . . . is a statement of faith not only insofar as it is *fides quae creditur* [that is, a statement about some theological object], but also in as far as it is *fides qua creditur* [that is, in the exercise of the subject].[18]

Unless commitment to the content of a dogma is supported by subjective assent, any discussion of it is hardly relevant. Hence, without an accompanying experience in response to the objective side of the statement, a profane student of religious beliefs is not on an equal footing with a person who, even though only implicitly, has accepted the grace of faith even 'before it is on reflection expressed in proposition'.[19] This latter person in facing a dogmatic statement can proceed, as it were, from faith to faith, *ex fide in fidem,* whilst the unbeliever (who also may be under the influence of the same grace) can, on the contrary, 'repress the truth' and push it aside.

A dogmatic statement, in its objective content can only be

regarded as 'successful' (that is, reaching its full shape), when this correspondence between *fides quae* and *fides qua* is achieved.[20] There is, in principle, no dogmatic statement which should not be an expression of faith from both its objective and its subjective side.

Now this approach to the *fides quae* aspect of Christian commitment will not be new to those of my readers who followed the earlier discussion on the act of faith.[21] There, of course, I had an axe to grind with respect to Rahner's *analysis fidei*, and I now have to point to a similar difficulty in this new context. My query will concern the actual connection between the *fides quae* and *fides qua*.

It will be noticed that the two contributions I am considering betray a certain hesitation regarding the objectivity of dogmatic statements. What they state is, on the one hand, objective because they are open to public discussion and, as we have just seen, they are not mere projections which 'objectify the subjectivity of the speaker'.[22] On the other hand, the believer who speaks is already a listener to God's word and is unwittingly in possession of the formal object of faith.

Therefore:

> What we call . . . a dogmatic statement in the strict sense is . . . merely a further development, an unfolding, of that basic subjective reflection which already takes place in the mere obedient listening to the word of God.[23]

Does this mean, then, that at least – in principle – a dogmatic statement, is, after all, a conceptual projection of a subjective faith, individual or communal? An affirmative answer is suggested when, further on, Rahner says that a dogmatic statement is 'determined by all the theological characteristics of the *fides qua creditur*'.[24]

In any case, the objectivity of the content of a dogmatic statement is of a particular kind. It is certainly not a statement of an objective fact which could be empirically verified. Neither is it, on the other hand, a mere projection of man's subjective state. The objectivity of a dogmatic statement seems to consist in the fact that its acceptance (even only implicitly) by the individual is conducive towards his salvation. A dogmatic statement, insofar as it is objective, renders the event of salvation present and brings man in his confession of faith into relationship with his own fulfilment in God. This is why in 'Dogmatic' Rahner can characterize this objectivity by attributing a mystagogical function to it and specify it in 'Dogma' as exhibitive or sacramental. Thus a dogmatic statement, in his view, remains for ever a means towards salvation, a milestone on man's road to it. It is a concrete beginning rather than an end. For what it objectively contains may show up a partial truth and thereby point towards the presence of the Mystery itself. It may evoke a grace-experience which, in its concrete and objective content, is the communication of the Mystery itself to the believer.[25] In other words: the *fides quae* of dogma in all its objectivity is a step towards an encounter with God.

One could say, therefore, that a dogmatic statement refers primarily to the objectivity of faith, even if this objectivity presupposes a subjective faith which it brings into effect, or concretizes those who accept it. Human subjectivity is at both the originating and receiving end of this objective process. Whilst the subject at the receiving end can be the individual believer, the subject from whom dogmatic statements originate is never a single person, but the community of believers. For dogmas are the decisions of the Church.

1.4 Dogma as the Decision of the Historical Church

We can take, lastly, the objective content of the Christian message as the communal expression of the Church's decision at a given time. Rahner, in fact in both essays mentioned, explicitly connects the objectivity of faith with the Church. Dogma is always an ecclesial decision, an ecclesial statement.[26] For the individual's expression of faith, however deep and strong the inner conviction, never amounts to a dogmatic statement. Not even the 'personal' infallibility of the Roman Pontiff can produce a dogma – he always acts on behalf of the whole Church. Hence the objectivity of faith is due, as it were, to a corporate personality, or rather to its testimony to the message of God's word, 'and this testimony takes place in the assembly of the believers, it originates from this latter, and is destined for it'; and the individual believer is encompassed by his community ' . . . since belief must take place in the Church, from the Church and towards the Church . . .'.[27]

Now Rahner applies the distinguishing marks of an objective faith to the communitarian act of the Church. First of all, just as the individual believer, so

> the Church is both hearer and preacher of God's revelation. The latter does not cease to be God's word because it is spoken by the Church . . . [28]

In other words, just as the *fides qua* of the individuum is, or should be, one with the *fides quae credendum est*, so it is within the Church as one body. Although 'a dogmatic statement is not identical with the original Word of revelation',[29] this word is embodied within it. Therefore, any activity of the individual on the second level of theological reflection always relates to the objective faith of the Church. This faith is already present and alive in the Church's commitment to the message. It is basically dogmatic.

Whilst

> . . . there is and must already be theology on account of the individual history of the faith of individual men

Rahner hastens to add,

> . . . confronted with a common spiritual situation which, being common, must always be grasped and understood again in common, the traditional message must always be grasped anew in common.[30]

Therefore, there must be a theology for which the Church herself is responsible. This is indeed a theology of a superior kind,

> in which the Church as a whole engages in theological activity through the bearers of her established *magisterium*.[31]

Briefly, objective faith is to be found in the doctrines and dogmas of the Church insofar as these are taught and dogmatized by a believing community. Nonetheless, Rahner does not pass over the influence of the individual believer and theologian on the coming-to-be of doctrine and dogma. It seems that he envisages this influence as being exerted through a kind of dialogue between the community 'with its superior kind of theology' and the individual. Thus, for instance, the theologian can express his faith in a statement. Yet this statement is at the same time a question to the Church 'as to whether she can make this statement her own or, at least, can support it as being a possible statement in the one Church'.[32] When such a statement is accepted by the Church, the individual will, along with the Church, be responsible for it before the ultimate *norma normans* (that is, in the message of the first witnesses), in the faith of the primitive Church, as grounded in Holy Scripture. Furthermore, in dialogue with the Church, the individual binds himself to her linguistic ruling (*Sprachregelung*), for in a dogmatic statement . . .

> there always occurs not only the manifestation of the reality to which it refers [that is, objective faith] but also a terminological determination of common linguistic usage. The definition of a dogma often consists just as much in fixing the common mode of expression as in distinguishing between the true or false propositions.[33]

With this allusion to dogma as *Sprachregelung* within a dialogue, Rahner does not intend to relativize its objective content, so that a dogma would be merely an ecclesial language game in which alternative formulations would be equally valid. What he is saying is that the reality referred to by these statements is infinitely richer than the terminology at the disposal of the community.
Hence,

> the historically conditioned, limited terminology lends historical finiteness, concreteness and contingence to the statements of faith itself, particularly in its theological form.[34]

Thus, while the individual believer or, rather, theologian, working this time on the second level of theological reflection, does his best to enter into the communal consciousness of faith in the Church, so he contributes actively 'towards the continual historical changes of the terminology of the Church'.[35] A dogmatic statement is the result of such a living and historical dialogue. It is within this historical dialogue, which engenders an objective dogmatic faith, that Rahner deals both with the possibility of heresy and schism[36] and, repeatedly, with the development of Christian doctrine.[37] For, according to him, just as is the case with a community built on dialogue, so its dogmatic decisions are thoroughly historical.[38] A dogma is not just the summary of past decisions, nor is it just a ruling for the present. It stretches into its own future.

In his 'History', more than in his previous attempts, Rahner indicates rules for a future development and is not afraid to predict the trend which it will take. Since we in our lifetime are experiencing this very same process, we can anticipate its future. This is possible if we reckon with the fact that dogmatic statements can be revised and purified from faulty decisions of the past. He even adds an explanation, which may offend traditionally minded theologians:

> ' . . . because the magisterium in its authentic pronouncements can err as it often erred in the past'.[39]

Furthermore, it is possible to predict the future progress of doctrines if we are willing to detach certain no longer useful underlying models of thought which have amalgamated with otherwise correct expressions of faith; if we are ready to improve their terminology and adapt it to *our* horizon of understanding; if we, like our predecessors when making new decisions, do not fail to revert to the origins of faith as a whole (*globales Glaubensverhältnis*); if we are willing to apply modern rules of hermeneutics not only to Scripture, but also to defined dogmas; if we are prepared to speak a new language in confessing the faith, and so on.

In going beyond the present situation we can expect from the future not so much a detailed progress in particular statements, but rather a gaining of new insights into the whole of Christian faith in a dechristianized world.[40]

This wholeness of Christian faith towards which the unfolding dogmatic statements strive is, for Rahner, no more and no less than the global Mystery of the God of revelation. Doctrines and dogmas are but signposts erected for the believing community of the Church, pointing to the all-embracing Mystery of God. They are mysteries within the Mystery for man's advance towards the Mystery. It is in this sense that they function as objective contents for individual faith.

1.5 Comments and Questions

This presentation of Rahner's thought has already been a commentary on his approach to the objective content of faith. I have selected four aspects from which to tease out his view, and in respect of each of these I could not refrain from putting questions arising from my slightly differing concept. Nonetheless, before trying to develop the latter, I must emphasize my basic agreement with his view on the scholarly work on the second level of theological reflecton, with his concept of doctrines and dogmas in relation to individual faith and, most of all, I agree with his assigning of the origins of dogmas to the activity of the Church. It is with this last point that I will make my own entry into the discussion.

In insisting on the objectivity of faith, one should recall my treatment of Rahner's anthropological conversion at the beginning of Volume 2. In those suggestions, comments and questions, I gave only a somewhat restrained welcome to his tenet that truths of divine revelation are only theologically valid if they can be meaningfully expressed in terms of the human predicament (that is, in terms of man's transcendental thrust towards the infinite Mystery of God). I ventured to radicalize this Rahnerian concept, maintaining that revealed truths are not first and foremost statements about God the Mystery, but about how God interprets man, mankind and its history. God is the subject of this interpretation, whereas man is its object.[41] Consequently, the question about the objectivity of faith, the contents of divine revelation, is a truth or truths about man from the point of view of God. The search for this objective truth of faith must, therefore, be directed to our own attitudes, to our active behaviour towards the world in which we live. Yet the measure, the ultimate criterion of this basically human truth, is its correspondence to God's interpretation of man. Doctrines and dogmas are man's efforts to express this correspondence correctly. And this, inevitably, is done in a social and historical process.

At this point, however, there is a need for a careful distinction between doctrines and dogmas. Although both try to grasp and explain this correspondence between human response in confessing the faith and God's revealed will for man, their ultimate sources are different. The subject of doctrines is the individual reflecting on his own and his fellow Christians' response to God's word, whereas the subject of dogmas is already the community acting as a whole, both as regards its own behaviour and its interpreting God's revelation. Of course, doctrines are not mere opinions thought out by individuals. They are proffered in their social context, they are acted upon, they mould the practical response of at least a small community.

On the other hand, the dogmatizing act of the community should not be made into a mystique (that is, in taking the community as a living person). When I speak of the Church's responsibility in defining dogmas, I mean simply that she fulfils the duty any corporate body with public authority has in legislating for its own survival, for the preservation of its own self-identity, and for the benefit of its members. Hers is the duty to safeguard and keep, foster, and unfold the attitude that is confessed and practised in faith.

Whereas the objectivity of this faith is mirrored in the practice of the faithful, its objective *expression* is in a happy balance between its doctrinal and dogmatic interpretations at a given time. I can, like Rahner, speak of an act of dogmatization which issues from the dialogue that takes place within the Church in her historical situations. This dialogue is between various doctrines, on the one hand, and the dogmatizing acts of the Church, on the other. It is a process which characterizes the concrete life of the Church, without making a mystique of it.

Now, leaving aside for the time being the active role of doctrines in this life-process of the Church, let me raise some points about her dogmatizing activity. It is, first of all, a historical *duty* of the Church to define dogmas as soon as the community of practising faithful becomes conscious of an all-embracing unity beyond the narrow confines of the local church. Faith itself projects the idea of the one and only Church, and this idea becomes, as it were, retroactive in an adherence to common traditions, in more or less general structures and organizations and, above all, in the need for legal rulings concerning the lives of the faithful. It is from the latter that dogmatization originates.

There is little doubt that the word 'dogma' was employed by the early Church in its legal sense.[42] This legislation refers, in accordance with the view which I am proposing, predominantly to the *praxis* of faith and only secondarily to views and opinions circulating in various local churches (that is, to doctrines). This, of course, does not mean that doctrinal points are irrelevant to dogmatization; indeed, they are important insofar as they influence the shaping of *praxis* or are an attempt to justify an already existing *praxis*. This is why, as a rule, a dogmatic decision of the Church is an answer to an existential threat to the life of the universal community in the possibility of error and is so overwhelming that it might run counter to the practice of faith or evacuate its content. Thus a dogmatic statement is usually a self-defence of the universal Church in a given historical situation. This circumstance alone justifies that authoritative pronouncements of a dogmatic statement can exclude by *anathema* some of the members of the community. But, having arrived at such a decision, the dogma itself is a new beginning which appeals to *all* the faithful, not so much for the acceptance of its own wording, as for the exploring of ever new ways in which faith can be practised (and expressed) within the framework of an ecclesiastical definition. Though dogma, in its true sense, originates in a definite historical situation, its function is to shape the future *praxis* of the believing community.

Now this approach to the basic nature of a dogmatic statement is one-sided. It does not take into account the often very regrettable history of dogmatizations; the violent wars they have caused, the bloodshed in martyrdom for or against the wording of a dogma. I have left out of account those political, social and economic interests which have made a very un-Christian use of defined dogma. For, as Paul Tillich says, there is a demonic potential in each and every defined dogma: it can be the cause of human violence. 'Dogmatism' is an epithet which every dogmatic theologian should fear.

These dangers are, admittedly, concomitant to each and every act of dogmatization. For legislating for a correct practice either engenders doctrines or is done in the name of doctrines: doctrines are the inevitable means of dogmatization. Thus, their use promotes the act of dogmatization by lending it a language in which to express itself. In this case, doctrines, as linguistic means, may fix the original intent of dogmatization to an idiom no longer apt to convey the dogma's original meaning. From this could follow that doctrines (and often dogmas gained by means of them) tend to live their own existence apart from Christian *praxis*. In this case doctrines may well result in a kind of re-duplication – they pronounce a dogma about a dogma – for the sake of the linguistic permanence of a previous legislation. In the first case one is liable to stray into an antiquarian dogmatism, and in the second to produce an unnecessary number of *meta-dogmas*.

Nonetheless, doctrines, despite their basic ambiguity, inevitably play a role in the concrete life of the Church. It is by their means that Christian *praxis* is able to avoid indifference: not every response that goes under the blanket of faith is admissible. Doctrines tell us, even if they seem to verge on the side of mere speculation, how this practice can be improved upon. Doctrines focus our attention on trying to grasp how God interprets man, in the realization of which the objectivity of Christian faith consists. To put it another way: doctrines 'realize' the objectivity of faith in the sense of insight and understanding, while dogmas 'realize' the objectivity of faith in the sense of promoting their practice. When these two aspects become one act of interpreting human life from the point of view of God, or rather, when a workable balance is established between them, then access to the objectivity of faith is opened up to us.

Now, I take Rahner's second level of theological reflection to be a scholarly study of the historical and social circumstances in which Christian doctrines and dogmas came about and how a workable balance was established between them. A major part of this study is what used to go under the name of the history of Christian ideas, or the history of dogmas.

But there is more to it than positive historical research. It is also a task of this second level of theological reflection to concentrate on doctrines, inasmuch as these promote dogmatic development. For doctrines and their system are open-ended, while dogmas in their wording – not in their effect on Christian *praxis* – are decisive. Yet, as various doctrines, sometimes in their dialectical opposition, have played their part in the coming-to-be of dogmas, so they continue to do now. They penetrate deeper into God's interpreting man, they even try to discover what God in himself is, he who wills us to act and to be in his own way. Considering Christian doctrines on this second level of theological reflection can lead us to a justified criticism of past dogmatic decisions, but it can also open the way for improving them, for putting them into different constellations in which a past insistence may lose its significance, whilst other hitherto neglected aspects may, if need be, become apt subjects for future dogmatization. Theology, on this second level of reflection, is about understanding the objectivity of faith which past decisions, according to their own light, legislated upon for the sake of Christian *praxis*.

Now it could be said that my comments and questions have not substantially changed the purview of Rahner's approach to the objectivity of faith. Basically, this is correct: my remarks are intended to be a commentary. Nonetheless, I believe that at a significant point I have deviated from Rahner's concept: for me, the question of objective truth in theology is not verified by the impenetrable presence of God's or man's mystery, but rather by the practical viability of Christian doctrines and Church dogmas. For, it seems to me, the question of verification in theology should be answered by the simultaneous presence of two factors. First, the objective truth of Christianity is, humanly speaking, embodied in the *praxis* of an integrated life enjoyed by a group of people who with courage shape their existence according to the doctrines and dogmas derived from the message of Revelation. Secondly, the objective truth of this faith is established by those who do not take these doctrines and dogmas as foregone conclusions, but rather as ever-new possibilities of human life; their commitment to them releases to an ever-increasing understanding and practical realization. If these two verifying aspects, the commitment and its open-ended freedom to live it, achieve a workable synthesis, the objective truth of the Christian faith is verified. It is as simple as the legendary truth of the pudding.

Access to this verified truth of Christianity presupposes, of course, an open-ended knowledge of its doctrines and dogmas. In what follows, unlike Rahner, I shall, as far as possible, avoid the appeal to mysteries within the one and only Mystery that is God. In concentrating on doctrines and dogmas I am certainly aware that these statements, at their heart, are mysterious and humanly inaccessible facts. Yet I do not share the view of Rahner's fundamental theology, according to which the inaccessible Mystery of

God 'draws' and fascinates human striving. For Wittgenstein's obligatory silence, in facing a recognized mystery, is valid for the theologian also; not however as regards those statements which, as real possibilities of action, have become part and parcel of the theologian's practical life. Progress in doctrinal and practical understanding was one aspect of my verification principle. One strives to understand a person to whom one is committed, for an ever deepening comprehension will change the quality of life accordingly.

In this third volume I intend to do precisely this, rather than struggling for a decision which might or might not lead to commitment. This was purportedly the scope of Rahner's *Foundations* on the first level of theological reflection. My own here is a reflection out of the commitment within which, with God's help, I stand. Nonetheless, in considering a pattern of Christian doctrines, my progress to faith from faith, from *praxis* to *praxis*, will be performed in dialogue with Rahner and for the Church, in whose responsibility of safeguarding and keeping, fostering and, above all, unfolding the faith we have a share.

This is why my first task will be to re-examine the concept of God, which – according to the objective truth of Christianity – is that of one God in three persons.

Chapter 2

God Revisited: The Doctrine of the Trinity

The great variety of religious experience means that each and every believer will have his own concept of God. The truth of this statement becomes all the more apparent when we see it exemplified in the writings of one particular author – Karl Rahner.

In my presentation of his work I have already tried to make my way to Rahner's God, as approached from his philosophical theology and as viewed in the absolute and abiding Mystery which underlies his efforts in fundamental theology.[1] In the various attempts at explaining man's existential and historical approach to faith there have emerged new aspects in the image of that God of whom man, in Rahner's view, always is in search.

I have neither time nor space here for trying to point out these shifts in Rahner's concept of God: one such attempt was the substitution of the word 'Mystery' for 'God'.[2] I am of the opinion that a similar shift occurs when Rahner faces the specifically Christian concept of God which is the Triunity of Father, Son and Holy Spirit, as known from revelation through the person and history of Jesus the Christ. We can say that God, as disclosed to Christian belief as a Trinity of persons, belongs to the objective content of ecclesial faith, to its inevitable *fides quae* pronounced in doctrinal and dogmatic statements, and is to be considered on the second level of theological reflection.

Now, if I remain consistent with my suggestion that the business of theology, its very subject matter, is man as interpreted from the point of view of his religious faith in God, it will be all the more important to work out as objectively as possible the image of *this* Christian God. It is a mirror that reflects the man of Christian faith and from which his self-interpretation takes its origin.

To reverse the procedure, namely, to arrive at this image from man's reasoned questioning, would set in place of God our own, probably distorted, *Doppelgänger*. The Christian God must not be a Feuerbachian projection of man's own self.

This is why in my Rahner presentation (and, as we shall see, despite him) I shall have to start with the doctrine of the Trinity within the one Mystery of God. My question is no longer on the level of shepherding man toward a decision for Christianity as a whole. It is, perhaps, on account of this that Rahner assigns a very modest place to Trinitarian doctrine in his *Foundations*. His first three chapters (*Gänge*), with the exception of formal Christology, anticipate at least in a questioning fashion, all the other characteristic doctrines of Christianity.[3] Then he tries to lead his reader (at the end of his fourth chapter) by way of his doctrine of grace to a general framework in which the full Christian 'experience' occurs. This general framework at the same time is an anticipative understanding of the doctrine of the Trinity. Though Rahner promises that 'there will perhaps be an opportunity to discuss the Trinity with our efforts to reach an understanding of . . . the incarnation',[4] his further dealings with this doctrine remain marginal. One might even say the fulfilment of this promise is an appendix, as in the *Glaubenslehre* of Schleirermacher. Rahner mentions it briefly in the epilogue of *Foundations* in offering a resume of his *brief credal statements*. It is a fact that beginners in theology today should not be fed at the outset of their access to a theology of decision (first level of reflection) with the intricacies of Trinitarian speculation, and indeed because the historical emergence of a Trinitarianism was preceded by, or went hand-in-hand with, developing Christology, Rahner's strategy might be correct. However, his remote predecessors, Augustine and Thomas (not to mention the Greek Fathers) plunged their readers at once, or very soon, into the consideration of this august mystery.[5] They may not have had the same concern as Rahner. Yet, if one is to go beyond his elementary level, one must at the beginning risk cracking the hardest nut (as Barth did in his *Church Dogmatics*) by speaking of the specifically Christian doctrine of God the Father, the Son and the Holy Spirit.

In starting my further Rahner presentation with this doctrine, I am going, as it were, to revisit Rahner's concept of God with which I am acquainted from his philosophical and fundamental theology, now considered as the subject matter of objective faith.

Only then shall I turn to Rahner's explicit and critical suggestions concerning the traditional Trinitarian doctrine, from which there will emerge a concept always hovering at the fringe of all our considerations of Rahner's theological thought: the Person of God in Trinitarian doctrine as significant for the whole of dogmatics.

In this third volume, however, I am not going to end each of my chapters with the customary comments and questions (as in the first two volumes). But the reader will not be spared them: they will feature later.

2.1 'Theos' in the New Testament and the Theological Concept of God

It appears from Rahner's late reflection on the *membra disjecta* of his contributions to Trinitarian theology that the concept underlying the same is summed up in 'Theos', an early article he published in 1950.[6] Any reader of this article, after having tried to understand the concept of God in Rahner's philosophical work and, at a later stage, its slight metamorphosis in the replacement of this concept by *the* Mystery, will feel that here we are dealing with a new image of God. This God analysed now from the *data* of the New Testament is someone who is capable of 'becoming', if not of changing, in history.

In addition, therefore, to the implicit natural theology as contained in his early works of *Spirit* and *Hearers*, Rahner affirms an exclusively theological concept of God. In order to maintain this he has, on the one hand, to go beyond the purview of Vatican I's dogma which insists on the ability of man's rational power to affirm God's existence and even speaks of a possible demonstration of the same without the aid of divine revelation;[7] and, on the other hand, he will have to show that the God of the Bible is not the God of metaphysics, but rather the one with whom we have to deal in the history of Jesus the Christ. The programme of a *theological* knowledge of God is not a metaphysical disclosure. It is a hermeneutics strictly connected with the revelation of Jesus the Christ. Indeed, its source is this historical event, this once-for-all happening unfolded in the faithful understanding of early Christian communities.

The thesis of Rahner's 'Theos' is that the God of the New

Testament is the Father of Jesus Christ our Lord, and not the neutral Deity of metaphysical reasoning.[8] This God is always the Father who, in a free dialogue with man through Jesus the Christ manifests who he really is. Biblical revelation is not concerned with his attributes, it speaks rather of God's 'attitudes'.[9] What is revealed is something that otherwise could hardly ever be known by man: God (that is, the Father) 'relates' himself in history to the recipients of his self-revelation. The 'Theos' of the New Testament is definitely a *personal* God who acts freely in man's history.[10] Just as man, so the God of revelation is free, historical and, at least in this relationship, is 'becoming' (*im Werden*).

Furthermore, while ever since the *Hearers* Rahner believed that man is capable of knowing God to be a person, the concept of a personal God in this context assumes a slightly different tone. For surely, there is a difference between concluding that someone unknown must be a person and knowing someone personally – that is, through the relationship which he has with another person or with us. Then, and only then, do we know him personally, *as a person*. It is this kind of knowledge of God which seems to be emphasized here as against knowing that God is or must be a Person. Now the 'personality' (*Personhaftigkeit*) which Rahner attributes to the God of the Bible hinges on three cardinal points:

(i)   that this God is a truly personal God who can 'relate himself' to man (in contrast to Thomas's metaphysics, where this relationship on God's part is only 'notional');

(ii)   that this is a God, who in gradually manifesting his relationship to man by taking up different attitudes to him, can also change (in contrast to the absolute simplicity and immutability of a metaphysical God);

(iii)   that he is a God, whose self-communication, by means of which he enters into a relationship with man, takes place according to three definite modes – the Father, the Son and the Spirit (in contrast to the absolute unity affirmed by a merely natural theology). This is why the God of the New Testament is the Father and not the divine essence or divine nature.

With this brief and summary presentation I am neither doing justice to Rahner's biblically-learned 'Theos' article, nor am I adequately representing the scattered hints in his later writings which implicitly refer to this image of God. It is to all appearances basically different from that of his semi-philosophical writings. In his later writings he makes no attempt to explain further the sketchy elements of a natural theology as indicated in his *Spirit* and *Hearers*. As we have seen, all the more importance will be attributed to the knowledge of God the Mystery, which has little or nothing to do with natural reasoning. It belongs to what I call a theological *Zwischenbereich* of fundamental theology. For my part I shall rather focus on whether the concept of God as it emerges from Rahner's 'Theos' article remains in Rahner's basically anthropological approach, or whether by going beyond, it gives us an altogether new and, in his words, 'categorical' knowledge of the God of revelation. To put it briefly: is this concept of God identical with the vague notion of unfathomable Mystery, or is it a concept which can be borne by faith alone in listening to God's historical self-revelation? Are we still in his anthropometaphysical approach (to which Rahner's fundamental theology belongs), open to man's historical experience, or have we reached a stage where not only is the attempt of human metaphysics to know God shattered,[11] but all human sentiment about a mysterious presence is overcome by an entirely different conception given to us in and through revelation?

As expected, Rahner's answer to these questions is not without ambiguity. On the one hand, by employing the blanket term of 'the Mystery' for God, he to a certain extent leaves the realm of pure philosophy where a metaphysical disclosure of God could be envisaged. Thus, in a lecture given in 1965 to a predominantly Protestant audience at Marburg he advocates a certain radicalism concerning the doctrine of God, even in Catholic dogmatics. This radicalism consists in the 'continual destruction of an idol, an idol in the place of God, the idol of a theory about him'.[12] As used here, *der Götze* (idol) is no doubt a tacit allusion to Barth's summary judgment on the God of natural theology, as are Rahner's following pages referring implicitly to the dialectical theology advocated by the early Barth. With Barth, Rahner is ready to accept that the God of whom we talk philosophically 'has already given Himself to us'; that he only 'appears when he is accepted simply'; that we can speak of him only, when he is already related to us, when he is the 'God for us'.[13] Yet, on the other hand, rational reflection in facing the alternatives of 'yes' or 'no' to God always remains a necessary presupposition to acceptance in faith: 'It is only preliminary: but it is a necessary preliminary', as the translator rather unskilfully renders his text.[14] There must be a preliminary advance of human reasoning on which this 'God for us' of revelation will impinge. This fact justifies, to a certain extent, the traditional structure of Roman Catholic dogmatics which begins its work with the consideration of God in himself and man's knowledge of him abstracting from his being a Trinitarian God: *De Deo Uno* precedes the treatment of *De Deo Trino*.

In the course of dealing with this image of God, I shall refer to elements, on the one hand reserved to faith alone and, on the other hand, to the remaining traces of the God of philosophers. Rahner's is a view that, in spite of an irenic attitude to a Protestant refusal to accept a metaphysical concept of God, maintains the balance between the latter and the God of revelation. His concessions to the Protestant approach can be summed up in the following hints:

(a)   even God as considered in his oneness by theology is God the Father,[15] as we saw in the 'Theos' article;

(b)   the natural knowledge of God as advocated by Vatican I is but a 'reductive element' in faith's approach to the revealed God (or, as Rahner says, 'within the total experience of God');[16]

(c)   the true God can only be known in revelation and in salvation history – the origin of our knowledge of him is in Jesus the Christ;[17]

(d)   revelation therefore did not proceed from God's one being to God's triunity:

> One could . . . more correctly say that the history of revelation first of all shows God as a person without origin, the Father, who has then revealed himself . . . within this relationship with the world as a self-communication, as the source of divine life processes [*Lebensvorgänge*] capable of creating persons. These life processes reveal their divine immanence characteristically in the economic Trinitarian relationship of God in Christ and in his Spirit which is given to us.[18]

(e)   thus creation itself is posited by God as an extrinsic condition in order that he can communicate himself to man:

> The beginning and the 'grammar' of the divine self-expression communicated into the void . . . the beginning of the Trinitarian self-revelation.[19]

(f)　the attributes of God's metaphysical being as treated in traditional Roman Catholic theology should be extended by the consideration of his free 'attitudes', 'dispositions', to join hands with the Lutheran *theologia crucis*.[20] Only God who in his freedom is the Lord, as also Barth affirms, can be the one crucified for us.

Now, as I have formerly observed, all these irenic concessions to a Protestant approach to God and our knowledge of him, seem to remain in harmony with a metaphysical disclosure of God, on the one hand, and with man's global experience of the Mystery, on the other.[21]

Their balance, to Rahner's mind, can and should be maintained. Thus his final plea to his Protestant audience is to maintain the unity of theology and metaphysical reasoning, in order to get at that fundamental experience of God, the Mystery, in which he can give himself as an answer to questioning man.[22]

But this will be precisely the point which my comments and questions will have to put to the test. For, despite Rahner's plea for a static metaphysical God, at the conclusion of his essays the concept of God which seems to have emerged, the God of revelation, appears to me as in a process of *becoming*.

> He really can *become* something in this history, precisely because (and in the final analysis not 'although') he is infinte and unchanging, the absolute power, capable of doing this.[23]

However, the poles of this 'becoming' are not quite clear. On the one hand, there is no difference between the *Deus in se* and the *Deus extra se*, for self-communication means that God wants to give himself as he in himself is. On the other hand, God is not simply identical with himself – that is, his unity is not simplicity (*nicht einfach-sein*). He *becomes* identical with himself which is, as Rahner says, 'the real content of salvation history', the mystery of divine love.

This paradoxical 'becoming' of the unchangeable and infinite

God can best be summed up in the doctrine of the Trinity and Incarnation. For this is the concept of God emerging out of his self-communication.

2.2 The 'Unity' of the Economic and Immanent Trinity

A full presentation of Rahner's dispersed remarks about the Trinity[24] would unnecessarily complicate my own presentation. As he never produced a fully-fledged dogmatic and systematic treatment on this subject, it will be quite sufficient to restrict ourselves to a most significant essay published in the second volume of *MS*, and translated into English by one of the best Rahner-scholars of the Anglo-Saxon world, Joseph Donceel. (It is a pity the English version does not bear the original sub-title which translates as: 'The Trinity as the Primordial Ground of Salvation History'.)

It is an essay within the overall scheme of dogmatics organized according to the 'process' of salvation history. To call it a *Grundriss*, an outline, is something of a joke for a work that had (by 1994) reached its seventh oversized volume and boasts as its authors the best names in the German theological confraternity. Nonetheless, Rahner's contribution on the Trinity seems to set the scene for the whole scheme of *MS*. The entirety of Christian faith is to be presented as a history in which man's salvation is accomplished. This history has a basis or foundation as well as an origin. Its basis is the specifically Christian concept of God, the Trinity, and its origin is God's first work, the creation as the pre-condition of man's partnership with God in grace. The history of salvation initiated in such a way will be fulfilled by the Last Things. If salvation has a history, so it has its primordial basis: the life of the Blessed Trinity.

This is why Rahner's Trinitarian doctrine, as proposed in *Trinity*, is not strictly speaking a dogmatic treatment but a systematic reinterpretation of the dogma (whose scriptural roots and development are, incidentally, skilfully dealt with by R. Schultze, J. Schierse and L. Scheffzyk in the same Volume II of *MS*).

Now, the actual method Rahner employs has three important features. Before giving a summary presentation of the Church's Trinitarian belief, he sets up, apparently by way of hypothesis, a principle for understanding the dogma: namely, the axiomatic unity of the 'economic and immanent' Trinity. I will come back to this presently. After the main lines of the official doctrine have been sketched (already under the viewpoint of his axiom) he proceeds to draft a systematic presentation of Trinitarian theology. It is here that Rahner attempts to work out the anthropological significance of Trinitarianism, and at the same time to criticize the terminology sanctioned by dogmatic tradition. This criticism (discussed in the next section of this chapter) questions the correct contemporary use of the word 'Person'.

Rahner's approach, therefore, is built around the 'axiom' of unity between the economic and immanent Trinity. From this rather theoretical viewpoint he tries to balance the objective content of revealed faith (the *fides quae* aspect) with its corresponding anthropological reference (as its *fides qua* aspect). And this is the main thesis of *Trinity*.

The context of this 'axiom' in itself is similar to Barth's.[25] God revealed in his word is God as he is in himself without revelation: a Trinitarian God in both ways; or (more in accordance with Rahner's own scheme) the God who saves us as Father, Son and Holy Spirit (economic aspect) is in himself the unity of these three (immanent aspect). Our juxtaposition of Rahner's name with the great theologian of Basle is not fortuitous. In this point at least, they seem to converge – also (as we shall presently see) in their cautious attitude to the use of the term 'present' in Trinitarian doctrine. 'The Trinity is a mystery of *salvation*' (that is, its revelation means that thereby man is saved owing to an action of God). If it were not so 'it would never have been revealed'.[26] From this it seems to follow that wherever salvation in its real sense occurs, in this event the Father, the Son and the Spirit in their unity are mysteriously present in the history of man. Were this real Trinitarian presence in our world the same as it is in the inner life of the Father, the Son and the Spirit regardless of the world, the content of our Trinitarian belief would be only a theoretical embellishment of theological faith: a *mere theory*. Whereas, however, in Barth's *Church Dogmatics* the coincidence between the *ad extra* and *ad intra* aspect of the Trinity seems to be entirely tied to the fact of God's self-revelation in word, Rahner's purview seems to be wider. Barth ties the unity of God *ad extra* and God *ad intra* to explicit revelation, and

Rahner seems to come to the same conclusion from his concept of salvation history. The truth of his *Grundaxiom* is argued from God's factual self-communication which (see Volume 2) is already manifest in creation, in man's engracement and his coming-to-faith. This difference between Barth and Rahner seems at first sight insignificant, yet it will affect their procedure.

What, then, is the reality of God's self-communication? If it means only the reaffirmation of man's transcendental awareness *about* the divine Mystery, then as yet no Trinitarian belief has been imposed on man. If, however, as Rahner concisely argues in the corresponding contribution to *SM*, self-communication means not just producing something by way of efficient causality, but also a unity between God and his creature, then God gives himself to man as he is in himself:

> The gift in which God imparts himself to the world is precisely God as the triune God, and not something produced by him through efficient causality, something that represents him. And because he is the triune God, this 'trinitarian character' also affects the gift and makes it triune.[27]

From this follows, of course, that the Trinity thus known to us in its economic perspectives (*quoad nos*) allows us to surmise how God is in himself (*in se*). Thus by God's self-communication a new relationship between God and the world comes into being, wherein God the giver and his gift are basically the same in a very real sense. Our acceptance of the Trinity in faith presupposes this unitive action of God, the Creator.

This framework of Rahner's argumentation is already well-known to us: it rests on the priority of uncreated over and above created grace,[28] on the possibility of proper, over against mere appropriated, relations of man to the three divine Persons.[29]

Rahner's view, as argued here, is underpinned by the category of quasi-formal causality that enables all men to live in a supernaturally raised order. It is Rahner's supernatural existential[30] which lurks behind this Trinitarian *Grundaxiom*. The means, however, by which he here attempts to establish his statement presupposes the very centre of Christology: the *hypostatic union*. In encountering the man Jesus we are not just experiencing a human subject, but rather one aspect of the intimate life of the

Triune God: he is God's self-utterance, his *Logos*. If it were not so, the humanity of Jesus would only be related to the one God just as any other created thing is – and not properly to the Logos of God. Thus the Incarnate Son would speak to us *about* the Godhead only in generic terms, and would not reveal himself precisely as the Logos of the Father.

> Here something occurs 'outside' the intra-divine life in the world itself . . . which belongs to the Logos alone, which is the *history of one divine Person in contrast to the other divine persons* . . . there has occurred in salvation history something which can be predicated only of one divine Person.[31]

Briefly, the incarnation of the Logos opens for faith a tiny aperture through which insight is gained into the inner life of God. Rahner is convinced that without such an understanding of the *hypostatic union* one would not be able to speak of the Incarnation in a real sense. This inner life of God will repeatedly be called the 'history' of the divine Persons.

We can take this interpretation of his as the major premiss from which not only Rahner's *Grundaxiom* is deduced, but in which his whole Trinitarian position is summed up. Therefore, the old dogmatic principle, originating from Anselm of Canterbury and defined at the Council of Florence, is broken at a most significant point. According to this principle, any action of God in the created sphere proceeds from the one and undivided nature of God and not from any one of the divine Persons.[32] Not so in the case of the Incarnation, insists Rahner, the divine Logos in Christ acts according to his proper manner as a divine Person. If it were not so, the Incarnation would not tell us anything about the 'history' of the Persons within the Godhead. It is an instance of God's so-called economic action.[33] Rahner proceeds to generalize this apparent exception: if it was possible for God, in the case of the Logos, to take up such an economic relationship with one creature (Jesus), then he can also do so in other instances. In the Incarnation there occurred a personal self-communication of God to a man, and a reciprocal relationship between Creator and creature was established. Could it not be the same in every man's engracement? Could it not be the same, or a similar, relationship affirmed in the sending of the Spirit?[34]

Now, to follow Rahner's argumentation would lead us into the intricacies of scholastic speculation which would unnecessarily burden my own presentation. His argument could be reduced to two main aspects: these we will now examine in more detail.

First, it is asked whether in the case of the Incarnation this 'exit' of God from the inner-Trinitarian circle has its unique and exclusive term in the human nature of Christ as united with the Logos, *or* whether this 'unitive exit' of God can be extended to the third Person also, to the Spirit, who in grace inhabits the just. In technical terms the question is about a possible distinction between the special relation of God *ad extra* through the Incarnate Son and a special relation through the Spirit and the just who through grace become adoptive sons: *filii in Filio*.[35]

The answer which upholds the first alternative (relationship of God to the Incarnate Son) rightly insists that the 'Persons' in the Godhead are distinguished not by their different perfection, but through their mutual relationships. Consequently, if the Son's work is the redemption of mankind and the Spirit's the justification and sanctification of man, they would differ in their respective perfection and not in their inner-Trinitarian relationship.[36] Therefore, in the 'engracement' of man the one Godhead and not the Persons are involved. Against this view Rahner adopts the second alternative in stating:

> [Although] the threefold God, as threefold possesses in his divine self-communication 'one relationship' to creation, but precisely a relationship which refers to him as *threefold*: each Person in his own way to the world.[37]

That is to say, if:
(a)   there are 'Persons' in the Godhead on account of their mutual relationships, and if
(b)   in any of these 'Persons' in God, by way of self-communication, appears to the world, then the 'mode' of God's appearing should not be according to the 'Persons' own perfection, but according to the previous (that is, inner-Trinitarian) relations between the 'Persons' in the Godhead.

To put it more simply: if God's action towards the world while being creative, is at the same time unitive, then God, the Father, in the incarnation of his Son and through the 'engracement' of man in the Spirit establishes a different reciprocal relationship with the world.

The second aspect follows on from the first. Rahner in his debate with the traditional language of the Church ascribes to St Augustine the view[38] that any of the divine Persons and not only the Logos could have become man. Against this he can point out: from the mere fact that one divine Person has become man, the same 'possibility' cannot be deduced regarding the other Persons.[39] Only God, the Logos, can become man and none of the 'other' Persons. For if through the Incarnation the inner-Trinitarian circle is broken, then the *manner* of this *must* happen according to the nature and mode of the Father's inner-Trinitarian relationship to the Logos. Only in this way can we be sure that God's self-communication through the Logos reveals something *more* than what we already know from reflecting on creation. Only in this way do we know about God in himself, otherwise the Incarnation would mean 'practically only the experience that God in general is a person, something which we already knew'[40] – no doubt from our philosophical approach to God the *personal* Mystery.

It is in this way that we can know more not only about God in general, but also about the Father, since this economic action reveals him as being of such a nature that he *must* express himself in his inner-Trinitarian Word and

> can express himself . . . freely, empty himself into the non-divine: because when this happens, that precisely is born which we call human nature.[41]

That is, since the Father necessarily expresses himself in his Logos, and if by his free decision the Logos becomes man then 'man is possible, because the exteriorization of the Logos is possible'.[42]

Such then is God's intimate life: the Father who is the source of all divinity is *by necessity* self-expressive. And, provided this intimate self-expression, which is the Logos, freely enters the created sphere, by necessity he can only become man. If the

Logos with the Father, and the Logos with us, the immanent and the economic Logos are one and the same, then God, the Father, has communicated himself to man in this world.[43]

Now this self-expression of God is not unique. It also happens in another instance where the inner circle of Trinitarian life is broken. Over and above the manner of God's self-communication in the Logos, God enters our history by the mediation of the Spirit who dwells in our hearts through the mystery of grace: 'The one God communicates Himself in absolute self-utterance [Logos] and as absolute donation of love [Spirit]'[44]. Rahner's line of reasoning here need not be repeated: we know it from his theory of the Spirit's in-dwelling man in grace, not in an appropriated but in a 'proper' way.[45]

Therefore, in these two actually experienced modalities of God's self-communication, the hypostatic union and man's coming to grace, we can grasp the content of the doctrine of the Trinity as immanent in God's own life and economically extended through man to the whole of creation.[46] This supreme Mystery is bestowed on man in order that he may be saved. Our human insight into the inner life of God as a 'history' not only gives the basis to salvation history, but allows us to believe in God who, by relating himself to us and to our history, is 'affected' by what goes on in our world: it makes a difference in him. He is a God who is the 'silent companion on our way', as Whitehead might have put it. From this insight of faith 'man understands himself only when he realises that he is the one to whom God communicates Himself.'[47]

Thus Rahner can say that the doctrine of the Trinity expresses the ultimate mystery of our human reality: 'This Trinity amongst us in salvation history as it reveals itself to us by deeds, is the immanent Trinity.'[48]

With this 'identification' the overall systematic access to the Trinitarian dogma is proposed, and Rahner is ready to address himself to the words in which this absolute Mystery was dogmatized by the Church's tradition. For the Church did her best to put into words what she believed. She confessed that the Father is God (the depth of Divinity), the Son is God (who meets us in Incarnation), the Spirit is God (who comes to us in grace) – and in these three only one God is given.

To express *this* concept we are told that one and the same Divinity (hence one 'essence', one 'substance', one 'nature') is given to us in the three 'Persons'[49]

The dogma is nothing but a conceptualized form of the primordial experience of Christian faith. Its content is not identical with its conceptual expression. Though consecrated by ecclesial usage, the concepts are human words which are intended as logical explanations of the meaning of the dogma. The dogmatic statement does not try to 'explain away' the mystery; the concepts used in it (such as substance-nature and hypostasis-person) are words only valid in the context of faith and obligatory in ecclesial parlance in order to enable a logical coherence in speaking of an experience in faith. A dogmatic theologian is not only at liberty, but has the duty, to re-think again and again the actual wording of the dogmas and to develop their contents.[50]

Thus their use is mainly a linguistic ruling of a historical human community. And this is why Rahner avails himself of this possibility of reinterpreting at least one of the terms of the dogma, namely, that of 'person', leaving alone 'substance-nature'. He will suggest, almost in accordance with Barth, a slightly divergent understanding of the word 'person' in Trinitarian theology: God is the one who lives in Rahner's three manners of subsistence.

2.3 Rahner's Anthropologocal Approach to the Trinity: Persons or Manners of Subsistence?

From the trend of Rahner's reasoning the reader could surmise that, even in his approach to the Blessed Trinity, Rahner will choose the line of anthropological theology. God's Trinitarian self-communication cannot exist without someone being addressed by it. And this addressee is the condition of the possibility of revelation itself. Thus, the Trinitarian dogma would be meaningless if there was not a corresponding experience in man. If it was not so, in confessing this dogma one would not be able to experience in it the nearness of the Mystery of God. In fact, the mysterious character of the Blessed Trinity underpins the mystery of man's own reality, elevated to a supernatural order: it radicalizes (as Rahner says) the all-embracing concept of the

Mystery.[51] From this anthropological undercurrent there follow two consequences for the theological interpretation of the Trinitarian dogma.

First, since being part of history, the concepts in which the addressee of the Trinitarian self-communication expresses his experiences are in continual change, it is likely that the wording of the dogma will be reinterpreted by the addressee. Secondly, since this Trinitarian self-revelation of God radicalizes man's own mystery, man is likely to re-live his experience according to the scheme of his own thinking. He can develop his own starting point towards the meaning of this supreme Truth. The motive, both in reinterpreting the concepts and in working out a new scheme of understanding, is anthropological.

Accordingly, Rahner chooses to reinterpret the concept of *hypostasis-person*, and not that of *essence-nature* of the same definition. The meaning of 'person' today is inadequate to denote the mutually opposed relations which, according to traditional theology, constituted the Trinitarian Persons.[52] Since Locke and Descartes the main connotation of the word 'person' is individual self-consciousness. Yet to understand three individuals in the Trinity would lead to the error of tritheism. Thus the language of the Church cannot ignore the definite change in the meaning of this concept[53] and the theologian, even if he retains the term sanctioned by ecclesial usage, must develop another meaning for it. His reinterpretation *now*, just as the Church's expression of it in the fourth and fifth centuries, stems from a common experience of faith: there is but one God, but one divine essence subsisting in the three *hypostases-persons*. When in our concepts we generalize this threeness by using the word 'person' for each,

> we do so subsequently to our experience. Our generalization is, *at least* at first, a logical explanation, not some new extra knowledge not included in the original experience. It serves only to remove a modalistic [54] misunderstanding of our experience.[55]

What the ancients must have experienced, as we do now, was their own salvation, as worked in the 'three manners of God the Father's givenness' – they stated three concrete ways of being given of one and the same God in the economy of salvation and, then, immanently, they spoke 'of the three relative concrete ways of existing of the one and the same God'[56]. These three concrete ways were expressed by the word *hypostasis*, which was subsequently latinized by the concept of person. Now, in our situation, and with our own changed terminology we could speak, as regards the economic Trinity, of three manners of givenness and, as regards the immanent Trinity, of three distinct manners of subsistence, *drei Subsistenzweisen.*[57]

For someone not versed in these technicalities, the theologians' debate seems to be a quibble about words. But what is really at stake is whether or not the believer can address the Father, the Son and the Spirit, *separately*, with a personal 'Thou'. Do these act-centres, these 'I's', in the Godhead correspond to a threefold Thou? Can we have a personal relationship with each of these three manners of subsistence, without reducing them to an impersonal 'it'? Or, if we are willing to advance from an economic-Trinitarian purview to the inner life of the Trinity, we might ask: are the three in the Godhead personally related to one another, so that the Son can say 'Thou' to the Father?

These questions are not merely speculative, they concern the awareness of Christian piety. And precisely this Christian piety may take offence at the theologian's reasoning according to which there are 'no three spiritual centres of activity, no three subjectivities and liberties', no three consciousnesses, but rather one consciousness in God that subsists in a threefold way.

> The subsistence itself is as such not 'personal', if we understand this word in the modern sense.[58]

and

> there is properly no *mutual* love between Father and Son, for this would presuppose two acts. But there is a loving self-acceptance of the Father . . . and this self-acceptance gives rise to the distinction.[59]

Hence, as Rahner affirms, it was only in an improper way that some of the ecclesial documents continued to speak of the inner-Trinitarian life in these terms, without taking account of later linguistic developments. To speak technically of such a 'mutual love' is inapt as regards the way in which later the Spirit is said to proceed from the Father and the Son as *one* principle, as their mutual love.[60]

Rahner's initial criticism concerning Christian piety, in which no Trinitarian awareness is discernible,[61] can rebound on his own proposal of substituting for the Persons the three manners of God's subsistence of givenness.

This is exactly what Rahner tries to avoid. For if, in accordance with his *Grundaxiom*, the immanent Trinity is the condition of possibility for the economic one, then man's situation in salvation history *is* Trinitarian. To the explanation of this in his own terms, he devotes a considerable number of pages, loaded with speculation of an anthropological kind. An understanding of his analysis of man's situation might give us an idea, if not of the mystery of the Trinity, at least of the way Rahner's mind works.

Man has an origin and a future (*Herkunft und Zukunft*). He is in history, but his spirit transcends to the infinite (*Geschichte-Transzendenz*). At the same time he is aware of his supernatural destination: he knows that God's grace is offered for his acceptance (*Angebot-Annahme*).

These pairs of opposites are not the same, yet they are self-involving realities. Origin-history-offer can be subsumed under the experience of knowledge and truth, while future-transcendence-acceptance are expressions of love. The first series is the condition of the second, and *vice versa*.

Now, just as in man's existence there is and always remains a dialectical tension between love and knowledge which *cannot be overcome*,[62] unless in a 'third and higher power to this duality' (that is, in the total reality of man), so a self-communication of God to man must present itself as a self-communication of absolute truth and absolute love[63]. There is at least an analogy between man's understanding himself in his own situation and our understanding of God's historical self-communication: the two modes of knowledge and love correspond to the givenness of the Logos and the Spirit in salvation history.[64] The oneness of this duality in man corresponds to the one divine essence. Now, in order to raise this analogy from the status of a mere parable to a more convincing understanding of the doctrine, Rahner widens the range of his own speculation. The truth man arrives at in history is not merely the correspondence of a human idea with an object in reality. It is rather the *lived* truth in which someone deploys his being for himself and others: manifests himself historically as faithful and reliable and makes this state irrevocable'[65]. Love, on the other hand, to which man in his future 'transcends', is the outgoing unselfish venture of man's life existing with the other and for the other in full freedom, and yet always expecting encounter and reciprocated love. 'It implies the will of its acceptance' and in the case of God, his absolute love 'creates the possibility of its acceptance and this acceptance itself'.[66]

God's one self-communication is the deployment of his being for us in history from its very origin (Father) – it is God's offer of himself in the manner of Truth (Son) and of its acceptance in love (Spirit). All this becomes definitive and irrevocable in man's experience of salvation history. The traditional 'missions' occur, become an event, in the unity of the one self-communication precisely in the different manners of the Son and the Spirit.

So much for the 'essence' of the economic Trinity. But if Rahner's *Grundaxiom* is valid, then from the missions we can draw conclusions about the inner Trinitarian 'processions': Christ, whom we encounter, is the eternal Son, the Logos of God, and the Spirit of whom we are aware is the eternal Spirit. The mysterious and unoriginate Father expresses himself in his truth for himself: the Son. It is the Son who is offered and accepted in love, and this love is the Spirit. This is why God can communicate himself in freedom *ad extra*. The immanent Trinity is the condition of this *free* self-communication of God. There is a real distinction between these three, in spite of their unity; there is a real communication from the Father to the Son and from both to the Spirit. And what is communicated in this process (which Rahner calls, paradoxically, the intimate 'history' of the Trinity) is the divine essence common to all three. Of course, the word 'communication' in this context (as any reader must have noticed) is different from what Rahner means by God's self-communication to the world. The difference between the two contexts, according to Rahner, seems to be the intervening fact of divine freedom. The self-communication within the Trinity is by way of necessity, that without is a free decree: the immanent Trinity does not have to become the economic one, but if it becomes so in revelation and grace, it must happen according to the three manners of God's subsisting in himself.

God is given to us in a threefold way, or as Barth would say, 'three times over'[67]. In these three manners of God's givenness to us the dogma of the Trinity affirms the three Persons of the one and the same divinity. We have one God in three manners of his historical self-communication. This 'history' of God is specific to Christianity. It is this specific concept of God which will concern us most in the comments and question of the next chapter.

Chapter 3

Comments and Questions: God in Process?

Theological journalism sometimes hits the nail on the head. From among the many newspaper reviews of *Grundkurs*, I happened to keep a cutting by Heinz-Jürgen Vogels. In *Rheinischer Merkur*, Vogels asks whether or not Rahner's three pages on the Trinity corresponds sufficiently to the norm of *sensus fidelium*; whether or not his image of the Trinity satisfies the prayerful mentality of Christian believers.

It is not so much the parsimony of the three pages that seems to worry Vogels, but rather Rahner's inverted commas regularly added to the word 'person' in the Trinity:

> Here you can read, of but one self, of but one personal pronoun, he, as addressed to God, and not of Persons who before any self-communication of God to the world know one another, as indeed appears from Mt 11:27. Rahner speaks of one, and only one in the Godhead to whom the word Person in its full sense can be applied. Does this attitude imply in practice that the pious Christian cannot say Thou to Christ as the Son of God, as to God from God; that he cannot in the Eucharistic presence address and adore a divine Person; that God is lonely and needs his self-communication to be accepted?[1]

Vogels is not alone in this quarrel with Rahner. Although a careful theological reader of Rahner's Trinitarian position would not jump to such dramatic questions, he is bound to be puzzled first and foremost by the virtual elimination of Persons in the Trinity.

Yet, over and above the many queries I could put to Rahner, in order to understand him, I should first concentrate my comments and questions on a more general level, that is, on the concept of God underlying the whole Rahnerian scheme, including that of the Trinity.[2]

This concept, as we shall see now (and in the following pages of this chapter), has a great deal to do with Rahner's identification of economic and immanent Trinity[3] and puts into perspective his cautious attitude to any reference to 'persons' in the Godhead. As I shall argue, this keyword, 'person', as understood in Trinitarian theology, casts a doubt on the viability of Rahner's concept of God, whereas a proper understanding of 'person' can either correct his view or suggest an alternative approach to a Christian concept of God. I shall, indeed, opt with Rahner for a God whose being is history and becoming not, however, in what he substantially might be but in what he is as a community of Persons.[4]

But before embarking on this position which will either correct or offer an alternative to Rahner's concept of God, I must say a few words about the literary *genre* or, as Rahner would put it, about the level of reflection on which our dialogue with him moves.[5]

3.1 The Systematic Position of Rahner's Trinitarian Doctrine

Theological commentators and critics often bark up the wrong tree – or, at any rate, this was my impression in glancing through a good number of articles concerning Rahner's Trinitarian position along with his concept of God. This holds true not only for journalistic attempts at reviewing in a few words a substantial book, like *Foundations*, but also for those who deal with these writings of Rahner as scholarly presentations of the Trinitarian doctrine. Thus, Rahner is seriously criticized from the point of view of the Church's dogmatic position and the *data* of the New Testament,[6] his wholesale references to Patristic and mediaeval literature are severely scrutinized,[7] and so on.

Why these authors miss the point is, I believe, the fact that Rahner, contrary to all appearances, does not pretend to write a scholarly treatise on the Trinity, not even in the second volume of *MS*. Like most of his articles, Rahner's Trinitarian reflections fall into the category of programmatic writings of a systematic kind. In them the conditional tense abounds, as if expressing a wish to work out his suggestions more thoroughly – elsewhere.

Nonetheless, these conditionals suddenly switch over to almost apodictic statements not intended, however, to point out something in positive historical theology (like the bulk references to the Greek *versus* the Latin model of the Trinity, to Augustinian or Thomistic sources, etc.) but rather aiming at the systematic place of Trinitarian doctrine in the whole of Christian theology.

As already mentioned earlier, the value of these statements is that of a systematic truth which emerges from the topic's position in the context of Rahner's overall thought.

In this latter respect, his Trinitarian position, despite the few printed pages dealing with it, is central. His is, we might say, a Trinitarian thinking which, as we shall presently see, concretizes itself in the mystery of Christ. Since the Trinity is always at the back of his mind, it would be a waste of time to look for minute *faux pas* of historical interest in Rahner's own presentation: the systematic interest remains dominant. Hence, other theologians in their reflections on Rahner's Trinitarian position find fruitful ground for a constructive dialogue with him – either by pointing out systematic inconsequences in his otherwise acceptable approach, or by contrasting it with other theological views. Of the first, T. Torrance and E. Jüngel[8] are good examples; as, for the second, are J. A. Bracken's two remarkable articles in the *Heythrop Journal* and A. J. Kelly's comparison of Rahner with process thought.[9]

These authors, *viz* critics, take on their opponent on his own ground. And this is the intention of my own comments and questions. Before proceeding with these reflections, however, I should clarify an aspect of Rahner's method in his Trinitarian doctrine which may have aroused some uneasiness in my readers. It concerns the very heart of Rahner's approach: the 'unity' of economic and immanent Trinity. What is the status of this insight? Is it a hypothesis set up by man in facing God's ultimate Mystery? Or is it, rather, a dogmatic conclusion at which man can arrive after having in faith accepted the revelation of the Father through the Son and in the Spirit, and after his attempts to grasp it by applying the method of Vatican I, comparing mysteries beyond man's comprehension?[10]

In the first case, Rahner's hypothesis, which by its very repetition becomes an unalterable *Grundaxiom*, is argued from an anthropological postulate of correspondence between divine revelation and the nature of its human hearers. In other words, the hypothesis is the result of man's attempt at putting explicitly into words what he already has, or is, in his own mysterious being: the implicit *fides qua* of man becoming *fides quae* in the Trinitarian God, indeed, the domestication of God's ultimate Mystery by the mystery of men.

In the second case, on the other hand, Rahner's *Grundaxiom* originates in the primary content of faith, the *fides quae* of our Trinitarian dogma which, by the anthropological illustration of the second half of his essay, is then tentatively made amenable for the *fides qua* of searching human thought: the *intelligentia fidei*. Briefly, in Rahner's approach does the anthropological tail wag the theological dog, or is it the other way round?

Where we should look for the genuine source of Rahner's thesis in 'uniting' the economic and the immanent Trinity is, I believe, in his underlying concept of the 'One God'. Here is the systematic position of Rahner's Trinitarian doctrine, and not that of Christology. Of course, without God's revelation in Jesus the Christ, we would have little or no inkling of the Trinity. Nevertheless, with the Trinitarian God in the background, or rather, with a hypothetical insight into his nature, we can understand *who* Jesus the Christ is. Only a circular argument such as this is open to a systematic approach to the God of Christian faith. As I shall argue, it will be significant that Rahner presupposes the nature of this God and does not seem to come to it *via* faith in Jesus in whom God *is*. The nature of this God is, as it were, an historical *a priori*.

3.2 God in History – or the Historical God of Christian Faith

One aspect of Rahner's concept of God may have become clear right from the beginning of my presentation: the God in whom we believe is not only the God of salvation history, but indeed his very nature *is* history. Yet history is not understandable without reference to time, and any being engulfed in time must be changing and becoming.

Such a being is of necessity relational. Now, if God is such a being, then we can speak with the exponents of Anglo-Saxon process theology[11] of a divine relativity as applied also to Rahner's concept of God. Can Rahner's concept of God be taken in their sense?

3.2.1 Rahner and Process Theology?

This concept is indeed the welcome suggestion of J. C. Robertson in comparing Rahner's and Ogden's theological schemes.[12] A. J. Kelly, pointing out Rahner's kinship with process thought, draws up the outlines of a Trinitarian doctrine, perhaps in a more differentiated way than does Robertson:[13] the two casts of thought with their respective terminology contribute to the contemporary relevance of this basic Christian confession of God. In spite of all his reserve, J. Donceel, who is obviously sympathetic to the project of process theologians, extends the parallelism between them and Rahner by drawing heavily on Hegel.[14] Donceel proposes from the remarkable mixture of these sources (adding Marechal as well) a, to my mind, panentheistic God of process theology which is, unbeknown to Rahner, now almost complete. We have not only a God in history but indeed a changing God of a Whiteheadian or Hegelian type – to the regret of Dom Illtyd Trethowan.[15] I could go on illustrating the gradual meeting of these two concepts of God by referring to other articles along the same lines, about Rahner's Christological thought.[16]

Without entering into a detailed discussion of process theology, let us try to see whether or not its central insight about the *bipolarity* of God is implied in Rahner's concept. This bipolarity means that God, in the abstract kernel of his primordial nature, is unchangeable while in his consequent nature he is exposed to new experiences within this contingent world. Under this latter aspect God can change, fulfil himself and reach the term of his own divine process.

Now, Rahner's thought has indeed remarkable similarities with this position. In his 'Theos' article he seems to indicate that the God of the New Testament is basically different from the God of the philosophers. Being the Trinitarian Father, as disclosed by the Christ, the *Theos* of the New Testament seems to be affected by whatever happens to man. It is, indeed, in Rahner's Trinitarian theology that we read a great deal about the divine life process extending even into the sphere of creation. In the incarnation of the Logos, 'something occurs "outside" the intradivine life . . . which is the history of one divine Person . . . '[17] and, at least at this point there is not a one-sided, but a reciprocal, relationship between the Creator and creature. The God of the Christians can relate to the world.

Nevertheless, Rahner stops short of going the whole way with process thought. For him, God, 'affected' by his world, does not mean that he 'experiences', 'receives' these contingent events in his infinite consciousness. Though Rahner's God in a sense relates to the world and somehow shares in its becoming, he would not say, like Ogden, that God in his love both gives and receives from the creature, that man is not only taken up into, but also contributes to, the divine life.[18] God is not only the basis of, but also takes part in, salvation history. This history, just as the creation of the world, is a contingent event of divine freedom. Thus Rahner would not agree with Ogden that the God of love must not, and cannot, remain on his own without his creation.[19] Rahner would not state either that, if God is indeed essentially love, he must of necessity pour out this love on others than himself. The reason why Rahner does not say this is that God in his Trinitarian being has already fulfilled his love. Nonetheless, it can be said that Rahner's underlying image of God is the God of process theology, without, however, this divine process being such that, contrary to our experience in the sphere of creation, it is not in time and cannot be regarded as in progress towards perfection.

Rahner's view remains dialectical: God

> . . . really can *become* something in this history, precisely *because* (and in the final analysis not *although*) he is infinite and unchanging . . . [he is] capable of doing this.[20]

For mere mortals Rahner's play with '*because* and finally not *although*' lies beyond comprehension.

An attempt should, however, be made at explaining why this final view, as poised dialectically between sense and nonsense, is a logical consequence of Rahner's overall systematic approach to the one God. Rahner, in his cumbersome attempts at finding a place for the treatise *De Deo Uno* and at reconciling the Catholic doctrine of One God with the God of the Trinity, maintains to the bitter end the validity and relevance of a kind of metaphysics in providing access to both the being and the concept of God.[21] Yet he must be aware that there is no metaphysics without a content. Human thinking in its access to God is already burdened with *a priori* positions – even in facing the Mystery and in listening faithfully to what it may disclose. The man of metaphysics starts from a *parti pris*.[22]

How we know this being, what sense we attribute to it must, by its very nature, be pre-theological. Now, if we compare Rahner with process thinking, in both we can discover such a metaphysical *a priori* (whether explicit or implicit). The 'being' of Rahner and the 'reality' of process thought are already structured by their own content before they are used in the doctrine of God. All the same, Rahner can draw the conclusion of an unchangeable God who is still historical, and the process theologians can conclude to a bipolar God who, by remaining one and the same, does actually enjoy change. Apply the same to the doctrine of creation: the Maker of all, though able to ground and steer history, remains free from and sovereign over time (Rahner); the Creator, on the other hand, who is essentially love, cannot but create in order that he may not remain solitary (process thought). Either way, metaphysical preconceptions assert themselves even if they do not act as the only factor in the business of theology.

Starting from similar presuppositions ('being' and 'reality') the two metaphysical schemes seem to diverge.

3.2.2 The 'Metaphysics' of Creation

My reference to the doctrine of creation comparing Rahner with process thought, is most relevant both for the similarity and dissimilarity in their respective concepts of God. The remote basis of their similarity is the basic problem they want to solve: how to capture the image of a God who, according to classical metaphysics, is the absolute and unchangeable and yet is felt and experienced in our changing time and history. He is the Creator of all, yet becomes part of our history, the silent companion on our way.

The above-mentioned metaphysical preconceptions prefigure their respective answers.

At first, however, both approaches are in step: this Creator God must be real and not only imaginary. God, his presence to and in the world, is presupposed at the outset. But where they differ is in how the *reality* of God is worked out in the context of their common basic problem. To put it briefly: whereas the process theologian's view of reality remains mostly empirical (in the sense of being open to experience) with an abstract superstructure, we might say that Rahner's view is abstract with an empirical infrastructure. That is: in process thought God is real because he can experience, expand and fulfil himself by creating a world (the 'consequent' nature of God), yet in such a way that at every moment of his own process he realizes himself perfectly. In this perfection God is recognized by abstract thought as absolute and unchangeable: the 'primordial' nature of God.[23]

Rahner's God, on the other hand, is worked out according to a reverse metaphysical scheme: God's being is at the edge or even beyond the horizon of our own reality whose ultimate condition of possibility he is. Whilst this initial position corresponds to the primordial nature of God in process thought, Rahner hastens to add a qualification which might at that point make it seem to resemble the 'consequent' nature of God. In his doctrine of creation, as we saw earlier, the Transcendent lets the world be not only by way of efficient causality, but also by way of his self-communication (*quasi-formal* causality). The result of the so-called 'creative act' is first of all man's being. Strictly speaking, this latter dimension of God's reality is the one which lets his presence not only be known but be experienced by man, his creation. This second dimension is what I meant by the Rahnerian infrastructure of God's reality. In process thought it could be said that the concrete 'becomes' abstract and the changeable unchanging; Rahner's concept is that the abstract 'becomes' concrete, the unchanging somehow changeable in time and history.

In whatever way these two schemes arrive at the concept of God the Creator, the final result again seems to be similar. First, 'being' and 'reality', an instance of which God is, is ultimately *bipolar* even in Rahner's theology. He speaks of an absolutely unchanging yet a historical God, just as process thought does of his primary and secondary nature. Second, the 'being' and 'reality' which we know and, in a way, experience includes God because they are included in God: Rahner's *quasi formal* self-communication of the Creator includes the creature within himself and process thought openly calls it *panentheism*.[24] Third, the means whereby one comes to know God and whereby God includes in himself this world is the same: it is history.

Whereas in my own groping attempts towards a more viable concept of God I shall appreciate these three points, it will be asked whether being or reality with which these two schemes work are not restrictive, falling short of an all-embracing transcendence. Granted, 'being' and 'reality' refer to a totality of what actually *is*. But beyond this totality there is the realm of what can be, or even could have been, of what is potentially in being or reality, and what is possible at all. God is not only the Creator as the supreme Being or the fulness of reality, he is the possibility of all possibilities. It is along this line that for faith in creation a slightly altered concept of God recommends itself.

3.2.3 Faith in Creation

The idea that creation, and consequently the concept of the Creator-God, is a matter of faith has been suggested by the severe criticism which all metaphysical schemes have undergone in the last two centuries. Theories of metaphysics which want to combine the absoluteness of God with his being in history are all the more vulnerable.

The metaphysics of Rahner and the process theologians in arriving at the concept of God are no exceptions. One could hold that God envisaged as the Supreme Being or the totality of what really is must be a static Absolute, an unchangeable and unalterable monolith for which any movement in history is but an imperfection. To place the infinite and omnipotent God within the maelstrom of history is unthinkable. In himself, he is God apart.

And this is exactly what Rahner wants to avoid at all costs. He must widen the field in which his inherited metaphysics of being moves. But in doing so, he stops short of abandoning the category of being.[25] The latter was criticized in the 1970s by W. J. Hoye in his small book with the strange title, *The Obfuscation of the Absolute Mystery*.[26] As I see it, the main complaint of the critique is that Rahner misplaces the notion of the Mystery with which he ultimately identifies the concept of God. It is for Rahner not so much in God himself, but rather in the communication of being on the level of creation, in the communication of his self in granting grace to created nature and in the fact of Trinitarian self-revelation of the one God. The Mystery of God to all intents and purposes consists in God's historicality. But such a concept, by necessity, limits the infinite, detracts from the power of the Almighty and at the end of the day reduces God to the horizon of the human spirit.[27]

Whether one calls God the Absolute Being or the One who *has being* in an absolute sense,[28] what we are dealing with is not the God of faith, but, according to Hoye, 'one of his strangest creatures'.[29]

Hoye's severe criticism of Rahner applies all the more to the scheme of process theologians. This is particularly the case when Hoye criticizes Rahner's doctrine of creation – indeed, his argument seems to apply to both – affirming that Rahner's concept of God cannot take account of creation *ex nihilo* as traditional dogma holds it to be.[30] The Being which God is in Rahner's sense should, according to Hoye, include in itself non-being or nothingness, the term from which creation in the dogmatic sense is to be thought out. The concept of God should be a synthesis of both being and nothing, for – to speak symbolically – only the God who, by bringing about being, conquers and takes on himself its contrary, can be infinite and all-powerful. This alone is the Mystery of God himself.

Hoye, of course, in this last assertion oversteps the boundary of the traditional doctrine of the Creator God. Nonetheless, his suggested counter position to Rahner (and to my mind to the process theologians) can open up an avenue along which I could still envisage the concept of God that faith in creation professes. For it is my opinion that creation is the subject matter neither of philosophy nor of fundamental theology but of faith. And so, consequently, is the concept of God which emerges out of this belief. The Creator-God of faith is a revealed concept. And at this point I want to part company with Rahner, in order to arrive at a similar conclusion to that of the process theologians. My thesis will be that the concept of God emerging from faith in creation cannot but be a God who is not only in history, but is in himself historical.

To support this assertion, however, I shall have to say what I understand by faith in creation and by the ensuing concept of God. Of course, in our access to this revealed concept of God we are involved in a circular argument. On the one hand, the dogma of creation is the result of man's reflection on his being in his world, on his active engagement in it from the point of view of faith in God; on the other hand, he has as yet no concept of this God, whom he prayerfully acknowledges as his Creator. He has to find him by subsequent reasoning.

Now, reason's function in fulfilling this task can be inventive, reflective or interpretative. By the inventive function of reason I can understand any conclusion about the ultimate ground of reality: to these belong *a posteriori* types of assertions about God in a rather primitive natural theology. Man's reflection might come to a more differentiated concept: it is ontological in the sense that it assumes a certain isomorphism (analogy) between the being of God and man's being. To this belong, in one way or another, Rahner's, and the process theologians', *a priori* awareness of God. Now, I submit that neither inventive nor reflective reasoning is capable of yielding that viable concept of God which emerges out of faith in creation.

The emergence of such a concept can possibly be the result of man's interpretative reasoning. By this statement I mean the self-understanding of man, who is engaged in a historical action within his worldly circumstances. This self-understanding is now seen from the point of view of certain events of history in which a possible sense and meaning is believed to be given by God to the totality of existence. It is to this possibility that man commits himself.

Phenomenologically speaking, faith is a surprising gift of awareness of one's own courage to act in this world according to this commitment. In reflecting upon this commitment, on the one hand, man will reinterpret himself and his whole world (belief in creation) and, on the other hand, seek to explore that 'possibility' to which he has unconditionally committed himself. I call this possibility, God the Creator. Briefly, in this faith and nowhere else, for the believer, God can become the event of his life.[31]

3.2.4 Towards a New Concept of God
In presupposing this situation of faith I shall try to work my way towards a concept of God using the elements I have learned so far

from Rahner's historical God, as compared with process thought and from Hoye's criticism of Rahner's approach. Let us begin with the latter. For faith the most important thing about God is neither the fact that he is *a* being (which inventive reason might assert) nor that he is at the fringe of our (transcendental) awareness (to which reflective reason may conclude), but rather that he proves to be the greatest opportunity in the unfolding of free human action. Faith reckons with this possibility and hopes to find God in it.

What Hoye has correctly seen in Rahner's references to the dogma of creation *ex nihilo* is that this possibility, God, on which one relies, is a correlate of a totality in which both the real and its opposite, nothingness, are encompassed. This is an insight with which man cannot deal. Inventive reason has no concept at all of absolute nothingness,[32] and reflective reason has but a vicarious notion of it: the absence of a perfection otherwise due, an unfulfilled potentiality, the loss of life and being. None of these gaps can be envisaged in the God one believes to be the possibility of existence in its totality.

Now, the *ex nihilo* part of the dogma of creation is an interpretative symbol for understanding in faith the Creator-God. Whereas our own reality is, so to speak, exposed to absolute nothingness without encompassing it, God's own hidden Mystery is conceived by the believer in creation as something in which absolute nothingness is not an impossible surd, as it is for man: it belongs to God's own reality. And just as man has power to deal with his own reality, so God is the power for whose creativity nothingness is, as it were, a possibility to deal with. In and through faith in creation, God's hidden Mystery can now, up to a point, be interpreted.

By interpretation I mean two distinct, though related, activities. In its more passive sense an object known by the knower is perceived with its appropriate attributes, and an agent known is characterized by apt predicates. In an active sense, the act of interpretation means also moulding and manipulating the known object. I am interpreted by someone who, knowing me, attributes to me various characteristics or in observing my acting makes various assertions about my behaviour. On the other hand, when I actively interpret something, I willy-nilly interfere with it. Mentally, at least, I recreate the object of my knowledge in giving it a new shape in the totality of my understanding.[33] Supposing this object of my interpretation is not known to me otherwise than as a possibility for my action, I shall be able to interpret it only in the first and passive sense. In fact, there is nothing I can 'mould' or 'manipulate', there is nothing which at the first moment could engage my knowledge, except the sheer imagination that moves me to further inquiry and action. The ways of an active interpretation concerning a possibility itself are closed.

Yet I can become aware, I can mould and manipulate my own further actions which I now understand from the point of view of my engagement with this possibility. When I say that the God of creation is a possibility of human engagement I mean the beginning of a process within us in which our interpretation of this possibility might or might not lead us to faith. Should this faith occur, it will inevitably attribute qualities to this possibility itself. Faith will sooner or later discover that this possibility, named God, is an agent moulding and interpreting our whole behaviour. It is a power, just as we have power actively to interpret things which surround us. Before it, we are struck with prayerful admiration that arouses the psalmodic praise of our thankfulness for having been created. As regards it, we further want to know what or who is this possibility.

Now, I submit that the attributes of God's infinity and omnipotence can only be understood by way of this interpretative reasoning. There is no objective entity confronting our knowing from which we could, as it were, 'read off' these attributes.

That we attribute to God *infinity* becomes obvious from our presupposition, namely, that this Creator-God of faith embraces a totality wherein not only that which *is*, but also nothingness is a possibility. We suppose that God, as an agent, actively relates to this totality which for us is unfathomable. In relating himself also to nothingness, he is indeed perceived as the Creator *ex nihilo*. He can, by supposition, 'mould' and 'manipulate' a world which is not yet given. We, on the contrary, can interpret in a passive or active sense a world that is already given. A similar reasoning can lead us to the attribute of God's *omnipotence*: being related to totality, everything – including nothingness – must be in his power and might.

But is this possibility, God, to which our devoted reason now attributes infinity and omnipotence, real, a Being which is absolute and supreme? Is this God, whom faith now thankfully adores, an irresistible reality, or is his infinite omnipotence a mere projection of our own active engagement with it? Inevitably, we ask what or who is the Creator-God of our faith. In attempting an answer my first step is to analyse God's omnipotence.

3.2.5 The Bipolarity of God's Omnipotence

There are two ways of asserting God's omnipotence. By means of reflective reasoning in metaphysics we might come to the conclusion that the Supreme Being and Ultimate Reality is the source on which everything depends. Just as power and might are our created perfections, all the more is the Creator in its own unfathomable way all-powerful and almighty. My conclusion is by an analogical postulate. But the question is, whether or not this conclusion can move and motivate our action. Faith, being *per definitionen* free, is not necessarily overwhelmed by this metaphysical reasoning. The believer, rather, reckons with an ultimate possibility of his worldly action and thus he can see in God the point of absolute dependence for what he does. Consequently, this presupposition will prompt him to speak of God's omnipotence in a different way, a basically different colouring, than that of usual metaphysical reasoning.

In order to illustrate this different approach of faith, for what it is worth, I shall now refer to an argument from etymology. God the all-powerful does not mean exactly the same as God the almighty. Whatever the etymology of these two words, power and might, it seems that even commonsense language attributes the first to living and free agents whereas the second can qualify any sort of immensity.[34] 'Mighty' for a mountain is a common qualifier, whilst a powerful mountain sounds either odd or means something slightly different. We speak of a 'powerful' ruler and when he is said to be 'mighty' as well we mean that his power can be imposed by force. Nevertheless, both are attributes of God, the all-powerful and almighty.

The divergence of the meaning of these two words gives us a clue to assuming in God a certain *bipolarity*. All-powerfulness belongs strictly to God as a living, free and personal agent, and almightyness to him as an infinite, immense substance – the abyss of his own reality.[35] If this bipolarity in God is admissible, I have reached a position similar to and, as we shall presently see, very dissimilar from that of process theology. The kinship of this view with Rahner's will also be obvious.

Faith can, therefore, assume two dimensions in the concept of God: the personal and the substantial. Now, I submit that God's personal reality is the primordial, and the so-called divine substance the consequent dimension. Whereas, for process thought, God's primordial nature is the abstract, the absolute and the unchangeable, for us God's personal side can be conceived as the more concrete (since it refers to God as an agent), as the more relational (since, being a free agent, he is believed to relate himself to his own possibilities) and as the more changeable (with regard to those relationships he has taken upon himself). God the all-powerful Creator of our faith can be the historical one.[36] On the other hand, in my effort to think of God in my own metaphysical concepts I must stretch the meaning of my words by saying that he is also real in a substantial way. This, in itself, would mean that God in his almightyness is absolute, changeless and eternal. To avoid having two, more or less conflicting set of concepts of God, I am faced with a decision between the God of faith and the God of metaphysical reasoning. However, for the believer in Creation it is a foregone conclusion. It is faith that rules our approach to God and not reflective reason. Hence, if reason envisages God in this substantial way, its conclusion can be interpreted by faith, thus: though God as a personal reality is historical through and through, he is also absolute, changeless and eternal in so far as he posits his own being definitively and irretrievably. This is God's unfathomable creativity which not only lets his creature be out of nothing, but also lets himself be in his almighty reality both encompassing being as well as nothingness. God the all-powerful person defines himself as the almighty source of all that is.

This, indeed, seems to be the way along which in the Judaeo-Christian tradition faith in God the Creator has developed. Creation is not envisaged as the production of a smaller reality by an immense and infinite one. The believer, rather, reverts to the imagery of the Old Testament, first to the category of 'making': God shapes the world, his creation and man in it.[37] But even this category turns out to be ambiguous. So the next step sums up

God's creating the world by his mere word of command,[38] then ordering it according to his own personified Wisdom.[39]

All these symbols of the creative act evidently go in the direction of that personal dimension in God as mentioned above. Or, to take another line of thought, which, though indirectly, refers to Israel's Creator-God: when Moses in the epiphany on Mount Horeb encountered God, his question was not *what* but *who* this God was: 'What is your name?' The question is about the person and not, as I might put it, about the substance of God. Though the name revealed to Moses in itself may mean Yahweh, the 'I am', the context of the epiphany suggests another meaning, 'I shall become who I become'.[40] His God will be identified in those free deeds which occur in the events of ensuing salvation history. A process is indicated here which proves to be the progress of God's self-revelation. All this, however, is only a symbolic expression of what I am endeavouring to conceptualize. Faith asks to know God's personal side, his freedom shown forth in events of history and encountered by man's freedom in moulding his own history. God's all-powerfulness manifests itself in historical events dependent on his sovereign freedom (which also includes the Creation of the world), rather than in the creative acts of his almightyness. He is the word that for man draws the line between being and non-being, between the possible and non-possible, between the permissible and the forbidden.[41]

Whereas all-powerfulness is the 'attitude' of a person whose authority is, for faith, undoubted, God's almightyness remains an abstract attribute, an inscrutable secret which the believer can fathom only by the further revelation of his ever-active *dabar*, his word. This is why in the Old Testament, God's absolute unchangeability is actively interpreted as his faithfulness to his own word. The faithfulness of God replaces the fear of man before the unknown almightyness of an otherwise faceless God. In this he gains only an inkling of the otherwise incomprehensible substantial reality of God.

3.2.6 The Bipolar Concept of God and His Creation
The concept of God toward which I have been groping is bipolar: the God of faith is a personal as well as a substantial reality. His infinitude consists in the fact that, for him, an infinite range of possibilities is open, and this infinite range includes non-being.

This is why God alone can be regarded as the Creator out of nothingness; nothingness is in his power. Yet as an agent in freely relating himself to a set of possibilities he defines his own substantial reality: he *de facto* becomes the Creator. The 'personal' is the *posse* of God wherein God's historicality can be envisaged. This *posse*, of course, should not be taken in the sense of Aristotelian potentialities to be actuated in order to fulfil the agent and make it more perfect. The One who *has* this infinite range of possibilities will not gain by realizing them. However, once a set of possibilities *are* realized (think of one of the possible worlds) not only do they gain existence and substantiality but God himself defines his own *substantia*.

The substance of God as posited and delimited, is not immediately accessible to the believer. *What* God is, is a matter of trusting faith in a Person *who*, it is hoped, is faithful to his own self-determination. It is this faith that overcomes the creature's fear before the whim of an almighty Being, which could annihilate man and his world once raised out of nothingness, which could force and coerce the creature. This is why trust in God's faithfulness solidifies itself in the attributes of his being absolute beyond change and alteration. In other words, these attributes of God, asserted formally with the logic of our reflective reasoning, are now understood by faith's interpretation as God's unfailing and faithful providence, guidance and authority. It is faith in creation rather than reason's logical conclusion to the Supreme Being in its personal omnipotence that can live with the almighty 'substance' of God.

Our insistence on *faith* in, instead of *knowledge* of, creation along with the bipolarity of God has its manifold significance for the whole of Christian doctrine. Indeed, I could affirm that the basic decisions in theology which rebound in its various fields are taken in the doctrine of creation. I mention some below.

As for the *idea of God* in a Christian sense, I shall see its advantage when I come to the doctrine of the Trinity. But before anticipating this central teaching of Christian theism I can see, even in concentrating on the one God, that this God cannot but be free and personal. In fact, the very 'essence' of the all-powerful God of faith is his free personhood. Thus I can state *a priori* that nothing, at least in the sphere outside God, happens without his freedom. That God creates of necessity, whether envisaged in the scheme of process theologians or coming near to it in Rahner's thought, can be excluded from the outset. Our world is due to God's free decision.

As for the so-called *act of creation*, faith would relegate it as secondary to any speculation along the lines of efficient or any other causality. Rather, I believe in the free Creator who *enables* the autonomy of this cosmos and, within it, the freedom of man. The faith of this free agent, man, does not suffer any compulsion or necessity when it proclaims the glories of the Creator God. Belief in him is a free offer to all and sundry, and not an inevitable conclusion. Until someone sees that the acknowledgement of the Creator in faith is beyond the category of necessity; but once freely accepted it is, more than necessary for a changed life here and beyond, since no one can force a creed with its first article on him. We are born free out of the freedom of God.

As for the *difference between* the Creator God and his creature, a faith in creation does not have to tread the laborious path of reflective reason. The latter, in order that it may speak of God, has in the very same act to deny any positive perfection we find in ourselves and in our world (*via negationis*), yet assert the same in an analogous way (*via assertionis*) of an unfathomable Supreme Being (*via eminentiae*). The believer in creation, on the contrary, perceives right from the beginning that his reality and his being an agent is of a totally different kind from that of God. Whereas in God the free and personal takes primacy and 'posits' the substantial, in our case it is *vice versa*. The substantial is given, the world's and man's *esse* is, as it were, 'thrown' into reality, out of which freedom and personhood emerge in the adventure of life. The knowledge of one's God runs parallel to the becoming of this life process.

As for the classical attribute of God's unchangeability, faith in creation is in a better position to state: *because* the God in whom we believe is changeable in his primordial personhood, he can be unchanging in his substantial reality; because God becomes in his own history, he is unchanging and eternal. In so putting it, I have changed the sense of Rahner's cryptic sentence:

> He really can become something in this history, precisely because (and in the final analysis not 'although') he is infinite and unchanging, the absolute power, capable of doing this.[42]

Yes, God is infinite and unchanging, because he realizes himself to himself in defining his substantial reality.[43] He can, however, *become* in his personal being. God as infinite and unchanging can preside over the flow of our history from outside, whereas God, once having decided to create, takes a part in our historical struggle. The difference is that we, in my view, have changed the terms of Rahner's statement – because God can change, he can also be infinite and eternal.

For this concept of God, I have had to invert the Aristotelian principle of *agere sequitur esse*: God is so because he acts so, and not *vice versa*.[44] I do not argue from what God is (*esse*) to what he can do (*posse*), but the other way round: since God, the all-powerful, acts (*posse*) he is so (*esse*); since the all-powerful says so it will be so. And, in fact, most of the contents of faith refer to things which are not yet part of a reality which we can experience – and yet trusting and relying on God's promises we commit ourselves to them as to undefined possibilities. Thus, for faith the *posse* of God prevails upon his one divine *esse*, and in this sense he is the God of history, not only of our own – but of his divine history.

At this point the reader might ask in what sense this suggested concept of God is different from the God of process theology and from the God of Rahner. As regards both schemes, I have avoided speaking of God in the category of 'reality' or 'being', instead I have ventured to speak of him as a *possibility*. Obviously, a metaphysically trained mind would see in this an *a priori* degradation of the God of whom I am in search. Yet, from the point of view of faith, the logical conclusion to an ultimate Reality or first Cause, an awareness of transcendental reflection disclosing God's presence, is of no use. Once the proof is arrived at, whether or not it is convincing, one can ask with some justification: 'So what?' Once, however, this God is perceived as a possibility of one's actions and behaviour there is a challenge to further action in faith. God is *the* possibility of man's existence. But does this argue that God *in himself* is nothing but a possibility?

This is what the believer at the moment of facing this possibility does not yet know, since only in his active engagement with it can God become *for him* a reality or being. Now, if encounter with this possibility constitutes the dawn of faith, it is justifiable to transfer this category to God himself. God as possibility has a wider range than what is real or beingful: it comprises everything which as yet is not, but will be; everything which might have been and will never be. Only in this manner can God be thought of as the point of reference to absolute totality.

Possibility in a metaphysical sense is the mixture of being and nothingness but, as applied to a concept of God the Creator, it is a synthesis of both in which nothingness is overcome not so much by being as such, but by a personal power of life. God as possibility of all possibilities is, if I may borrow Nietzsche's phrase, the absolute 'will to power'.

In having this concept of God, I should not be worried by my kinship with the process theologians. As we have seen already, the bipolar God I am advocating is in no need of creation, since he is absolutely free. In the event of creation, however, the Creator lets a reality be which is by no means structured like his own: it is 'thrown' into being that it might become personal on its own, whereas God, the through and through personal agent, defines his own substantiality in terms of his freedom. The only isomorphism, or analogy, between God's reality and that of created man is to be found in the predicate of freedom: God's is the freedom of the Creator and man's is the freedom of the creature (and not a created freedom). This Creator is in no need of creation, since in positing himself in his own substantial reality, he is already his own history.

That this God is his own history means that he is, as it were, always in the making. His inner history is his own Trinitarian life. In this respect, the doctrine of the Trinity is the best, if not the only safeguard against the thesis advocating the necessity of creation. And once the need to create is no longer valid, at least the danger of pantheism is fended off. The so-called panentheism which characterized the thought of the process theologians, and was also attributed by some to Rahner, can be made harmless. Though God in himself is in his own Trinitarian history, the history of the world which he creatively enables is not his own. Though it is initiated by God, it is carried out by man, whose reality is structurally different from the 'reality' of God. It remains to be seen, *how* and *to what extent* God will take part in this, for him, 'alien history'.

The question is whether or not this safeguard – that is, the Trinitarian constitution of the one God – is correctly entailed by these two theologies (namely, the one I proposed and that of process thought). Taken as a whole, this doctrine – in its classical form, which presupposes the distinction between an economic and inner or essential Trinity – is missing in process thought. But is it correctly entailed in Rahner's theology, the kinship of which with the former I have tried to maintain?

3.3 The Trinitarian History of God?

The idea that God can be conceived as history in himself can shatter our traditional concepts of him. The manner of coming to this possible understanding was the event of Jesus who was believed to be the Son of God. Furthermore, his life, death and resurrection left the believer convinced that in a certain form Jesus, after his departure from history, lives on in the community of the faithful and even in the individual believer's heart. In a threefold experience he now knows *who* God is: the one God of the Jews is now the Father, the Son and the Holy Spirit. The axiomatic formula by means of which this threefold attribution of the *one* divinity was traditionally expressed came about through the assumption of an immanent Trinitarian life which, though independent from our ongoing history, must somehow correspond to historical faith in the Father, the Son and the Spirit. Rahner's further interpretation of this correspondence between the 'history' of the immanent and economic Trinity finds expression in his *Grundaxiom*.

3.3.1 The Twofold Reception of Rahner's *Grundaxiom*
We have seen that the unity between the economic and immanent Trinity was at the very centre of Rahner's doctrine. These two are one, since the immanent Trinity is the *sine qua non* of Trinity revealed. Now, Rahner's thesis is greeted by Torrance and Jüngel as a step towards an ecumenical consensus between the Catholic and Protestant churches. There remains, however, a doubt whether Rahner, in view of his Trinitarian *Grundaxiom*, has in fact radically re-thought his concept of God. Torrance, for instance, tries to locate an abstract and still speculative element in *Grundaxiom*; an element, as Torrance says, which arises first

of all from Rahner's endeavour to envisage this unity as resulting from

> . . . a logical movement between sets of concepts taken from offi-
> cial declarations of the Church and with an underlying desire on
> his part finally not to break with scholastic formulations of the
> dogma.[45]

However, it is not this conformism that troubles Torrance, but the fact that the immanent Trinity is assumed by Rahner to be the necessary condition of possibility for God's free self-communication' – that is, of the economic Trinity.

Torrance suspects a fallacy here, when he continues:

> Is this not a confusion between a necessary movement of thought
> (a logical necessity) and a kind of 'necessity' arising from the fact
> that God has freely and irrevocably communicated himself to us
> in the Incarnation once and for all in such a way as to make any
> other possibility unentertainable for us?[46]

Contrary to this, Torrance holds that the economic Trinity is not the means of enabling the knowledge of the immanent Trinity but is the very same thing as the immanent Trinity.[47]

The other Protestant reviewer, E. Jüngel, is just as appreciative as his Scottish colleague. He raises, however, two important points which might clarify Rahner's mentioned persistence with scholastic formulations. First, the concept of divine substance (*Wesen*) cannot, with the assumption of the *Grundaxiom*, be thought of as abstracted from the 'history of God's threefold reality'. And, this 'history' is indeed Rahner's immanent Trinity. Secondly, from the above, according to Jüngel, the impossibility of any natural knowledge of God would follow.[48] And this will be understandable in view of Jüngel's later thesis, according to which the only way of knowing God at all is through the history of Jesus the crucified. Confronted by the cross, one cannot entertain any concept of God other than the Trinitarian.[49]

Rahner's Protestant reviewers are, though with some reserve, satisfied with the *Grundaxiom*. However, not so the opposite camp of Catholic theologians who vehemently contest the point which pleased their Protestant counterparts. Since their main complaint centres around Rahner's (according to them) arbitrary criticism of the use of 'Persons' in Trinitarian theology, I shall refer only to their reception of the *Grundaxiom*. These Catholic critics seem to be uneasy about Rahner's glib identification of the two Trinitarian aspects. Their reasons, as we shall presently see, are taken from the maintained validity of a metaphysical approach to God.

Marinelli, for instance, doubts that Rahner's argumentation rests on a sound metaphysical basis. The point on which Marinelli illustrates this deviance from sound Thomistic principles is, indeed, Rahner's trump card for assuming his *Grundaxiom*. It arises from the question why only the Logos could take flesh and not the Father or the Pneuma.

Now, Rahner argued: since the Incarnate Logos is taken for the self-expression of the Father, he must also be of such a nature (*worthaft* – Logos-like) in the intimate life of God. Therefore, by necessity, the Logos alone can incarnate and manifest a trait in God's hidden nature. Aquinas, according to Marinelli,[50] was of the same opinion; however, with the great difference that in relying on his own metaphysics he did not claim a necessary nexus, but only argued the *de facto* convenience for the incarnation of the Logos. Consequently, the economic Trinity (as manifested by the Incarnate) is not necessarily the same as the immanent Trinity. Rahner's argumentation is, as Marinelli states, unequivocally anti-Thomistic.[51]

It is a hard accusation from a camp with an almost excessive veneration for Thomas Aquinas. It presupposes that the nature of the *one* God can be known by a metaphysical conclusion: that is, by natural reasoning, whereas the same reason as illuminated by faith can add its non-metaphysical arguments, *ex convenientia*. This latter reasoning is of a supernatural kind. Hence we cannot know for certain that *only* the Logos was able to take flesh, and there is no necessary *nexus* between the economic and immanent Trinity. Rahner's contrary assumption of a necessary *nexus* will reduce the transcendent, and in itself immanent, divine life to our history. The result is that 'there is no immanent Trinity beyond the economy of salvation'.[52]

The same consequence seems to be drawn by Hoye: following the logic of Rahner's concept of God as the Mystery that shares its own being with us, the immanent Trinity will not only be united but *must* coincide with its own economic aspect. In fact, Rahner does not unite the two, but rather reduces the immanent to the economic Trinity. In this case, according to Hoye, God's Trinitarian self-communication means the gradual admission of man into God's being with the result that at the consummation of the *visio beata* not only the triunity of God's action in history will be the matter of human experience, but also the threefold distinction of the Father, the Son and the Spirit in the immanent Trinity.[53]

As I see it, Rahner's Trinitarian doctrine is poised uncomfortably between two, Protestant and Catholic, positions. The first of these welcomes the ultimate unification of the economic with the immanent Trinity, but dislikes this unity being a unity in difference: for us pilgrims on the way, the economic logically postulates the immanent. The second of these positions welcomes the gnoseological postulate, but dislikes the final unity in which it results.

In whatever way we see it, Rahner's is a halfway solution which may turn out to be the result of wishful thinking: he wants to have his cake and eat it. And this precisely is the source of my own uneasiness in dealing with Rahner's *Grundaxiom*.

3.3.2 The Meaning of God's Trinitarian Self-revelation

For my part, I am not going to choose the line either of the Protestant or the Catholic critics of Rahner's Trinitarian doctrine. My appeal is, rather, to the concept of God which I have tentatively developed in a previous sub-section of this chapter.

However, in order to do so I shall have to ask a somewhat speculative question. What was God's purpose in revealing himself to man in history as the Father, the Son and the Spirit? That is, I ask what is the meaning of God's Trinitarian self-revelation?

I hold that the revelation of the Trinity as a salvific truth for man (on which Rahner correctly insists) is not meant to manifest the threeness of the one Godhead in itself – that is apart from our world – but rather the true concept of the *one* God's reality as *ultimately personal* and thus *relational*.

This thesis can be put another way: the primary purpose of God's Trinitarian self-revelation is not that God is three, but rather the incomprehensible unity of the Father, the Son and the Spirit. Strictly speaking, *the* Mystery is not that there is but one

God. Neither is it that this one God is active in salvation history as the Incarnate Son or as the Spirit working in our hearts. It is, rather, how this God can be one and the same in the ineffable unity of the Father, the Son and the Spirit. The meaning of the Trinitarian revelation is the 'how' of this oneness in God's own reality. I maintain that this is a oneness neither of simplicity (inventive reasoning can assert it with ease), nor of mutual love (reflective reasoning can guess it by starting from the phenomenon of interpersonality), but of a *koinonia*, a *communion* whose pale counterpart we experience in our own desire for the fellowship of human beings. God's reality as revealed to us hints at the Mystery of his oneness in communion.

This, however, does not explain the whole of my alternative view. Indeed, I have so far seen only its outline. Yet this is sufficient to suggest why, or in how far, this Trinitarian self-revelation can be a *salvific truth* for man.

In it, not God himself is given to us but rather a Copernican point of faith, from which we are able to reinterpret our own reality. By means of this reinterpretation the believer acquires a definite task for his free and creative action in history: he is enabled in and through the altered view of reality to re-fashion his life in its various relationships. In trusting God's word that reality, other than that which we experience, is ultimately personal and relational he will face new possibilities on his way to salvation. He will live in loving memory of Jesus who was the Christ and in the fellowship of the Church and will thus find and define his new personhood in facing God who freely related himself to the world in the incarnation of his Logos and in the mission of his Holy Spirit. In the believer's basically changed view of reality, in his commitment to act accordingly, can be seen the salvific nature of God's Trinitarian self-revelation.

In this changed vista of a new life, man's relationship to the God of salvation will also change. His aim, to put it simply, will be not so much to *know* God, as to be *known* by God within a personal encounter. For there is a difference in kind in concluding to the fact that God must be a person and in knowing God *personally*. The first is the conclusion of reflective reasoning, since any positive perfection in the reality we experience can be attributed to God, whilst the second presupposes a living interaction between those who meet. In a friend encountered I learn to know him inasmuch as I am known by him. In such an encounter, as we shall presently see, not only do two individuals meet, but in and through the encounter they *become* persons. Thus the basis of man's salvation is the possibility of this divine-human encounter in which he becomes a person before God and God becomes personal for him.

One can know many things in the cold objectivity of logic, yet it is a different kind of knowing when one is confronted with a subject in a mutually active relationship. One may know someone as a potential friend or foe, but the quality of one's knowing changes radically when events prove the encountered to be indeed friend or foe: one has then perceived a different kind of reality, the reality of the personal.

This, I believe, must have happened with the apostles in their intercourse with the living Jesus, and again when, gathered together in the early Church, they could confess that Jesus is the Lord. For them the human individual, Jesus, had 'become' a divine person. The insight which was yielded to them was neither the knowledge of the Father, the Son and the Spirit, nor of their own 'proper' relationship to these three, but rather of the nature of that reality, in the confrontation with which they began to be different persons. In this kind of encounter, I believe, they saw that the ultimate, as well as primordial, in God's reality is the bond which unites persons (both divine and human) in an ineffable communion.

It was, perhaps, in this sense that the revelation of the Father, the Son and the Spirit never seems to have affected the truth about the *one* God in the early Church. It was not a mathematical problem for the early Christians to equate the three with one and *vice versa*. Nor did they have to devise fancy terms like 'transcendental oneness' to fend off the charge of polytheism. What no doubt they were convinced of was that in the encounter with Jesus, within his Church, their life, their personality had been changed. This, I believe, prompts Peter to speak of the Christian's experience as sharing, being *koinonos* in divine nature (2 Pet 1:4). He does not speak of an abstract nature, *physis*, of the Godhead, but rather of a communion between God and man, by means of which the newly-born human person is now taken into those relationships in which the encountered other lives, whereas the encountered takes upon himself the lot of the human other in its entirety. Man in his own reality can never become the sharer of God's own reality. All the same, I can speak of a deification, a *theosis*, in the sense of being engaged by faith in the dynamism of God's self-revelation through Jesus and the Spirit. Its meaning is that the divine reality is personal and relational. And in this sense, too, is salvific.

Of course, the value of our alternative view of the meaning of God's Trinitarian self-revelation can only be seen when we further expand its implications in the other fields of a theological system: in strict Trinitarian doctrine (which I shall briefly outline below), in the doctrine of Jesus the Christ and his redemption, in the doctrine of the Church and of the eschatological fulfilment. Here, however, I shall have to restrict myself to a restatement of my initial stance. Trinitarian belief that responds to God's Trinitarian self-revelation gives us the sense of taking part, not by ourselves, but as a human communion of persons (the Church) in those relationships which Jesus the Son of God had with his Father and the Spirit, as well as (which is more important) in those relationships by means of which the Son of God related the reality of God to our world. This participation is the basis of our becoming persons before God. Out of this newborn personhood we begin the process of interpreting our own selves and our world as a personal reality. As A. J. Kelly wrote in his most perceptive article: 'The revelation of the Trinity assures man of the ultimately personal nature of Reality', within which the

> presence of God in the Incarnation has a personalising effect on man engaged as he is in activities and processes of making his world . . . for the reality of the world is ultimately personal.[54]

3.3.3 The Status of the 'Two' Trinities

It is now, with this approach to the meaning of God's Trinitarian self-revelation, that I am in a position to modify Rahner's doctrine.

First, in pleading for his *Grundaxiom* he argued that through the Incarnation and through the coming of the Spirit we know *more* about God than that which we knew before. This 'more' does not refer to our knowing of God as personal 'since', as he says, 'we already knew it'[55] but, apparently to the inner

Trinitarian life of God (the immanent Trinity). What I, on the other hand, affirmed is that God as personal can only be known through the experience of the three-faceted God, the Father, the Son and the Spirit.[56]

Secondly, this fact will alter our concept of the immanent Trinity as well as its relation to the economical experience of the same. I shall affirm that there is only a *theoretical* link between the two. There is neither a coincidence between the two Trinities, nor is the experience of the economic Trinity meant to reveal the existence of the so-called, immanent Trinity.

Now, such theory is an inevitable accompaniment of any historical process which serves as a matrix for the understanding of what we experience, or of which in faith we are convinced. A theory is like paradigms and models in science, or parables and metaphors facilitating our grasp of historical events. None of these is without an element of abstraction. If, therefore, I hold that the distinction between the economic and immanent Trinity is such a theory, I am speaking abstractly,[57] I shall need to be aware that such an abstract discourse is exposed to the danger of forgetting the matrix of original experience. All the same, *abstrahentium non est mendatium*. The question remains: what is the status of this abstraction, and consequently, how do the two 'Trinities' relate, once they are distinguished? Rahner's *Grundaxiom* serves precisely this task. To explain, however, how I understand this relationship, the *transitus* from one to the other and their *nexus*, might land me at cross purposes not only with Rahner's view, but also with those authors who were critical of his Trinitarian doctrine.

First of all I would maintain that the distinction between the two Trinities is something arrived at by believers themselves, since the doctrine of the immanent Trinity is not a directly revealed fact of faith. It was not the mission of Jesus to reveal beyond the one God the immanent Trinity of the Father, the Son and the Spirit. Knowledge of this immanent Trinity is the result of a laborious process of human living and thinking *vis-a-vis* the personal and relational reality of God. For the believer in Jesus faces a drama in which not only mankind, but also the Three play various parts. The Father sends the Son and the Spirit; he gives up his only Son for our sake; he accepts, as we shall see, the Son's propitiatory sacrifice; his 'anger' is expiated by the obedience of the Son; he is prayed to by the Spirit crying out in our hearts, while only in this Spirit can we say Jesus is the Lord (1 Cor 12:36). These Trinitarian roles not only run in a dramatic plurality, but at times seem to be extending each other's work, or even seem to be conflicting among themselves. The believer, living in faith with this unordered mass of experiences, is challenged to make a virtue of his need in producing a viable theory along the lines of which he can reasonably speak and think of God's triunity. This, I believe, is the matrix of the distinction between the two Trinities. While what is called the economic Trinity is the concrete and graspable fact of Christian belief, the immanent Trinity is worked out by a process of trial and error, as early Church history witnesses; its status is that of a theory which will inevitably emerge. With this, I am now in a better position to establish their relationship.

3.3.4 The 'Two' Trinities in Relationship

Rahner's *Anthropologische Wende* is clearly felt in his arguing for the *Grundaxiom*. He tries to ground, in a transcendental way, the threefold experience which faith has in relation to the event of Christ. By reflective reasoning he is then ready to transfer the historical experiences of faith to the necessary inner structure of God's being. In this transcendental sense alone will the immanent Trinity have life and history apart from the world. But once this inner-Trinitarian history is postulated, he will reverse the coin: knowledge of the so-called economic Trinity is only possible if there is a distinctive threefoldness in the inner life of God. The immanent Trinity is the *sine qua non* – the condition of possibility of the economic – on a gnoseological level. This is their relationship.

This insight can thereafter be 'anthropologized', as it is in the second part of Rahner's essay. As we saw earlier in this chapter, its point of arrival is the mysterious and unoriginated Father expressing himself in *truth* for himself in the Son, and this truth being embraced in *love* by the Spirit.

The analogy of man's coming to truth and love can now be magnified into the infinity of God's intimate life. The distinctions gained in our history are transferred isomorphously to the 'history' of God apart from the world. Thus, the traditional formula of the early Church, as Torrance remarked, must emerge at the end of this anthropological speculation. God's inner-Trinitarian history must be, *mutatis mutandis*, similar to the events of salvation history which we can experience. In this part of his essay Rahner is, on Augustinian lines, attempting to find *vestiges* of the inner-Trinitarian life in our own worldly or spiritual 'experiences'.

K. Barth, in his arguments against the *vestigia trinitatis* of Augustine[58] would also be against Rahner, provided he assumes a link, accessible to metaphysical speculation, between the alleged threefoldness of human experience and the Trinitarian faith.[59] And this is exactly what Rahner seems to do: from the threefold experience of the economic Trinity he postulates, as its condition of possibility, the existence of the inner Trinity.

This is the reason why I have suggested that the assumption of the inner Trinity is a theoretical construct which inevitably accompanies man's encounter with the Christian message. It emerges as a possible interpretation of the experience of faith. After I have accepted the meaning of the Trinitarian revelation as a whole, I can (and must not) find analogies of God's supposed inner-Trinitarian life. Analogies do not lead *ante factum* to the assumption of the immanent Trinity. It is everybody's right to read into human nature's constitution analogies, or to discover Trinitarian traces in basic human relationships for this assumed belief. But the often artificially perceived threeness in these cannot be regarded *a priori* as created traces of God's triunity. With these premises, *pace* Barth, Trinitarian 'analogies' can be useful in order to illustrate the believer's action and way of life, which has been raised to a higher power owing to the fact that he believes. He can commit himself to the revealed personal reality of God and undertake to re-fashion himself, his society and the world, in order to make it one, despite its plurality: he aims at the realization of oneness within human fellowship living in a personalized world. In this partial achievement, as motivated by Trinitarian revelation, we can attain a weak reflection, as in a mirror, of what the oneness of the Trinitarian God might be.

If indeed the link between the economic and the immanent Trinity arises out of the theoretical interpretation of Christian experience, then my position is nearer to those critics who object to Rahner's apparent deduction of the immanent from the economic Trinity: the connection being rather *ex convenientia* than by way of transcendental reasoning. This might be so but, if we examine more closely Rahner's and his Thomist adversaries' views, we shall find that both are founded on the same basic presupposition: their starting point is the absolute necessariness of an unchangeable divine substance which is accessible by way of natural reasoning. It is the firm and immovable substratum of those relationships which constitute the Persons. It does not, as it were, dissolve itself in the Persons' dynamic relationality.[60] If my view about the concept of God is correct, it is God's 'substance' which is being constantly 'posited' by the relationship of the Persons and not *vice versa*. God's relationality, as perceived by faith, enables the believer to speak of an unchanging divine oneness. God is always in the making: he is what he wills to be.

In assuming, therefore, the necessary and immovable divine substance, Rahner and his Thomistic objectors are at one. Their difference consists in the status of this divine substance. While in classical theism this divine substance is all we can know about God's being and the rest is a matter of faith, Rahner speaks of the same as a *structural unity* according to which the divine 'Persons' share the divine being. From this follows that Rahner's three 'modes of subsistences' (= Persons), as it were, borrow the necessary character of that monolith of divine substance, so that one can but be (*ad intra*) the source of divinity (= Father), another but its expression (= Son) and the third but their loving union (= Spirit). This is why in Rahner's view, apart from the Son, the other Persons not only *ex convenientia*, as in Aquinas, but by logical necessity, cannot incarnate. That his strict Thomistic adversaries maintain the contrary view follows from the assumption that the inner-Trinitarian processions are by the way of necessity, whereas God's action *ad extra* is entirely free. Not only the Son but each Person could have become Incarnate. This is not so in Rahner's view: though divine action in the non-divine sphere is in itself free, it is subject to the structural necessity that prevails in the inner-Trinitarian processions.

Here I should ask against both views: do I have to maintain the inner necessity of God's intimate life process while granting him freedom only in his acting in the non-divine sphere? Could I not hold that God is unfathomable *freedom* both as regards his immanent life and as to his dealing with our own history? He is not only free in his self-communication to the world, but also in what he is and wants to be in himself. Since God's primordial reality is personal and relational, he is, whether *ad intra* or *ad extra* the unbounded freedom.[61]

As we have already seen earlier in this chapter, Rahner's Protestant reviewers have maintained this unbounded freedom of God and, indeed, recognized in it his absolute transcendence. Yet at the same time, I have observed an undoubted tendency to diminish, or even to eliminate, the distinction between the two Trinities. This is not because they (like Rahner) argue from the economic to the immanent Trinity, but because the former is simply God's self-revelation: there is one God, and man can have no concept of him other than the Trinitarian. More precisely: apart from Jesus Christ and his cross all other approaches are blocked for our inquiring reason, since only Jesus and his history contain the right concept of God. This means that any anthropological approach to God is *a priori* denied.

I wonder whether this view is tenable, for, as I hold, there *is* an access of reasoned human action to God apart from his true Trinitarian being. The very possibility that there is an Ultimate beyond all possibilities on account of which we can act, gives us a certain idea about God. To put it another way: that man finds himself able to act upon this 'possibility of possibilities' implies the hypothesis of an agent to whom personality can be attributed. And this attribution does not require a Trinitarian or Incarnational revelation. One could say that in his active search man *expects* such a personal encounter *before* it actually occurs.

This latter view, however, should not be regarded as a premiss for a logical or transcendental disclosure of God's existence. It remains a vague attempt on man's part to personify or hypostatize this ultimate possibility of his action. Indeed, Jewish believers also had to assume a certain plurality in their approach to God, in his relating himself to his people in the angel of Jahweh and in speculations about the creative divine word, the divine Wisdom.[62] For them too, thinking and praying commenced from historical events as interpreted by faith in election and creation, providence and salvation. Thus a pluralistic view of the Godhead and perhaps even a Trinitarian revelation have a prehistory in biblical belief. This was eventually confirmed by the event of Jesus the Christ. One could not argue that these intimations of the Trinity are altogether invalid. Neither are the attempts of a religious mind, even outside Jewish revelation, to arrive at a concept of God which is an appropriate basis for the coming of Trinitarian belief. For the religious mind inevitably assumes a divine 'what' and acting upon it invests it with personal qualities. Granted, this mode of person-ification is not a logical premiss for the encounter with the triune God: that happens only after the 'leap' of faith. For faith first acknowledges the true personhood of God in the event of Jesus the Christ and then the believer is called to presume, even if only theoretically, an inner-Trinitarian life which is not exhausted by God's relationality to the world. The religious mind has at least a hint of a 'what' or of a 'who' to which it attributes the contents of divine self-revelation.

However, to identify the approach to this 'what' or 'who' exclusively via the cross of Christ (as, for example, Jüngel does) seems to me an illegitimate reduction of the Christian message. It would imply first of all an all-pervading *possibility* of God, within *and* outside his intimate life. Now, in view of my bipolar concept of God, the assumption of a God who by his very nature is capable of suffering and dying, is only admissible on certain conditions. God is possible in the personal and relational pole of his reality, whilst he is unchangeable and therefore impassible in that which he defines and 'posits', the substantial pole of what he is. Even in dying on the cross God is not dead, but remains that which he wants to be forever. As I shall try to explain later, the death of Christ on the cross can mean the death of the Logos, even the suffering of God in his personal reality. Yet, his one-for-all defined substantial creativity triumphs over and above the nothingness of death. Death as viewed from the resurrection is forever disassociated from sheer annihilation; the Son's passion means glory. If my hypothesis of God's bipolarity is correct, then 'one of the Trinity suffered and died' holds true, provided it means the death of God's Logos in his personal reality.

3.3.5 The Immanent Trinity?

The question mark in this sub-title does not indicate a doubt about the inner-Trinitarian life of God. Yet, once the theoretical status of the immanent Trinity has been acceptably argued, it sig-nals the incomprehensibility of a truth which we have to maintain. We are called to believe that the God of the Christians is Father, Son and Holy Spirit, since it is in this way that we encounter God acting in history.

The immediate object of faith is the economic Trinity alone. Nonetheless, in order to defend this threefold confession from the charge of polytheism, I have to assume, beyond the history of God's Trinitarian dealings with his creatures, a sort of 'history' of God in himself. I must speak correctly of the life of God, apart from his acting in our history. Since it is not directly revealed, all my attempts to state something about the immanent Trinity will be theoretical and abstract. As Torrance has written, the immanent Trinity 'infinitely transcends the grasp of our minds'.[63] All the same, it opens up the possibility of

> . . . union and communion . . . far beyond creaturely existence – which is another way of describing *theosis*. It is precisely there . . . however, that we are restrained . . . from transgressing the bounds of our creaturely being and inquiring beyond what is given through the Son and the Spirit . . . [64]

In speaking of the immanent Trinity I am, along with Rahner and his predecessors in theology, in danger of this transgression. Yet, instead of choosing the way of silent adoration I shall have to tease out some ideas from what is given to us in God's Trinitarian self-revelation. And indeed, this is the concrete matrix of the outline which follows below.

If the meaning of this self-revelation is that God is a personal and relational reality in encounter with his creature, I cannot simply state that beyond the economic Trinity of our immediate faith there is an immanent Trinity. The verb 'becoming' is apt for both. In the sphere of our innerworldly experience the Trinitarian God has become a reality and is becoming all the time when men and women are drawn in to God's intimate life. But does this becoming valid also apply to the divine sphere? A strictly metaphysical approach would deny this possibility: the predicate 'becoming' is regarded as an imperfection and therefore cannot legitimately be transferred to the Supreme Being.

Yet in my argument in this section, I am striving to convert this concept of God into the more dynamic and active one which I know from revelation. I have even avoided characterizing this concept with the Thomistic tag of *actus purus*. Though this latter conveys a kind of dynamism and activity, its qualification, *pure act*, can be mistaken for the monolytic and unchangeable Deity which hovers in the background of all metaphysical considerations. If, therefore, I agree that the revealed concept of God is basically different from this metaphysical conception I shall have less difficulty in envisaging the 'becoming' of the immanent Trinitarian life. Furthermore, freedom, in which I have seen God's unalterable quality, cannot be visualized without such a dynamism, even when God is not considered in relation to the creature. This is why I have to assume a certain becoming in the life of God's inner-Trinitarian life: the immanent Trinity is not, it comes to be, it is an event in the divine sphere.

Does, then, this event-character of God's intimate life imply temporality? The 'happening' which may characterize God's dealing with us cannot be transferred to the immanent Trinity without qualification. God's life is eternal. If I understand eternity as timelessness, I cannot speak in any meaningful sense about 'becoming' in God. Time can be regarded as a mere sequence of events in which the present, abandoning the past, reaches towards the future. In this sense, there is neither becoming nor time in the inner life of God. Yet time can also mean a synthesis of these three moments in one and the same act of becoming. This is, in a genuine sense, eternity. Hence, I can speak of an eternal becoming in the life of God. Or, to be more precise: there is an eternal becoming in the personal reality of God, whereas I can speak of God's substantial reality as becoming eternal. The first refers to the personal pole of God who defines himself in the manner in which he chooses to be active, while the second refers to the way in which he posits his own substantiality – his attitude to himself and eventually to the world. I perceive these 'attitudes' as his immovable attributes, his omnipotence, his eternal simplicity, etc.

In trying to describe adequately the inner-Trinitarian life, I first have to appeal to God's eternal becoming in which his personal reality is being defined as Father, Son and Spirit, apart from the economic manifestations. In order to understand better what is meant by God's personal becoming, I am thrown back again to the notion of personhood.[65] This repetitiousness will be excused if I now recall that an underlying personalism has guided my dialogue with Rahner, influencing the present discussion with some insights from process theology.[66] My concept of God's personal reality as well as of his bipolarity can, despite their modified use in my context, be appreciated from these sources. I believe that, through a correct adaptation of these terms, I can reach an adequate counterposition to Rahner's model of the immanent Trinity.

3.4 Towards a Model of the Immanent Trinity

In making my way from the Trinity, as confessed in its economic manifestation, to the inner-Trinitarian life of God, I shall have to clarify the concept of personhood and apply it to God's personal reality. I shall be considering, in other words the inner-Trinitarian 'processions' and their relationship to our created world.

3.4.1 The Concept of Person

Although Rahner in his own dealings with the concept of person (divine and human) claims the authority of mediaeval tradition lead by Thomas Aquinas, his basic approach to the understanding of personal reality betrays more of a kinship with the Enlightenment and German Idealism, especially that of Hegel. As I have stated before,[67] for Rahner the personhood of God hardly goes beyond the postulate of God's free and absolute subjectivity, just as human personality is laid bare by man's transcendental openness. This is why he feels himself forced in his *Trinity* to reinterpret drastically the divine 'Persons'.[68]

As we have already seen, the so-called modern view of personhood makes Rahner substitute the awkward 'modes or manners of subsistence' for Trinitarian 'Persons'. It seems to me that thereby his own Trinitarian position is weakened, not only from the point of view of traditional devotion to the triunity of God and its supporting traditional speculation,[69] but also as regards what he wants to achieve in his *Trinity*, namely the raising of the hypothesis of unity between the immanent and economic Trinity to the status of a firm Trinitarian principle. Surely Torrance is right when he states:

> If we cannot use 'person' to speak of the intra-Trinitarian relations of Father, Son and Holy Spirit, then we cannot use it to speak of real personal distinctions within the economy of God's self-communication to us in salvation history either.[70]

Hence, even more cogently, he asks:

> If so, then has he not severely damaged his basic axiom that the 'immanent' Trinity is the 'economic' Trinity and *vice versa*?[71]

In fact, I believe that Rahner's attempt at reinterpreting the 'Persons' in the Trinity, when all its implications are examined, is a mistake.

This is why my tentative counterposition suggests another interpretation by reversing the question: it is not the Persons in the Trinity who will first have to be defined in a different terminology, but the underlying divine essence or substance.[72] To say, however, that the whole of divine reality, including its substantial pole, is ruled by what is personal in God, also requires a changed approach to the notion of personhood. For what personal reality is cannot be disclosed from any being's solitary self-consciousness whereby it is related to itself. My only insight into the 'personal' is obtained through the fleeting awareness of awakening love or hate between human selves insofar as this *between* can radically change the subjects in encounter and allow them to *become* persons in the mutuality of their interrelationships. The prelude to this becoming a person is the basic sociality of conscious human subjects, and its fulfilment is either the hardly attainable communion of persons or its contrary – the irretrievable isolation of a person with the consequent loss of selfhood, in hatred. Briefly, both love and hatred are personalizing factors in human life.

This view of personhood does imply, on the anthropological level, that man himself is not yet a person, although he has the possibility of becoming one. It gives a new twist to common-sense parlance that counts as persons those with whom we have no special acquaintance. This I regard as improper usage, as compared to the person and persons which may subsequently emerge from such relationships. One *becomes* a person by meeting one's fellows, as I said, in love and hatred. Furthermore, it is incorrect to speak of persons in encounter without any qualification; we should rather speak of such an encounter which enables men and women to *become* persons. Of course, this elementary encounter takes place at the dawn of human life, perhaps already with one's mother in the womb, and in early childhood within the family. Hence, it is a mistake to hold that every conceived and potential human being is a person. There is obviously another sense (on an advanced level) in which I can speak of an encounter between persons. This presupposes the success or failure of the elementary encounter and takes place when men and women who have already become personal meet. This encounter of persons might deepen in the social and communal history of their respective personhood, as well as enhance and widen the respective fellowships in which they have become persons. On the elementary level I can speak of the coming-to-be of the *primary* personhood, whereas on the advanced level I can best characterize the further becoming of persons with a word borrowed from biblical usage: *covenant* is the deepening event of advanced personhood.

3.4.2 The Personhood of God

These anthropological preliminaries are not meant to underpin a logical reasoning which would lead me to the doctrine of the immanent Trinity; they serve to create a terminology by means of which I can speak of the becoming of three Persons within God's personal reality. For this is the way he reveals himself to us: Father, Son and Holy Spirit. In fact, God's personal reality consists in the coming-to-be of these three.

If personhood is to be understood – neither as the highest perfection of being as such, nor as the peak of consciousness, but rather as an interrelationship – then I cannot envisage the one God, who reveals himself as personal reality, without a counterpart. He cannot be a solitary God. On the contrary, the personhood of God arrived at through metaphysical reasoning or, as God as *the* Mystery who *has being*, as in Rahner's later insight, could remain alone in his solitariness. Now, the question is: how are we able to speak of definite persons in God's personal reality as perceived in the revelation of Jesus the Christ?

Granted, in the sense of my definition of personhood, God could be regarded as personal inasmuch as he lets his creature become a personal counterpart of its Creator. From this position, however, it would follow that in himself God is not a personal reality unless he creates: he *must* create in order to become personal. Yet along this line of reasoning, which is indeed that of the process theologians, I could at most argue for the different roles the one God assumes in his venture into the realm of the non-divine and sum up these different roles with the traditional names of the three persons. In this way, however, I would *not* be lead to an adequate doctrine of the immanent Trinity.

But there is another way, which I have suggested by my description of personhood. I have distinguished a primary and a secondary becoming of the person. Just as the infant who becomes a person in his or her immediate relationships before going on to be further personalized in the wider circle of society, so I could envisage the coming-to-be of the Father, the Son and the Spirit. In the relationship which emerges between the personal God and his creation I can speak only of a secondary personhood, whereas faith – though only theoretically – can envisage the immanent Trinity as the process of primary personalization in the life of God.

This insight can be illustrated by the experience of a specifically Christian faith. In coming-to-faith the believer is said to become 'new creation' (a new personality). This process cannot mean primary but secondary personalization. Nonetheless it comes about by a correlation between the believer and Jesus Christ whom he acknowledges as the Son of God, the Father. Thus the believer's relationship terminates not exactly to Jesus or to God the Father, but to the relationship of the two. And this is on account of which the believer is made capable of acknowledging Jesus as the *Kyrios*. The question remains how he will understand and explain his own capability of confessing Jesus as the Son of God, and how he will perceive that relationship on account of which Jesus *is* the Son of God, the Father. In any case, the believer is now able to see that the divine Persons emerge from this relationality.

If, indeed, relationality is that out of which persons arise, and if God is believed to be personal, it is easy to see the coming-to-be of at least two persons. And so it was in the course of history. The third Person of the Godhead was, in a sense, a 'latecomer'. The temptation to confess a duality in God was recurrent. It was also motivated by man's experience of evil and of his own impotence in facing the sovereign freedom of God. This experience engendered fear of his wrath, or even divided the Deity into two sources of good and evil. This kind of fear is active and present in the Old Testament and even rebounds in the New.

Now, New Testament revelation in its message overcomes this fear, for the relationship of these two is perceived as an unfathomable fellowship, constantly defined by the two and consummated in mutual love. In the belief of this communion of love between the Father and the Son, a third is implied. For what irrevocably seals this fellowship of two freedoms if not a third defined as everlasting love? The God of the New Testament is not revealed as the two in relationship, but also as an ineffable communion, qualified as love. Faith, though indeed only theoretically, cannot avoid personalizing this loving fellowship within the intimate life of God, even apart from its relationship to the creature. That it is indeed, as the in-between of the Father and Son, a person on its own, and not just a quality of their relationship, or a power which holds them together. It is also surmised from this belief that only in sharing this loving fellowship, in the Holy Spirit of God can we say 'Jesus is the *Kyrios*' (1 Cor 12:3). The believer's new personalization, the new creation, cannot emerge from an a-personal relationship. Hence the belief that the Holy Spirit, like the Father and Son, is the third Person of God's triunity.

I do not propose to discuss in exactly what kind personhood can be attributed to the Spirit. Is the Spirit a person in the very same way as the Father and the Son are? Or, does personhood apply to him only in an analogous sense?[73]

The answers to these questions depend on the analogy with which I try to visualize the communion subsisting between the Father and the Son. The best of these, I find, is still that of the intimate community of husband and wife. This community in its persistence cannot be explained by the partners' free decision alone. It is often the case that their covenant is kept alive by the free will of a third party. And this third party has a life and freedom of its own: it is a person such as, for instance, the parents' offspring, or God, in a Christian marriage, making the union not only permanent in the partners' intention but also irrevocable. One could also speculate that a human love relationship arises out of the meeting of two 'I's', whereby the 'I' encounters the 'Thou' in the 'We' of their fellowship. This 'We' is not only an in-between of the couple's relationship: it is, though not quantitatively, more than the two persons together. However, these analogies miss one important point: in the meeting and loving encounter of human beings, there arises but a covenantal unity between two who have already become persons on their own in their primary personalization. Theirs is but a covenant, and the common 'We' they pronounce is, at the most, that of a collective personality and not itself a person.

By applying these personal analogies to the personal reality of God, I should be able to envisage the coming-to-be of the Trinitarian Persons out of their primary, and not their advanced, personalization. This requires an even higher degree of abstraction which I shall nevertheless attempt to outline.

The God of revelation is a personal, hence relational, reality. This means infinite possibilities, including that of nothingness. Tradition named it 'abyss', the *pelagos* of the unfathomable Divinity. Out of this abyss there emerges a relationship, with its opposite: two persons in relationship, whom I call the Father and the Son. They mutually define one another: sonship cannot exist without fatherhood and *vice versa*. However, their relationship itself is not yet qualified, unless they define it as irrevocable love in its mutuality. This mutual love is not to be envisaged as two acts meeting somewhere in the in-between of the already existing relationship, but rather as a personal force which holds them together. Though this love takes its origin from the Father and the Son, it has a definite role within the Godhead. It defines itself as the inseparable communion between the two – it defines the persistent love-relationship and thereby an unceasing fellowship. I speak in traditional terms of the *spiration* of the Holy Spirit from both (*patre filioque procedit*) within the *eternal becoming* of God's personal reality. This is what I might call God's primary personalization: the divine Persons arise out of their mutual relationship in which each is defined by the relationship to the others, while out of the same relationships each define according to traditional parlance, his personal 'role' within the life of the Godhead.

As regards the bipolarity of God, however, as I have already argued above, the inner-Trinitarian history of God is not yet complete: there is another aspect of God's becoming. The divine Persons do not only *define* each other and define themselves in their personal roles, but their free mutuality *posits* or delimits God's substantial reality.

This 'substance' of God is the ontological unity and oneness of his nature, similar to that irrevocable loving unity of the Persons in the Holy Spirit. However, the ontological unity of God's nature is not identical with the Pneuma. Yet it could not have been posited without the qualifying mediation of that Person who subsists in the mutuality of love between the Father and the Son. Thus, the ontological oneness of God, posited by the Three will be perceived by faith as eternal fidelity, of a God who is love.

3.4.3 The Triunity of God

The Christian image of God is that of the Father, the Son and the Holy Spirit in their ineffable oneness. This insight presupposes the Church's doctrine on the Trinity and is at the background of Rahner's *Theos* article. The way to this image is not by means of human reasoning but through man's listening to divine revelation and reflecting upon faith corresponding to it. In my cumbersome dialogue with Rahner and his critics I have been implicitly led by a model according to which this image could gradually emerge. Now is the time to sum it up.

According to Rahner we have assumed a human experience corresponding to this faith. This experience, however, was not directly of God, looming at the edge of man's transcendental horizon. Nor was it disclosed in the mystery of his self-revelation, but in the *history* of human salvation beginning with man's *faith* in creation and ending in his commitment to a still outstanding fulfilment which has been promised to him. In this span of history God has appeared to mankind neither as a supreme being nor the fulness of reality, but as the paramount *possibility* for men and women as free agents in search of their salvation. God, his existence and essence is not to be guessed or concluded to, but to be *encountered* as we meet another person. This means that the content of revelation as perceived by faith refers to *who* this God is and *how* he is the possibility of salvation. Briefly, God's self-revelation, beginning with creation, is about his being a person related to human history.

In reflecting on this experience Rahner is justified in speaking of the common element between the emerging image of God in himself and the corresponding experience of faith: God is history, or there is a history within God's life. Although he wants at the same time to maintain the eternal changelessness of the Absolute, his manner of speaking is such that I felt myself justified, inspired by the process theologians, to interpret God, in his immanent *bipolarity*. To bring these two approaches (Rahner's and the process theologians') to the image of God together is by no means artificial, provided I can amend their vistas. God is a free agent in facing his *infinite* possibilities in which he can realize himself. He is not, he constantly *becomes* in his personal pole of being. And in his 'becoming' God 'posits' that which and how he, in his substantial pole, unchangeably wants to be.

Now, the same history manifests God himself through the story of Jesus the Christ in the threefold fashion of being his Father who in faith becomes *our* Father and in his Spirit abiding not only in the assembly of the faithful, but also in our hearts. In the experience of faith in the personal God of salvation is implied what Rahner calls the *economic Trinity*. However, to conclude from this the so-called *immanent Trinity* is possible neither from their partial identification (Rahner: the second being the condition of possibility in knowing the first) nor is it a matter of direct revelation (the immanent being simply the same as the economic Trinity). It remains always speculation: there is but a *theoretical link* between the two.

Nonetheless, this speculation allows us to figure out the 'history' of God without and with creation. God's history is twofold: out of his personal pole there emerge those relationships which constitute at least two in the Godhead, traditionally called Father and Son, Source and Logos. I name them, *pace* Rahner, 'persons', since personhood is neither the peak of conscious egohood nor is it the highest perfection of being. To be a person is becoming oneself in relation to another. It is more in the category of possibility (since it is always in the making) than in that of being and reality. It is the emergence of *Thou* enabling the *I* to become. This becoming, however, is not without qualification. In God the relationship of Father and Son is held by the communion of Love, or, as we said, by their common *We*, traditionally called the Spirit of love. This is God's timeless but eternal becoming in his personal pole. Along with it, as an adjective of this last emergence, is posited God's constant and irrevocable substantial quality also to be freely manifested in case of his self-revelation. This is why the purpose of God's self-disclosure in creation, in grace and in final sanctification is not the revelation of the three but their 'personal unity',[74] their communion in unbounded Love.

It is this love which is the hidden content of our experiencing God as personal; it is the centre of our faith in being created; it is this love which in an advanced personalization encounters the already personal God in grace (that is, grace works through a deepening sense of that communion in which one is already engaged. Man can become one with the personal God *because, and in the measure that*, he has found his unity in the relationship with his human fellows); it is this love that, in encountering Jesus of Nazareth, will make us confess him to be the *Kyrios*, the Lord, one in being with God.

Chapter 4

God Incarnate: The Doctrine of Jesus the Christ

Every road in Rahner's thinking leads through the Mystery of Christ to God. The closeness of God's Mystery to man would not be a matter of concrete experience without the presence of the God-Man, Jesus the Christ. The self-communication of God that constitutes man in a supernatural order would be void without its divine and human objective, and the Word of God that becomes in man's faith the word of human acceptance would not be understandable unless the doctrine of the Incarnation is assumed. In order that man may be a mystery to himself, he must share in the divinity of Jesus Christ. Rahner's whole theology has, as he likes to say[1], an incarnational structure. In it God becomes human in order that man may become divine.

Yet it is a most difficult task to present Rahner's Christological thought in a unified way. Indeed, a short glance at his published work[2] or perusal of the 145 pages he devotes to Jesus the Christ in his *Foundations*[3] might frighten anyone who tries to tackle him at this centre of his theology. It is also remarkable that amongst the ever-growing secondary literature on Rahner, there are but few monographs analysing his Christology as compared with other aspects of his writings.[4] Nonetheless, attempts at briefly formulating Rahner's position in books dealing with modern Christology are more numerous.[5]

Neither these authors nor I have an easy task in attempting a systematic presentation of Rahner's doctrine. I shall begin by following the guidance of W. Kasper who, at the outset of his own Christology in his *Jesus the Christ* gives an overall summary of Rahner's views,[6] which may guide the procedure of my own Rahner presentation.

Since my approach to Rahner's theology in this volume is doctrinal, I shall first sum up Rahner's critical attitude to classical Christology, after which the question will inevitably arise of the systematic centre of his own position. In my answer I shall, despite the comparative silence in *Foundations*, defend the view that the underlying systematic principle organizing Rahner's position on Christ is his theory of symbolism. For, in my view, the implicit application of this theory gives rise to the thoroughly anthropological 'message' of Rahner's Christology and its own biblical verification.

Although in presenting Rahner's position I shall not be able to avoid critical hints at his Christ interpretation, I shall devote my conclusion to an overall reaction to Rahner's view, from which the outlines of an alternative approach to Christology will emerge.

4.1 Method in Presenting Rahner's Christology

Lucidity in presentation and wide-ranging scholarship seldom go hand-in-hand, especially in Germany. From among the many Christologies since the publication in 1964 of W. Pannenberg's *Jesus God and Man,*[7] in my view Kasper's work, published in 1976 (the year of Rahner's *Foundations*), admirably unites these two qualities.[8]

Hence, I shall borrow, by way of introduction, a summary view of Rahner's Christology from Kasper's book.[9]

4.1.1 Kasper's Summary View of Rahner's Christology

The category under which Kasper characterizes Rahner's position on Christ is, forseeably, its anthropological orientation: *eine anthropologisch gewendete Christologie.*

The general problem of Christological belief is how to account for the fact that one ascribes an unsurpassable meaning to a man who, as an individual, once lived in human history. Is this significance something that can be attributed to this man on account of his being at the same time God? Since in this age of modern humanism the repetition of the early formulations of this belief is not an adequate response, Rahner undertook, with many of his colleagues, to find his way to a Christology in the contemporary setting.

His starting point is man's transcendental orientation to the fullness of reality as perceived in the form of an all-embracing mystery. Man, now defined in his essence by this transcendental thrust, strives to realize his own mysterious self. The highest form of this human self-realization is the Incarnation of God in Jesus the Christ.

Rahner wants his Christology to be a radicalized anthropology and at the same time maintains, unlike others, that this highest realization of humanity has been uniquely achieved in the case of Jesus.[10]

This approach, on its negative side, suggests a critical attitude to traditional dogmatic tenets in Christology and introduces a demythologizing tendency concerning beliefs about Jesus the Christ. Yet, on the positive side, it allows access to the doctrine of Christ, as it were, 'from below' – that is, from the point of view of an anonymous faith in Christ which is in search of the God-man. It goes from the implicit to the explicit. Rahner's Christology is in fact an extension of transcendental theology, as applied to the actual relationship to Jesus the Christ as lived in the beliefs of the Christian churches. His investigation is guided by man's transcendental orientation towards God's Mystery. The condition of possibility of this human search is a historical event as realized in one concrete person. Before, however, giving a proper name to this person, Rahner calls him the 'absolute bringer of salvation' or the 'absolute Saviour'.[11] In this 'person' man's destiny is concretely achieved, since he is the one in whom God's absolute and irrevocable acceptance (*Selbstzusage*) of mankind is complete. In this manner, God is in Jesus of Nazareth. From this it should follow that Jesus the Christ is the unique and concrete possibility of our being human.

Kasper presents this transcendental disclosure of the Idea of Christ (the absolute bringer of salvation) as the quintessence of Rahner's Christology.

But, he hastens to add, this approach

> . . . is often misunderstood, as if Rahner wished to derive the content of Christology *a priori* from human thought . . . Rahner's transcendental method may not be made to approximate to Kant's. Rahner in fact warns us against the illusion that a transcendental Christology could be made to work by methodological abstraction from the historical Jesus Christ. Only as a second step does he consider the transcendental conditions of this perception, and then as a third step reveals the Christ-idea

as the objective correlative of the transcendental structure of man and his knowledge.[12]

To put Kasper's summary into an even more compressed form: in Rahner's Christology, every man and woman by their being human has the capacity to arrive at the Idea of Christ (= transcendental Christology). Who, however, this Christ is, is the matter of a previous (and *a posteriori*) encounter (= categorial Christology). Whereas transcendental Christology can hit upon the idea of the Incarnation, Rahner does not mean to say that every man and woman will acknowledge its concrete counterpart. This possibility is gratuitous and by no means necessary. But once this realization becomes an event, the

> problem is not that something like that does in fact happen, but how, where and when one is present of whom all that can be asserted.[13]

This latter seems to be the task of a categorial Christology. Thus, Kasper, in summarizing Rahner's doctrine, insists first of all on its anthropological character. Most of it belongs to the field of fundamental theology. Since in the latter,[14] the transcendental method dominates, he will, secondly, characterize Rahner's Christology as one built up 'from below' – an ascendent kind of Christology. Thirdly, Kasper sees the whole procedure of Rahner's doctrine on Christ within the interaction of the transcendental *versus* the categorial.

One wonders if Rahner would agree with this summary of the method he has followed in the many thousands of words of his Christological reflections. Do Kasper's three points mean that an anthropologically-oriented Christology of necessity approaches the doctrine of Christ 'from below'? Is this anthropological substratum the foundation of, or even an *a priori* reason for, this doctrine?

Furthermore, if Rahner's Christology is expanded in the tension between the transcendental and the categorial then precisely which aspects of our whole Christological conviction are to be taken for the categorial? Are, for instance, Christological dogmas categorial facts to be reflected upon transcendentally or is the categorial rather the Christ-image of the Bible? In the welter of words of Rahner's reflection on Christ the reader can hardly follow one line of argument.

4.1.2 'Descending' and 'Ascending' Christology

Many years ago, when trying to come to grips with Rahner's fragmentary early publications on Christology, I thought that his approach could easily be summed up by presenting it from two angles: a Christology 'from below', on the one hand, and 'from above' on the other. The first would stand for Rahner's efforts to make the Mystery of Christ palatable for modern man, whereas the second would discuss the explicit Christological beliefs of the Church. At that time these two were familiarized by Pannenberg with the terms 'ascendent' *versus* 'descendent' Christology.[15] The second begins with the divinity of Christ, with the concept of the Incarnation as central, whereas the former rises from the historical man, Jesus, in encounter with man to the recognition of his divinity. It is 'ascendent' Christology which is concerned with Jesus' message and fate and leaves to the end the concept of the Incarnation. Given this distinction, it seemed obvious that Rahner in the systematic presentation of his thought, unlike Pannenberg, opted for both.

It was, however, 'Basic Types', written in 1971, which threw doubt on the above simple scheme. First, Rahner was aware of, but re-names, these two types of Christology; for him, the descendent line is metaphysical, whereas the ascendent type of Christology builds on salvation history. However, in the way Rahner characterizes these two types the lucidity of Pannenberg's distinction is lost. For there is a third element overlapping both: it is Rahner's transcendental Christology. As we shall see later in this chapter, it is neither 'ascendent' or 'descendent': it is, rather, meant to express the basic unity of the two types which, on their own, can come to different conclusions.

To avoid this disunity, Rahner in 'Basic Types' argues their interdependence: 'descendent' and 'ascendent' Christologies mutually condition one another. The former, as he puts it, has a

> . . . secondary and interpretative character. It may again and again in order to achieve intelligibility [*um sich selbst zu verstehen*] and to justify its own propositions, be forced to return to the quite simple experience of Jesus of Nazareth.[16]

Ascendent Christology, on the other hand, will find its usefulness of the other 'as the necessary criterion for rightly understanding the assertions it contains'.[17]

Now, the reason for this unity in difference is that the two types come together, as it were, from different directions in the 'Idea of Christ', that is, in the God-man, the absolute Saviour in whom God's definitive and irrevocable acceptance (*Zusage*) of mankind has become an event. Transcendental Christology, as sandwiched between the two main types, has to express this central conviction.

Without entering into Rahner's concept of transcendental Christology, I should note its methodological position. It is, I believe, in *Foundations* where this concept and its role has been finally crystallized. Formerly, one might have understood this approach as a kind of foreknowledge (*Vorgriff*) of Christ before any acquaintance either with the Christological dogmas or the concrete encounter with Jesus the Christ. In this way the criterion of an *a posteriori* faith in Christ would have been understood as the *a priori* and transcendental idea and not *vice versa*. Not so in *Foundations*.

Although Rahner can affirm that the 'Idea of Christ' can emerge in so-called anonymous Christians, as well as in non-Christian religions,[18] he hastens to add that an *a priori* Idea of Christ can only arise owing to a historically prior and actual encounter with him: 'We always reflect upon conditions of possibility for a reality which we have already encountered.'[19] Accordingly

> ... a transcendental Christology ... does not begin with the presupposition that we know absolutely nothing in our historical experience about Jesus as the Christ, as the absolute Saviour;[20]

the 'Idea of Christ' is the product of

> a transcendental Christology ... which asks about the *a priori* possibilities which are found in man or for an understanding of the dogma about Christ, arises in fact only subsequent to and because of a historical encounter with Jesus as the Christ.[21]

Further, the 'Idea of Christ' 'cannot by definition be produced and constructed "from outside".'[22] It always refers to something concrete and historical, it explains the mutually conditioning elements of, what I call, 'ascendent' and 'descendent' Christologies. Both speak of a relationship of God through Christ to man and this relationship has to be such that it fulfills man's transcendental thrust.

There is, therefore, a certain circularity implied in transcendental Christology, and I shall not be wrong if I illustrate Rahner's whole methodology as follows:
(a)   encounter in faith with Jesus the Christ;
(b)   the Christological doctrines interpreting the same;
(c)   transcendental Christology which makes the ensuing relationship for man acceptable.

Without any doubt (c) will be of paramount importance in Rahner's Christology forming, so to speak, an empty mould to be filled with elements of (b) and (a). Both the concrete encounter and the doctrines will finally be accepted by means of transcendental Christology as their condition of possibility (c). It is a theological attempt to speak about the Mystery of Jesus the Christ.

4.1.3 Presentation of Procedure
From the medial position of transcendent Christology I am entitled to start from either (b) or (c) – from the concrete encounter as the 'ascending' line or from the doctrines about Christ as the 'descending' one of Christology. For Rahner, both ways will appeal to the 'Idea of Christ'. It is not a criterion either for the truth of Christological dogmas (b) or for man's encounter with the concrete shape of Christ as it emerges from the Bible and is preached to us by the Church (a). Transcendental Christology is a methodological device which helps us to understand and to follow Christ in a life's engagement.

And indeed Rahner's developing thought on the Mystery of Christ, whether it was a defence and/or a criticism of Christological dogmas in his early articles, or the summary and/or evaluation of Biblical data about Christ, pointed in this direction.[23] Hence it will be defensible if in my presentation I do not start with transcendental Christology, but rather show how gradually Rahner felt himself forced to go this way. In what follows in this chapter I shall present him almost chronologically. My starting point, therefore, is neither (c) nor (a): that is, neither the concrete encounter with the 'categorial' Christ nor with the 'Idea of Christ' of transcendental Christology, but the dogma of Chalcedon. The descent of God, his coming near to us in Christ is the point where my dialogue with Rahner's Christology begins.

4.2 The Reinterpretation of Chalcedon

For any theologian with a claim to orthodoxy, the launching pad for Christology is the dogma of Chalcedon. In 451 AD, after centuries of wearisome debates, the Church arrived at an apt summary of her Christological faith.[24] In Jesus Christ the unity of two 'natures' (*physeis*), divine and human, was achieved in the one 'person' (*prosopon*) or concrete subject (*hypostasis*) of the Logos, the second divine Person. These two natures are unmixed and unchanged. The *asynchytos* and *atreptos* of the formula exclude the possibility that, as a result of the Incarnation, Jesus Christ will be a being between God and man. The togetherness of the two natures is such that Christ is not divided, not separated, *adiairetos*, acting now as a man and then again as God. Nor can the two natures ever be separated. Christ was and remains truly God and man. His being is *achoristos*.

This, however, is a technical description of *what* Jesus Christ is. The term selected to express this ultimate subject was the 'Person' or 'hypostasis'. The whole unity was later referred to as the hypostatic or personal union. It is hypostatic insofar as the same being is the ultimate subject of all qualities and actions. It is a personal union because this subject unites the two otherwise separate natures.

4.2.1 The Limits of a Dogmatic Formulation

In the conclusion of his authoritative work on the early history of Christology, A. W. Grillmeier agrees with Rahner that the dogma expresses the 'ancient tradition in a formula corresponding to the needs of the hour'.[25] This means that neither the use of the terms nor their exact meaning was definitive. They were to be employed in further Christological thought and to be filled with a content later to be developed. Rahner, for his part, states in 'Christology' the dogma of Chalcedon 'was not an end but a beginning'.[26] We cannot get away from it altogether, yet we can go beyond it. The general reason for this is obvious to both Rahner and Grillmeier: we cannot encapsulate the Mystery of the Christ in a single dogmatic definition. The act of faith goes beyond these static sounding Greek terms, it needs an ever-developing reinterpretation. As we shall presently see, Rahner's future Christological thought is in a way a challenge to, as well as a reinterpretation of, the dogma.

Rahner's main quarrel with Chalcedon's formula in its historical emergence is that it was too little and too late to adequately emphasize Christ's salvific mediatorship. It was too late in view of the fact that in the wake of post-Nicene controversies there became established in the mentality of the Church's Christological belief an underlying mythical feeling, of which the Council was not able to rid orthodox faith. The Incarnation was envisaged according to the, so-called, Logos-sarx schema (a by now dubious catchword introduced through the early writings of Grillmeier: the divine Logos saved man in becoming flesh). In this concept, the humanity of Christ has tended to be, if not a mere appearance (docetism), at least a lifeless instrument in the hands of the Godhead acting through it. The *anthropos* in the union of the God-man is not really the mediator. It is like a workman's overall which the Saviour-Logos puts on in order to accomplish the job of mankind's salvation.

'The representation of a god's becoming man is mythological', as Rahner repeatedly says, 'when the "human" element is merely the clothing, the livery, of which the god makes use in order to draw attention to his presence here with us . . . '[27] To be sure, Christian orthodoxy immediately before and after the Council tried to ascribe an independent validity (*Eigengültigkeit*) to Christ's human nature. But was not this only a nominal concession to a mentality and devotion which in the past produced Apollinaris (who allowed the Logos to substitute for Christ's human spirit), at the time of the Council an Eutyches (who, in the God-man, allowed the human to be absorbed by the divine: monophysitism), and soon after Sergius of Constantinople (who attributed only one divine will, or operation, to Christ: monothelitism)? Does not this state of affairs argue that the two natures formula of Chalcedon was but an empty compromise which paid mythical dividends in subsequent history and even up to the present day?

This is why Rahner explicitly puts the question:

> Is it possible from the basic Chalcedonian doctrine itself actually to evolve the account . . . how far Jesus can be the Mediator between us and God?[28]

Thus, Rahner's main concern in Christology, if I may so put it, is not Christological but soteriological. To ask about the mediatorship of Christ is to ask about man's possible salvation. It is from this point of view that he radically reinterprets the Chalcedonian formula by isolating its validity and even reducing its content to the bare minimum. Instead of involving myself in his intricate argument, peppered in 'Christology' with innumerable question marks, I shall *anticipate* his *latest* Christological summary in *Foundations*. Here, too, the same concern is apparent, when he states:

> The real incarnation of the Logos is indeed a mystery which calls for an act of *faith*. But this should not be burdened with a lot of mythological misunderstandings.[29]

This is why Rahner, in summing up his review of classical (Chalcedonian) Christology, first of all isolates the validity of the ancient formula:

> The legitimacy and the permanent validity [of this latter] lies . . . in the fact that when it is presupposed it prevents Jesus unambiguously from being reduced merely to someone in a line of prophets, religious geniuses and reformers, and from being incorporated within the course of an ongoing history of religion.[30]

At the same time, Rahner tends to reduce the content of the dogma to its religious point of departure: the doctrine entailed in the dogma of the hypostatic union says of the God-man no more and no less than, 'the interchange of predicates in both an ontic and a logical sense; because one and the same Logos-subject or person or hypostasis bears both "natures" substantially'.[31]

This, according to Rahner, is the ultimate kernel of the dogma and its ultimate meaning is to maintain the doctrine of *communicatio idiomatum*. This formula as 'the official teaching of the Church' is in itself not adequate for further development, yet it remains a last critical norm 'for any further trials to express the very same truth'.[32]

How does Rahner try to express the same truth? Briefly, I can sum up at least the principles of his attempt at developing this, in itself isolated and reduced, standpoint in three catchwords: dynamic union, real becoming, and 'ontological' unity.

I shall try to describe these three, for the time being, without regard to their soteriological significance, yet in relation to the mainstream of the Church's Christological thought.

4.2.2 The Dynamic Union

It was Leontius of Byzantium who, in the sixth century, in defence of the Chalcedonian formula, found an ingenious solution between a resurgent monophysitism and a persistent Nestorianism.[33] The monophysites disliked the formula because to them the hypostatic or personal union still presupposed a duality in Christ. No more were the Nestorians satisfied because, in their eyes, hypostatic or personal union was as good as a simple oneness in which the divine absorbs the humanity of Christ and inevitably leads to monophysitism or monothelitism. Now, Leontius propounded the theory that the human nature *before* the union had no hypostasis or concrete personal centre of its own (*anhypostasia*); however, after the union had taken place the human nature was personalized by being united with the Logos (*enhypostasia*).[34] With this, in my view, a new perspective emerged in the interpretation of Chalcedon. The attempt to resolve the paradox of the unity between two concrete natures was no longer a matter of mental acrobatics. Thus, Leontius opened the way to considering God's becoming man as a dynamic act of *union* instead of trying to think about a possible *unity* of two ready-made natures.

Rahner's Christological speculation, it seems to me, is built (though unwittingly) on the presupposition of Leontius. He too, conceives of a dynamic *union* between the Chalcedonian two natures instead of trying to fit the two components into a state of *unity*: the act of union (*die einende Einheit*) is one thing and the resultant unity (*die geeinte Einheit*) is another.[35] The advantage of this proposal is that we are able to envisage the Incarnation and the Logos incarnate on two levels. With Cyril of Alexandria we can speak of a dynamic union, of God's real becoming in Jesus the Christ, whereas with the Chalcedonians (those who wanted to implement the correct but perhaps exaggerated insight of Nestorius)[36] we can attribute a certain autonomy (*Eigenständigkeit*) to the man Jesus, on the level of the resultant unity.

Hence, to an extent hand-in-hand with Leontius of Byzantium, Rahner is on the side of Cyril in admitting a certain becoming of God's nature (*physis*) in the Incarnation. Yet, in order to safeguard this view against a monophysite misunderstanding, Rahner allows for a certain subjectivity, an *energeia* in the created nature of Jesus.[37] It is here that the question of unity again arises. What is the force working in this dynamic unification? Contrary to all expectation, it is not the personal Logos of God who thereby 'breaks' the enclosed Trinitarian circle, or, as Rahner later termed it in *Foundations*, 'the point of unity'[38] is going to be God's creative self-communication. This is the basic paradigm of the Incarnation and its minor case is: God creating the world of man. An opening is made from the Mystery of the Incarnation to the mystery of man. The means is creation.[39]

4.2.3 God's Real Becoming

In his comprehensive survey of the hypostatic union in scholastic speculation, P. Kaiser[40] devotes an important chapter to Rahner's theory of the Incarnation. In fact, in summing up his research, Kaiser holds that Rahner's approach from the pattern of creation to the theological understanding of the Incarnation, is one of the most viable in contemporary theology. Decidedly, this is Rahner's basic insight. Indeed, already in 'Christology', he indicates the direction he will take beyond the problematic formula of Chalcedon.

'Christological considerations', he says:

> have led the way back to the more general doctrine of God's relation to the creature and allowed Christology to appear as the clearly unique 'specifically' distinct perfection of this relation.[41]

Hence, he asks:

> Would it not be possible to go further without abandoning classi-

cal Christology and make use of the concepts in terms of which the relation of created things to God is conceived?[42]

There is, of course, nothing very new in this statement. After all, did not the comparison between creation out of nothing clinch the early Arian disputes about the divinity of Christ? The Logos was begotten not made, but his human nature, his *sarx*, with which for our sake he united himself, was *created* by God. Whereas in the anti-Arian controversies of Athanasius, the concept of creation was used to illustrate by way of contrast God's becoming man, Rahner is going to use this same notion as the source, the point of unity, of the act of Incarnation. For him this concept of creation is God's creative act which enables the creature to exist in its relative autonomy, yet in such a way that it can remain totally dependent upon God. Thus the unity achieved in the Incarnation is the superlative case of creation. This, therefore, is Rahner's basic insight:

> We must conceive of the relation between the Logos-Person and his human nature in . . . this sense that here [i.e. in the general creature-Creator relationship] both independence [i.e. in the autonomy of human nature] and radical proximity equally reach a unique and qualitatively incommensurable perfection, which nevertheless remains once and for all the perfection of a relation between Creator and creature.[43]

The reason is, again in Rahner's own words:

> It is only in the case of God that it is conceivable at all that he himself can constitute something in a state of distinction from himself. This is precisely an attribute of his divinity as such and intrinsic *creativity*.[44]

This, however, is only the bare framework of Rahner's theory. Admittedly, he says that by duly emphasizing the specific nature of God's intrinsic creativity in the case of the Incarnation, we might already imply the content, the *what* of the dogma (that is, the hypostatic union).[45] But theology also has to seek the how of this event: *how* God unites himself specifically with one human being in such a way that in this Creator-creature relationship not only the created term is changed, or comes to be, but God himself is affected. If God himself does not change how can we really speak of the salvific value of the Incarnation? Rahner's motive is, again, soteriological when he asks whether such an Incarnation would

> have helped us at all, both when we take seriously the proposition that he [the Logos] became flesh and when we take seriously . . . that by becoming flesh he remained immutable and intact?[46]

Referring to the Scythian monks who earnestly affirmed that 'one of the Trinity suffered death', Rahner thus puts the key question about the Incarnation: *how can an, in himself immutable, God change and become flesh?* His theory of the Incarnation is a response to this question.

In explaining his position in 'Christology', he proceeds, so to speak, *per modum negationis*. We cannot envisage God's active union with man in such a way that he unites himself with a ready-made human nature. Instead, the traditional adage recommends itself – *ipsa assumptione creatur*; in the very fact that God unites himself with a human nature the latter is also brought about. This view is more on the lines of Rahner's thought, since according to it, God not only enables a human nature to be, but also constitutes it in such a way that it can be assumed into unity with the Logos. Nevertheless, this understanding of the adage can be misleading. It can still be asked, on the one hand, is Christ's humanity the same as ours and, on the other, does the thus assumed humanity affect the one who has assumed it? The dreaded danger of monophysitism is still lurking in the background.

There remains, however, a more correct sense in which the phrase *ipsa assumptione creatur* can be explained. The dynamic act of union (*die einende Einheit*) is the self-same ground out of which a total diversity from God (that is, human nature co-essential with our own) as well as the substantial unity with God can be brought about.[47] This means that the dynamic union is strictly the basis which makes the human nature existent and at the same time the ground on which this different nature is united with God. This view seems to have a double advantage: first, in substituting the dynamic union for the concept of static unity, Rahner has changed the main question concerning the Mystery. It is no longer that in an act of faith Jesus as God and man is asserted and then in a subsequent act of faith the *unity* of God and man is confessed. The real question, rather, is *through what is* the Logos constantly and permanently united with the manhood of Christ?[48] The content of the dogma, which is the hypostatic union, is already present at this first level of the dynamic union and need not be asserted in a second act of faith concerning the resultant unity with the Chalcedonian adjectives 'unmixed' and 'remaining'. Secondly, it follows from this that in the dynamic uniting of the two natures, God can remain in his immutability, whereas the resultant unity is genuinely the sphere where he truly comes to be in what he constitutes apart from himself. With this proviso, God the unchangeable can truly be said to change.[49]

In the light of these premisses, Rahner can later, in *SM*[50] and also in *Foundations*, undertake a cautious but firm reinterpretation of the 'is' statements of our Christological belief.

> For when we say Peter is a man, the statement expresses a real identification in the content of the subject and predicate nouns. But the meaning of 'is' in statements . . . in Christology is *not* based on such a real identification. It is based rather on a unique, otherwise unknown and deeply mysterious unity between realities which are really different and which are at an infinite distance from each other. For in and according to the humanity which we see when we say 'Jesus', Jesus 'is' not God, and in and according to his divinity God 'is' not man in the sense of a real identification. The Chalcedon *adiairetos* (unseparated) which this 'is' intends to express it in such a way that the *asynchytos* (unmixed) of the same formula does not come to expression . . . [Hence] the identity which they suggest but do not really mean is not excluded clearly and early enough by an explanation given sometime later.[51]

The test of Christian orthodoxy (which has become a shibboleth), 'Do you believe that Christ is God?', is not altogether correct since the *is* in this test and the expected answer to it express for us an unfathomable mystery: the 'becoming' of God in Jesus the Christ.

I can now see that Rahner's improvement of the Chalcedonian formulation depends on the viability of the idea of God's becoming in the Incarnation of the Logos. Whereas in 'Christology', I do not find a clear-cut explanation of this idea (already known to us from Rahner's approach to the Trinity). In his essay 'Incarnation' it emerges, if I may say so, in its Hegelian 'clarity'.[52] The conclusions of this article will then be summed up in a more simple form in *Foundations*.[53] The problem is how to uphold the divine immutability while speaking of a becoming in God. Whereas the first half of this dilemma has to be maintained not only as a metaphysical truth but also as a basic statement of faith, the second is needed for an adequate explanation of what the Incarnation means. For it is not enough to say of this mystery that God becomes and changes *in the other* which he produces. This would mean that in the Incarnation the divine does not change in step with the human and developing life of the man Jesus, although God through his Logos is united with him. In this case Christ's humanity would not, strictly speaking, be a self-communication of God to man, but only a mere instrument of the otherwise unchangeable Logos of God. In order to resolve this impasse, Rahner introduces a non-translatable twist in his German grammar. God, the unchangeable, can become not *in*, but rather *on* the non-divine reality which is the human nature of the God-man.[54] Thus, the Incarnation is an event that happens to God himself, however, only in the sphere of man. In fact, it is contrary to the movement as imagined by adoptionism, in which the history of one man is taken up into the divine. If not elsewhere, Rahner here advocates a descendent Christology, whether he acknowledges it or not.

This descent of God is underpinned by a kenotic-sounding Christology and, to my mind, an almost Hegelian dialectics. Both vehicles are a danger to orthodoxy. Rahner's recurring allusions to biblical texts portraying the manhood of Jesus,[55] which describe the self-emptying as well as the exaltation of Christ, suggest his liking of kenoticism. Yet Rahner's Christology is not kenotic in the sense that the Incarnation means the self-emptying of the divine, the Logos of God renouncing his divinity, or at least the attributes relative to it. For Rahner's kenotic tendency is at the outset combined with an Hegelian element of dialectics:

> The basic element [*Urphänomen*] according to our faith is the self-emptying [*Selbstentäusserung*], the coming to be, the kenosis

and genesis of God himself who can come to be by becoming another thing, derivative in the act of constituting it, without having to change in his own proper reality which is the unoriginated origin.[56]

This does not mean, of course, that God *must* change in emptying himself in such a way. The basic element in the Incarnation now seems to be the same as it was in creation: God

> brings about that which is distinct from himself, in the act of retaining it as his own, and *vice versa*, because he truly wills to retain the other as his own, he constitutes it in its genuine reality.[57]

This dialectical statement, which insists on God's love in giving himself away refers to creation: Rahner speaks of God's power as Creator out of nothing – this is his sovereign possibility. Yet this is only a

> derivative, restricted and secondary possibility, which is ultimately based on the other primal possibility – though the secondary could be realized without the primal.[58]

The primary possibility is the Incarnation.

Precisely out of this *parallelism between creation and Incarnation* can emerge the danger of equating the two doctrines, unless Rahner can save himself by a dialectics obviously dependent on Hegel, whose very words he employs. He adopts Hegel's self-alienating God, who as the absolute subject lives in himself and produces the world through his self-differentiation. Yet, how can this 'other' (whether man or the manhood of Christ), established by God, after it has become radically over and against God, again be united to God?[59] Can he explain the essential difference between the God-man and ordinary humans? Instead of going through the whole history of religious thought as Hegel did, Rahner seems to be satisfied with a verbal solution. He jumps directly from God's 'being himself' in 'the other' to God's unity with the other.[60] The trick he employs in 'Incarnation' is the verbal change of the Hegelian *Selbstäusserung,* the adequate rendering of which is beyond the capacity of the English language.

The first sums up the minor case of the creation and the second refers to the constitution of Christ's manhood. The first is also the radical self-emptying of God in man, his creature, whilst the second is God's self-utterance within the emptiness of man's world (that is, man created is by no means God; the manhood of Christ as created is 'somehow' God). Of Christ he says:

> This man is as such the self-utterance [*Selbstaussage*] of God in its self-emptying [*Selbstäusserung*] because God expresses himself when he empties himself. He proclaims himself as love when he hides the majesty of this love and shows himself in the ordinary way of man.[61]

I might interpose here that otherwise there is the danger of Christ's humanity being only the 'garb of the divine'! But, to continue . . .

> That there are other men who are not this self-utterance of God, not another way of being God himself, does not affect the issue. For 'what' he is, is the same in him [that is, Christ] and us: we call it human nature. But the unbridgeable difference is that in his case [Christ's] the 'what' is uttered as his [God's] self-expression, which it is not in our case.[62]

That 'what' of human nature being equal, it is the 'how' of this divine self-communication in the case of the Logos and of us that makes all the difference.[63]

From this the essential trend of Rahner's theology of the Incarnation becomes obvious. Once the Incarnation is subsumed under the notion of creation, both are to be ascribed to the *becoming* of God who is both immutable in himself and, in a way, changing. Hence, it seems that this becoming of God as regards creation can only be envisaged in the same way as the Logos becoming man. By its very nature the Logos is the self-utterance of God, whether within the life of the immanent Trinity or in the world created by divine generosity.[64]

From this it would follow that creation, if it is freely decreed by God, is – or, rather, aims at – the creation of man. God's self-alienation (*Selbstentäusserung*) into the non-divine *must* be in accordance with his self-differentiation (*Selbstäusserung*) in the

Logos. With this the anthropological turn of his doctrine of the Incarnation will be easily understood. Rahner states:

> We could now define man as that which ensues when God's self-utterance, his Word, is given out lovingly into the void of god-less nothing. Indeed, the Logos made man has been called the abbreviated Word of God. This abbreviation, this code-word for God is man, that is the Son of Man and men who exist ultimately because the Son of Man was to exist. If God wills to become non-God, man comes to be, that and nothing else, we might say. Hence, Christology is the end and the beginning of anthropology. And this anthropology, when most thoroughly realised in Christology, is theology.[65]

In Christ, indeed, we are supposed to encounter *man*, as he really *should* be, free and independent, because he totally depends on God. 'Christ who is most radically man and whose humanity is the freest and most independent not in spite of, but because of its being taken up, by being constituted as the self-utterance of God.'[66] Does, however, this encounter really tell us *who* this free person is?

4.2.4 The Resultant 'Ontological' Unity

Whilst the outlines of Rahner's doctrine of Christ are taking shape, one would also expect the emergence of the concrete God-man whom one is called to encounter. Yet is it enough to state that Jesus must be the highest realization of all creation? We must also ask *who* this creature is. This aspect, in my view, is anticipated by Rahner in the so-called consciousness Christology. The working out of such a Christology presupposes the distinction between the dynamic union and the resultant unity in the God-man.

As we have already seen earlier in this chapter, Rahner assigned the point of unity not to the personal *energeia* of the Logos in becoming flesh, but rather to the creativity of God who can constitute, posit, the other by becoming one with it. Once the Logos has, indeed, become flesh, and only then, can we speak of Christ's *human* consciousness. In other words, whereas in the act of union Rahner's thought is focused on God's creative dynamism and the humanity remains in its creaturely passivity, the state of unity (constantly and permanently maintained by the former) can be characterized by the free activity of the man Jesus who, in his human subjectivity, is or becomes conscious of himself. Rahner can now ask about the free I-centre (*Ich-Zentrum*) of the God-man. Is it here that Christ's free human autonomy can be witnessed by man encountering him? With this starting point the way is open to a genuinely ascendent Christology.

Having it both ways, descendent and ascendent, is not a privilege exclusive to Rahner. A conflation of the Cyrillian tradition of the divine becoming human with the post-Chalcedonian tendency towards an emphasis on the independent validity of the manhood is implied in the method of every Christologist with a claim to orthodoxy. One can be a Cyrillian and a moderate Nestorian at the same time. It is only a question of how one accomplishes the welding of these two opposite traditions. If my hypothesis is correct, Rahner is aiming for this, first of all by means of his early attempts at a consciousness Christology. It is, I believe, already prefigured in his essay 'On the Eternal Significance', published in 1953, a year before 'Christology'.

This essay is still permeated with Rahner's doubt whether the Chalcedonian formula is capable of fending off the resultant crypto-monophysitism prevailing in the Church. Though the *achoristos* (that is, without separation) of Chalcedon, the eternally remaining Godhood and manhood of Jesus is professed, do we attribute any significance to him as man on his way towards fulfilment? Rahner asks, almost passionately,

> where is the clear knowledge, expressed in ontological terms, of the fact that it remains eternally true to say that no one knows the Father except the Son and those to whom he wishes to reveal it: he who sees him, sees the Father?[67]

Even man's eternal fulfilment in the beatific and immediate vision of God is mediated through Christ's humanity. This mediation can only be understood if, as some twenty-four years later, Rahner states, 'We assume that the human nature of Jesus is a created "subjectivity" at least in the sense of a created will, created *energeia*.'[68] But, if Christ eternally remains human, and thus intercedes for us in his glory, then his human nature must be permanent in its integrity: a free, self-conscious and, if I may so add, world-conscious human being.

The problem of how this consciousness can be captured by theological means seems to concern Rahner at the outset of his early essay on Chalcedon in 'Christology'. As I have demonstrated, the pivot of his interest here was the mediatorship of Christ which does not allow the humanity to be a lifeless instrument (otherwise he 'would simply be a mediator to himself').[69] One would, therefore, necessarily have to assume two moral subjects, at least in a psychological sense, in the state of unity, in order to conform to the Chalcedonian two-natures formula. It all depends on what we understand by these two moral subjects in Christ. Now, a moral subject implies an existentially independent I-centre in the man Jesus and the Logos.[70] If this is so, then

> the human nature of the Logos possesses a genuine, spontaneous, free, spiritual, active centre, a human self-consciousness, which as creaturely faces the eternal Word in a genuinely human attitude of adoration and obedience, a most radical sense of creaturehood.[71]

It is self-moving, *autokineton*, with genuine freedom, as Cyril also was to admit after having advocated the becoming of God's *physis*.[72]

Now, this position is threatened by the traditional view that this self-conscious human nature is possessed by the person of the Logos who, right from the beginning of Jesus' life, communicates to his human nature the gift of the Beatific Vision and, in a way, is omniscient.[73]

To Rahner's ear nothing sounds more mythical than this tenet: it would diminish the autonomy of the human in Jesus. For indeed a man already in possession of his fulfilment, seeing the ultimate truth, cannot freely develop towards his goal, not to mention that such a chimerical being is capable of suffering, unless pretending to do so. It would mean again that Jesus' humanity would only be

> the material and the instrument, the recipient of commands, and the manifestation of the single personal centre of freedom. But this is not the case of Jesus.[74]

Rahner takes up this difficulty again in *Foundations* pointing out the monotheistic leaning of this traditional tenet: it leaves Jesus the Christ with but one will, and this is the divine. Such a view

> would overlook the fact that the man Jesus in his human reality exists with a created, active and 'existential' centre or activity *vis-a-vis* God . . . he prays, he is obedient, he makes decisions and in a process of genuine historical development he also has new experiences which surprise him . . . to overlook this is basically to have a mythological understanding of the Incarnation.[75]

Therefore, to maintain the genuineness of Christ's humanity, room must be left within his life for development and achievement.

In 1962, to counter this difficulty, Rahner undertook the drafting of consciousness Christology; this was to become his essay 'Consciousness'. This draft was, later, more cautiously reflected in *Foundations*.[76] To forgo the intricacies of the former,[77] it is sufficient for us to see that Rahner presupposes (with tradition, indeed), on the level of the dynamic union, the factual and ontic presence of the beatific vision in Christ, which gradually comes to the surface of his reflexive consciousness in the state of unity. With this, he avoids the pitfalls of an unorthodox approach, which, willy-nilly, reduces the God-man to an initially ignorant but indefinitely developing human being. This alternative would be adoptionism in a psychological sense.[78] No, as he asserts, the vision of God is not communicated to the man Jesus in objective terms which could then be dominant in his human subjectivity as his life goes through the cross and Resurrection. Consciousness in the man Jesus has a history.[79]

In regard, then, to the alleged beatific vision and 'omniscience' of the pre-Resurrection Christ, Rahner can apply the principles of his metaphysics of knowledge. No human knowing has an immediate vision of objective being. Neither is human consciousness immediately a reflected awareness of man's existent self. Yet we are aware of 'something'. We can become conscious of our being directed to the horizon of our self-transcendence. As will be recalled from Rahner's epistemology, this horizon is objective, but not objectifiable. It arises from what he now calls man's

Grundbefindlichkeit,[80] or his basic ontological constitution. As we go on experiencing our world, this consciousness becomes more and more reflected. Now the 'beatific vision' of Jesus the man arose from his own *Grundbefindlichkeit*. The latter was basically identical with every man's self-transcending capacity, yet different from it insofar as Jesus' being was in unity with the divine Logos. Therefore, 'deep down' in his very being he was always conscious of this union, though this knowledge remained unobjectifiable.[81] Thus, Jesus the man could become more and more aware in his *human* centre of self-consciousness of the *divine* person he always was from the beginning. In the state of unity Jesus could, as it were, gradually 'catch up' with the true personality he had always been.[82]

On the ground of this kind of *enhypostasia* Rahner could attribute an immediate vision of God to the man Jesus, but he refuses to call it 'beatific' before the Resurrection.[83] From this point of view, the 'omniscience' of Jesus is also understandable. Any man (and all the more Jesus) can enjoy, at least a potential omniscience, since his orientation is self-transcendent. It embraces the fullness of being: and with it also, the divine.

So much for the free and developing consciousness of Jesus which is guided not, as in our own case, by the all-embracing horizon of being, but more intimately by the ontic, unobjectifiable presence of the vision on account of the hypostatic union. The horizon of being and union with God are at least isomorphous realities. Both convey a certain kind of immediacy of man to God. Both allow for a developing consciousness to be definitively, and irrevocably, fulfilled at the end. For Rahner's Christology this view is of paramount importance. His introduction of consciousness Christology, as one could surmise, smoothly connects the doctrine of Christ with his scheme of an anthropoontological world view.

From the foregoing it has become apparent that, for Rahner, consciousness is not an entirely psychological phenomenon: it belongs to 'being-present-to-self' (*Beisichsein*), to the ontological constitution of man's being.[84] The categories, with which in Christology he tried to overcome his uneasiness about the Chalcedonian formula, later became ontological ones, on account of his consciousness Christology. By the time of *Foundations* this insight seems to have been firmly established in Rahner's mind.

The Chalcedonian formula, as he says, is conceived in *ontic* terms; it is an ontic Christology which operates with the help of concepts such as 'nature' and 'hypostasis', as derived from the *world of things*. However, Christology in ontic terms can be translated into an *ontological* Christology '. . . whose concepts, paradigms of understanding . . . are orientated . . . towards the original identity . . . of being and consciousness'.[85] In other words, it is not the conception we form of things that rules our Christological terms, but being, the meaning of which we conceive in our consciousness. Only by this translation from ontic to ontological can we envisage Christ's human consciousness in its human development and becoming, because it presupposes in him as in every man, though in a higher degree, a basic ontological constitution, a *Grundbefindlichkeit*: the original unity of being and consciousness. In the case of Jesus this unity basically originates in his hypostatic union with God.

Thus, on the level of unity I can speak of human consciousness in the God-man. Yet it remains to be seen whether all that is implied in this consciousness can supply the answer to the question *who* this person is whom man encounters as Jesus the Christ. I can now see *what* are united – I have already seen *how* this union can be envisaged – but *who* is the person who establishes such a developing plurality in unity – the person who controls, integrates and directs this being in all freedom? Does this person coincide with the function of unifying and integrating the many aspects of human being? Is this 'person' the one ready to be encountered as the personal Logos of God whom the faithful can address with a personal Thou? Rahner was successful in establishing the possibility of talking of Jesus' human psychology, of assuming a human I-centre which is consubstantial with ours. This I-centre is Jesus' consciousness, as it were, 'engraced' with his developing capacity for the vision of God. In a sentence: Rahner speaks of the *human person* in Jesus the Christ. The divine must remain in the background as a force enabling the union of the two natures just as – though to a minor degree – God's grace enables man's union with God. In the man Jesus, God comes near to man, insofar as he allows *the man* Jesus to become God and man. In encountering this man Jesus do we come nearer to the Person of the Logos? What I shall have to ask, querying Rahner's criticism of Chalcedon, is how in his

Christology (apart from God's becoming) the Second *Person* of the Trinity can enter the sphere of our created human life? The answer, I shall argue, is in Rahner's theory of ontological symbolism.

Beyond his critical views of traditional Christological beliefs and consciousness Christology, it is symbolism which allows and underpins a systematic doctrine of Christ.

4.3 Systematic Coherence: Symbol and Christology

Rahner's Christological thought is indeed pluralistic. As I have shown earlier in this chapter, different ancient traditions were conflated in his intererpretation of the dogma (for example, the Cyrillian trait and the *verus homo* of Chalcedon) and various philosophical thought patterns contributed to the further theological explanation of the Mystery (for example, the theological insight of kenoticism and the Hegelian dialectics of 'becoming'; the recurrent use of his own metaphysics of knowledge has helped his ongoing speculations). In presenting and discussing these various layers of Rahner's writings it has not been possible to address every single difficulty which may have emerged at the various stages of his approach to the doctrine. Yet his Christology is of real value only if it eventually results in a *systematic coherence* that collects the different strands of his thought into a more or less unified whole and can be used as an appropriate basis from which the main Christological questions can be answered. Hence, I shall have to explore, under this aspect, the underlying system of Rahner's Christology: a task, in the jargon of Lonergan, of 'systematics'.[86]

Now, systematic coherence within a partial branch of theology (for example, that of Christology) can only be arrived at through an insight which, as a principle, not only holds together the various (sometimes divergent) elements of the same subject matter, but is able to situate it in the whole of theology. From what I have seen, in Rahner's Christology there are several candidates for such a principle.

I could take, for instance, God's 'becoming' as the point of systematic coherence in Christology. Without it, Incarnation could not in Rahner's terms be envisaged. As we recall, on the level of dynamic union through the Logos, God can really become united with human nature. This 'becoming' of God is the condition of possibility for the dogmas of Ephesus and Chalcedon defining the state of unity between the divine and the human in the person of Jesus.

So I could take as a similar principle the coherence of creation and Incarnation which was obviously at the back of Rahner's Christology. Both presuppose divine causality which is not only efficient but also God's self-communication, that is, a quasi-formal bringing about of something different from God. The same insight could even be narrowed down to divine causality which alone is able to posit a being which is one *with* God in its difference *from* God. I could even specify this insight by saying with Rahner: the more a created reality (like the world, like human kind, and like the humanity of Jesus Christ) depends on God in its very constitution, the more it is independent and autonomous in its freedom.[87]

I could situate, as indeed the later Rahner did in the *Foundations*, the various tenets about Christ in an evolutive view of the world which reaches its peak in mankind whose history is directed to the man with whom God has already united himself, and in whom we can perceive God's merciful acceptance (*Zusage*) of our race.

All these principles could be, of course with due distinctions, taken as grounding the systematic coherence of Rahner's Christology. Why I do not think that any of these is sufficient is the fact that they are, on the one hand, explanatory premises to explain some aspects of the mystery of Christ and, on the other, are not meant to locate Christology in the whole of theology. There is, however, another Rahnerian insight which may ground this systematic coherence within Christology itself, as well as in its relation to other branches of the whole of theology. It is Rahner's theory of the symbol.

At first sight his article 'The Theology of the Symbol' (1959) is not an essay in Christology. Rahner's plan seems to have been more ambitious, namely, to work out the philosophical and theological meaning of symbolism as one of the key notions of the whole of systematic theology.

Rahner wrote:

> The whole of theology is incomprehensible if it is not essentially

a theology of symbols, although in general very little attention is
paid, systematically and expressly to this basic characteristic.[88]

We shall see that Rahner's 'Symbol', in aiming at the coherence
of the whole of theology, will give us a framework in which
Christology, too, finds its systematic coherence.

4.3.1 Philosophical Symbolism

Rahner's philosophical theory of the symbol is by no means new.
Like Tillich and others,[89] he insists that beyond the conventional
signs, which only point to the symbolized, we have real symbols
(*Realsymbolen*), in which the symbol participates in the reality of
what is symbolized. The question is, how to explain this 'participation', both on the philosophical and theological level. To
anticipate his conclusion, he will propose as a generally valid
ontological statement that every being, *qua* being, is of itself
symbolic, because it necessarily 'expresses' itself.[90]

Let me, then, first look at his philosophical arguments for this
thesis. They are connected with his own analysis of being from
the point of view of the age-old metaphysical problem of the one
and the many. Although it is a firm tenet of his general metaphysics, as borrowed from St Thomas, that being means oneness
(*ens et unum convertuntur*), Rahner carefully distinguishes
between two kinds of oneness: being, as considered in itself (*an
sich* or *ontisch*) can be one in the oneness of simplicity. In this
sense the capacity to symbolize cannot belong to the structure of
being.

But there is another kind of oneness beyond this ontic simplicity. In an *onto-logical* consideration being, including the
being of God, is of a dynamic character, because the ontological
meaning of anything that is, is to be present-to-self (*Beisichsein*).
To be present-to-self, according to Rahner, 'independently of any
comparison with anything else, means to be plural in one's
unity'.[91] Being is a process of self-realization which, for Rahner,
means self-fulfilment as well as self-expression.

Thus, a being symbolizes insofar as it fulfils and expresses
itself in 'another' by making this 'other' than itself its own;
therefore, the symbolized reality is the 'other' of the symbol and
the symbol is the real representation of the symbolized. In this
way, symbolized and symbol achieve a unity in multiplicity, and

this unity is what Rahner means by a participation characteristic of *real* symbolism.

What this general philosophical approach to symbolism pre-supposes, as he cautiously says, is that the plurality in the unity within a dynamic being is not always the sign of finitude, of the weakness of a being (*Seinsschwäche*). It can also be, as in Tillich's words, the power of being as shared, though in infinite difference, by God and man. I can remark at once that this abstract description of real symbolism does not go much beyond the analyses of *Spirit* and *Hearers*. It is based on the concept of being as proposed there: finite being by knowing and willing infi-nitely tends towards, but never succeeds in overcoming, the ontological difference, whereas the infinite and the absolute *has* overcome this difference. Thus, Rahner also differentiates between symbolism and analogy. While a real symbolism belongs to the very structure of being, 'as the self-realization of a being in the other'[92] (even if it is not exactly indicated 'for *whom* this self-realization in the other expresses the being and makes it present'), analogy is related to the human perception of *the way* a being is symbolic in itself. That a being is symbolic is presup-posed, but that a being is analogical emerges from knowing the various types of self-realization of each being in itself. Briefly, to be a symbol means dynamic possession of being, which at once implies the question of analogy about the way of being a symbol. The basis of analogy is symbolism, yet symbolism as such is known by analogy: both terms are tied to one another.

From this would follow that the being which is capable of sym-bolizing becomes, by means of analogy, open and accessible to its environment. Thus, men can communicate with one another insofar as they are capable of expressing themselves, and in expressing their intimate selves they, though analogically, can be known to others. In this way, human intersubjectivity is created: an intimate feeling of, say, sympathy and love realizes itself in gestures, words and deeds of two persons in encounter. The result is personal knowledge. It is this kind of fulfilment which Rahner has in mind. However, this will be better explained in the fol-lowing section on theological symbolism.

4.3.2 Theological Symbolism
Rahner's whole interest in examining the problem of symbolism

was theological. It was, it seems to me, the typically Roman Catholic devotion to the Sacred Heart of Jesus that prompted him to work out his general theory of symbolism.[93] Yet, beyond the allusions to the philosophical problem of the one and the many, the theological part of Rahner's theory of symbolism will be exemplified in the Christian commitment to a Trinitarian faith. The Trinity is the supreme instance where faith can assent to the most perfect oneness realized in the threefold plurality of the divine Persons. In other words, Rahner's starting point is the 'highest being': the Trinitarian God.[94] If this is accepted, we cannot but affirm a certain plurality within God which cannot be a weakness but is pure perfection.[95] It is on the grounds of this perfect plurality that Rahner can speak, first cautiously, then freely, of God's genesis, his coming-to-be. In this way the the theory of symbolism will throw a new light on his systematic Christology.

I have described earlier in this chapter the important role Rahner has attributed in the understanding of the Incarnation to 'becoming in God'. This, as I suggested, Hegelian undercurrent of his thought cannot by itself be taken as the point of coherence in his Christological system, unless from the background of his theory of the symbol. It is here that the genesis of God affirmed in 'Incarnation' becomes more understandable. In explaining himself Rahner can claim to follow the tradition of 'early systematic theologies' of their Logos-speculations.[96] According to these, the Word (as a reality of immanent divine life) is begotten by the Father as the *image* and *expression* of himself and remains the Father's necessary self-knowledge and self-possession. Where Rahner differs from this traditional speculation became apparent in three points:

(a)   he interprets this inner Trinitarian process ontologically, that is to say, as the presence-to-self (*Beisichsein*) of an existing highest being, namely the Trinitarian God;

(b)   he takes the image and self-expression, now standing for the generated Word, as being the 'other' yet united with the Father. From this he concludes, 'the theology of the Logos is strictly the theology of the symbol in its supreme form';[97]

(c)   only in third place, and depending on the two former points, does he speak of a 'movement', of a 'genesis' within God's Trinitarian life.

Because the Logos is the real symbol of the Father on the level of knowledge, and because knowing is a dynamic activity of self-consciousness, Rahner can speak of an ontological coming-to-be within God. It is God in his own 'history'.

Now, the difference between the generation of the Logos and the Incarnation, according to Rahner, is in the freedom of God in relation to these acts. 'Because God must express himself inwardly', he *might* and *can* express himself outwardly 'in a created utterance *ad extra*'.[98] The emphasis in this statement is on the 'might' and 'can', in order to stress the freedom of the *Creator* God. At the same time, however, the same sentence implies that, if and when this self-expression *ad extra* occurs, then it is a free continuation of the inner Trinitarian process. In other words, it is not God's movement *ad extra* which is the condition of the coming-to-be of the Logos, but the other way round: that God expressing himself within his own life conditions the possibility of creation.

With this, however, I have not yet reached the exact concept of the Incarnation; it only indicates the coherence of creation and the event of the Incarnation, that is, the coming-to-be of Christ's manhood. Yet, in this perspective, it is already understandable that for Rahner the 'production' of this human being, Jesus, is the highest instance of God's genesis freely extended *ad extra*, whereas the creation of man and his world, as we have seen, is a lower case of the same movement. God enables the creature to be the 'grammar of the Incarnation', or 'when God will not be God, man comes about.'[99]

In all this, I am on familiar ground as traced by Rahner's meditative article on the Incarnation. In reading 'Incarnation' and 'Symbol', one hardly perceives the difference. Yet, with the assumption of the notion of symbolism, the various strands of his thought come to a systematic coherence. The act of dynamic union which is the source of the Incarnation is symbolic: it is nothing else but the Father's self-symbolization in the 'other', the Son, in the inner Trinitarian life. Now, this Logos can express himself freely in the humanity of Christ. The latter, in turn, is the real symbol of God's life for mankind, whereas mankind, in view of the fact that the whole created reality takes part in the concrete and historical making of Christ, can in its turn become the symbol and presence of the Logos and ultimately of God the

Mystery. The created world (in the event of the Incarnation), on the one hand can reach its *pleroma*, its fullness, in Christ[100] and thus, on the other, is no longer merely a remote hint at its divine Cause. Its self-transcendence is *radicalized*, and can become the symbol of God's coming near to his creation.

Since the Incarnate Christ is part of this self-transcending world, his human consciousness is shaped not only by the Logos dwelling in him in the form of the hypostatic union, but also by the history of mankind. Thus, in Rahner's system Christ cannot but be the mediator between the hidden God and man in need of salvation. Christ is the absolute revealer of God and the absolute mediation of salvific grace: salvation and Incarnation are basically one. Symbolism works both ways – from above and from below.

I have with this reached the systematic kernel of Rahner's Christology. His theory of symbolism allows him to synthesize the various traits of current Christologies – by giving them a common ontological substratum. But what is more, Rahner's understanding of symbolism permits him to speak about the Mystery of Christ from two directions: from above and from below – either by deducing the possibility and the mode of Incarnation from his ontological concept of the Trinitarian God, or by raising man, faced with Jesus, to the mystery of the Incarnate Son. By means of symbolism a bridge is built not only from God to man but, more importantly, from man in search of the true God, the Mystery. That in this speculation the personal traits of the Father and of the Logos have not gained specific contours does not seem to disturb Rahner; he has definitively established the possibility of an anthropological Christology. It does not seem to be the Incarnate Logos in this particular man Jesus who has a salvific message for man. *Before* the Jesus of the Gospels had uttered a word, *before* he had gone the way of his destiny, the Incarnation itself had a salvific message for mankind. Just as the Incarnation is now understood in an anthropoontological way, so salvation is an anthropoontological offer of grace for every man and woman.

4.4 The Anthropological Message of the Incarnation

At the end of 'Incarnation', Rahner wrote:

Anyone, therefore, no matter how remote from any revelation

formulated in words, who accepts his existence, that is, his humanity . . . as the mystery which hides itself in the mystery of eternal love . . . such a one says yes to something which really is such as his boundless confidence hopes it to be, because God has, in fact, filled it with the infinite, that is, with himself, since the Word was made flesh. He says yes to Christ, even when he does not know that he does . . . *Anyone who accepts his own humanity in full . . . has accepted the Son of Man, because God has accepted man in him.* When we read in Scripture that he who loves his neighbour has fulfilled the law, this is the ultimate truth, because God himself has become this neighbour. He who is at once the nearest to us and the farthest from us is always the one person who is accepted and loved in our nearest and dearest.[101]

This rhetoric is, I would say, the sum total of Rahner's Christological message. It is, in fact, substantially *the* doctrine of Christ on which he takes his stand. His understanding of the dogma of classical Christology, his radical reinterpretation of Chalcedon, serve only as a secondary and remote control in order that he may remain on orthodox ground, whilst preaching about and witnessing Christ in the hope of leading man to an encounter with Jesus of Nazareth, is its primary purpose.

Rahner's Christology, I believe, is basically a theology of *witness*, and in my further presentation of his Christology later in this chapter I shall be gathering together several strands of his thought under this heading.[102]

These aspects of Rahner's Christological writings, then, in whatever coherence among themselves and from whichever starting point they are presented, would seem to reveal the single-mindedness of a very complex thinker; the Mystery of Christ to which Rahner personally commits himself, has to be conveyed whatever the cost. The passage quoted at the beginning of this sub-section witnesses his Christological mystagogy – his bearing witness to Christ.

In quoting this passage I have anticipated the themes which, in my view, make up the contents of this message. Thus Rahner, in his witness, can point out to the man outside faith ('remote from any revelation') that his existence is a mystery in which *the* Mystery is hidden; that to exist is to accept one's humanity in boundless confidence (that is, in full) since it was accepted by God in the Son of Man; that one's personal relationship with one's neighbour in its depths is already an acceptance of *the* Neighbour, the nearest and dearest, Jesus the Christ. Within all these experiences there is an anonymous pointer to the 'Idea of Christ', which turns out to be 'The Universal Bringer of Salvation' or the 'absolute Saviour'. Moved by this idea, man is in search of an identifiable 'Person' in all his concreteness. In short, the transcendental Christ must somehow correspond with Jesus of Nazareth encountered categorically in the history we all share.

At this stage I shall avoid laboriously collecting the ways and means by which Rahner, at various stages of his writings, lets the *a priori* Idea of Christ emerge from his speculations. It should be sufficient, in the first place, to see the emergence of the Idea of Christ in the context of his theology of witness. If my hypothesis is right, namely that Rahner in his whole work – especially in his Christology – is not so much theorizing about, as witnessing the essentials of, Christian faith, then I should consider what such an activity involves in general, and as regards the Mystery of Christ in particular.

4.4.1 The Concept of 'Witness'

In 1972 Rahner prepared for a symposium in Rome the paper which he eventually published as the article 'Witness' in *Investigations*. The article is hardly ever quoted and is sketchy, yet at the same time is illuminating both from an anthropological and Christological viewpoint. As I shall suggest later in this chapter, the theology of witness is strictly connected with Rahner's theory of symbolism.

In general, witness happens through the mediation of the word. The latter, however, can only be a truly witnessing word if in it not only the subject matter designed by its conceptual content is conveyed to man, but also the self of the witness is somehow communicated in full freedom, in order that it may evoke the corresponding answer. In this general framework, witness means the fulfilment in an encounter of an interpersonal relationship.[103] Hence, the basic structure of witness runs parallel with the theory of *real* symbolism: the man who reads the symbol 'shares' in the reality symbolized, and thence by self-symbolization reaches a certain fulfilment – he 'comes into his own'. Or, to put it in Rahner's words,

> the understanding of such a communication by the other [leads] to a state in which each party is orientated towards the other, a state which must ultimately be called love.[104]

For various reasons the article avoids ontological terminology and uses personalistic categories. Yet the ontological background is present in Rahner's mind. What we call Christian witness, as a concrete act of encounter, occurs exclusively within the context of revelation. This means that the witness and the person addressed are in some manner in the situation of grace, which is not only 'given' *in abstracto* but also modifies their human consciousness. For both of them, this situation can be experienced, whether explicitly or implicitly: it takes place within the individuals' awareness of man's mystery and is disclosed to them in the transcendentality of their knowledge and freedom tending towards the Mystery that is God. When these individuals encounter one another as free persons their communication becomes an intercommunion in which not only their respective ego is being witnessed to, but also that grace which is the impetus of their 'radicalized' transcendence towards God. Therefore, the witnessing communication of one person to the other is only possible if both are implicitly or explicitly related to God's love, and God accepts (*bejaht*) both subjects involved in this encounter. Witnessing (when the encounter really 'succeeds') as Rahner says, is a witness also to the grace of God.[105]

The ontological background here is not yet eliminated from Rahner's analysis; without the self-transcendence of the parties involved in the encounter, no witness is possible. And the self-transcendence of the parties is not a movement of each separate individual. It is concretized by two factors.

First, it is not to God that man initially 'transcends', but to the other, whose existence is equally enveloped by the Mystery. Secondly, in describing this encounter, Rahner underlines the historicality of witness itself: the witnessing encounter has to 'succeed', and for those involved in it, it is a venture, a *Wagnis*. This is because the Mystery of God is approached by man in *hope* and not in sure knowledge. Witness is based on a promise, and not on certainty.[106]

But this hope of the Christian has a certain object which Rahner also ventures to name: in general, it is the correspondence of what man aims at in his self-transcendence and of what is objectively and concretely promised to his hope. The object of this hope is the promise of the vision of God, as borne by the inner impulsion (*Getragenheit*) of man's self-transcendence towards this goal, which is grace or the *Pneuma*. Yet the manifestation, the historical confirmation of the fact that this goal is attainable in its exemplary success is man's possible encounter with Jesus of Nazareth.[107] Thus, on the one hand, witness in its concrete historical circumstances is an engraced event (or even a witness to grace) and, on the other hand, the content of such witness is a pointer to the reality of Jesus. The first can be taken for man's experience of the transcendental, and the second for his encounter with the categorial Christ.

What characterizes such an encounter in which Christian witness occurs is that the parties – owing to the insecurity of their mutual commitment – will indeed be in search of a concrete man. This man is no longer just a pointer to the God of man's self-transcendence, but a man most radically committed to God's life, a man whose life and death has reached its ultimate achievement insofar as his acceptance of God has been manifestly accepted by God. With this implied reference to the cross and Resurrection, Christ is the absolute witness, as well as the ultimate content of all engraced human witness. He is the faithful witness of the Apocalypse.

4.4.2 The Transcendental Idea of Christ

Having anticipated Rahner's concept of witness, I am now in a better position to present briefly, and to understand, his most characteristic idea in Christology. For, by keeping in mind that the transcendental Idea of Christ emerges in a specifically Christian dialogue between persons, I hope to avoid the danger of the misunderstandings of some other presentations.[108] The search for Christ and eventual encounter with the concrete person is not an altogether private affair. It cannot be deduced transcendentally, that is, in an *a priori* way. Neither is this idea interwoven with man's solitary self-knowledge, it emerges in man owing to his cosmic and historical situation. This seems to be the basis of Rahner's later 'description' of the absolute Saviour or universal bringer of salvation in *Foundations*.

> We are applying this title [that is, *Saviour* in an *absolute sense*] to that historical person who appears in time and space and signifies the beginning of the absolute self-communication of God which is moving towards its goal, that beginning which indicates that this self-communication for everyone has taken place irrevocably and has been victoriously inaugurated.[109]

Though in the original German the above description is more concise, I shall here try to explain briefly the English version by W. V. Dych.[110]

It is, first of all, clear *where* this concept of the absolute Saviour emerges and to *whom* this idea occurs. It emerges in the 'time and space' of ongoing history, hence it must be about an *event*. It happens, furthermore, to human subjects who are free, who live in intercommunion amongst themselves in this concrete world. It occurs, as Rahner says, 'to the freedom and intercommunion of the many cosmic subjects'.[111] Thus, we cannot speak of an individualistic *idee fixe*: the emergence of the idea is communitarian (embracing the whole of mankind) in a world whose history is governed by human freedom.

Secondly, the *mode* of its occurrence is such that it presents itself as a challenging offer for acceptance to those whom it addresses. This offer, too, is meant for human freedom – it is a genuine possibility, an alternative, at least, for 'the relationship which the spiritual creature [man] assumes towards it'.[112] The idea formed of the event depicts it as objective, as factually given, man's choice being restricted to its acceptance or rejection. It presupposes an ongoing historical dialogue between God and man, the situation of question and answer, offer and acceptance.

Thirdly, the content of this idea is not only God's historical self-communication, but precisely as it appears in the dialogal situation between God and man. It will appear in a historical personality in whom the free dialogue between God and the human race reaches a point of *breakthrough*. What does Rahner mean by this breakthrough? He seems to mean, on the one hand, that in this person God's self-communication is already given unambiguously, successfully and victoriously so that the 'irreversibility of this process has become manifest in and in spite of the ongoing dialogue of freedom' between God and mankind.[113] It is the climax of God's clear-cut promise of salvation, on which neither God nor mankind can go back. On the other hand, this is a breakthrough because what the movement of God's self-communication has intended to achieve, namely mankind's acceptance of God's offer, at least by one historical personality, has already been accepted. This person is thus the very manifestation of God's challenging offer to be accepted by the whole of mankind.

This personality is the absolute Saviour, the bringer of salvation in an absolute, irrevocable and unsurpassable sense. In him the desultory divine-human dialogue has become what it should be: it has reached its essence.

Yet, on account of the above description of the absolute Saviour, Rahner goes a step further in cramming even more content than it might appear into this idea. Thus, in fourth place, the absolute Saviour (that is, man's idea of him) suggests that he is the beginning as well as the end of a movement of God's self-communication proceeding from its past to its future. That is to say, the Idea of Christ 'lives in virtue of its end' – lives its present as borne by its future, as the cause as well as the goal of the dynamic 'history of God's self-communication moving towards its goal which has reached its climax in the event by which it became irrevocable'.[114]

Although I ask myself how such an idea can bear all these attributes without itself dissolving into the thin air of wishful thinking, I hasten to add that Rahner's intention was to use it only as a limiting concept (*Grenzidee*). Its function is heuristic: in various forms the idea of an absolute Saviour was prefigured on the fringe of his anthropology. In his book on the humanity of revelation, F. Greiner traces Rahner's idea of Christ, the absolute Saviour, back to *Hearers* and tries to outline its development in the later works – not, however, including *Foundations*.[115] Greiner's viewpoint, of course, is not Christological, but he examines the relation of transcendentality and history in Rahner's writings, and his final question is whether Rahner is able to find a place for the historical event of Christ in his overwhelming transcendentalism. Therefore, in order to simplify my own presentation I shall, broadly speaking, follow Greiner, even if I do not agree with him on every single point.

Greiner is right in affirming that the whole of *Hearers* is an implicit attempt to show how the subjectivity of man is bound (*hingewiesen*) to history in which, beyond the transcendental disclosure he is capable of, he has to reckon with the event of God's self-revelation in Christ. He must be 'on the look out' for concrete history and listen to the word that eventually comes to meet him in the Word of God in order that his transcendental thrust may be fulfilled.[116] The necessary orientation to the Word in history is equivalent to the heuristic idea of Christ: it is a beginning of man's truly *historical* existence. Thus it is that the transcendental method in theology, in implicitly aiming at this *conversio ad historam*, does not leave man in the solitude of his religious subjectivity.

In the gradual construction of his view on the supernatural existential, Rahner soon comes to the insight that this religious *a priori* is totally dependent on an ongoing history as marked by the presence of Jesus Christ in it. He claims, therefore, that any account of man's religious striving has to start from concrete history, in which this revelation of Christ has occurred. Thus, in the concluding part of his 'Christology', he already envisages the possibility of an *a priori* transcendental Christology with explicit references to *Hearers*. He speaks of 'an *a priori* sketch of the "Idea of Christ" as the correlative object of the transcendental structure of man and his knowledge'; this is possible and even necessary, although he acknowledges that such 'an *a priori* Christology' would only 'offer a kind of formal schema of Christ to the Christology which bears the message *a posteriori*'. Even if such an *a priori* schema came to be on account of grace which should be the grace of the *real* Christ, it would owe 'its existence to the real object *a posteriori*'.[117]

Thus, even at this early stage, Rahner's idea of the absolute Saviour is undoubtedly something that relates man to history and is, in some way, dependent on it. At the same time, it has a, so to speak, subjective function: in it man's *obediential potency* comes to its highest achievement. This openness to God's disposal is supremely realized in the hypostatic union of Christ.[118] In other words, in the idea of the transcendental Christ, man is referred to concrete history, even if Christ in the flesh is not yet encountered. This is the Christ-Idea in outline.

Nevertheless, in the middle period of Rahner's work, this outline gradually grows in its new anthropological importance, chiefly in his articles 'Incarnation' and 'Evolutionary View' and in his book *Hominisation*. The keynote is now not so much man's transcendental subjectivity as his *ex-static* nature:[119] man finds himself in what he is not, namely God. He is someone 'who never succeeds in encompassing himself because the finite can only be surpassed by moving out into the unfathomable fullness of God.'[120] Thus, man attains his fulfilment

> when he adoringly believes that somewhere there is a being whose existence steps so much out of itself into God, that it is just the question about the mystery utterly given over to the mystery. He must believe that there is a being who is the question which has become unquestioning, because it has been accepted as his own answer by him who answers.[121]

Man in this situation, to which Rahner refers as his potential God-manhood (*Gottmenschlichkeit*) cannot deduce, but surmises the reality of Jesus the Christ. If it is so, then he is well served by the Christ idea which is now an ideological means in his search for the real Saviour. This Christ idea is then cherished up to and in his *Foundations* where faith in Christ emerges from man's evolutionary self-transcendence, in which the whole of the cosmos, and man in it, surpass their own nature and contribute to their advance onto a higher level of being.

By the time *Foundations* was published (1976), the principles were known by means of which this evolutionary world is explained, and therefore I need not repeat them as regards man's coming-to-be out of the material cosmos. It is enough to recall that in 'Evolutionary View' Rahner regards history as 'led by free cosmic subjects' (man) in continuation with the evolutive cosmic process, in which the higher achievement is not only prefigured in the lower, but guides it in its becoming more (*Mehrwerden*) than itself. Thus, man, who has come out of the development of the material cosmos, must have been prefigured in matter, at least as an idea guiding its leap forward (breakthrough: *Durchbruch*) to consciousness. Matter, regarded by Rahner as frozen spirit,[122] has a basic tendency towards the spiritual which is 'awakened' in man. In the same way, before man becomes in fact the being to whom God's call in grace (which is the grace of the categorial Christ) is addressed, there is in him a 'frozen' idea about Christ through whom he is called to a supernatural destination. The idea of Christ is both implicitly anticipated and is moving man towards his real goal – the explicit recognition of Christ in this individual, Jesus of Nazareth. In 'Evolutionary View', Rahner can call this idea 'the decisive existential factor of man's life.'[123] Christ is the *entelechy* of the world process as well as of free human history.

In 'Evolutionary View' of 1964, and the almost parallel 1970 essay on the setting of Christology in the modern world,[124] all the elements of the 'definition' of absolute Saviour in *Foundations* are given almost verbatim.[125]

I will now return to my attempt at explaining this definition, to show why Rahner claims this idea to be the beginning and the end, past as well as future, cause as well as goal of our acquaintance with Christ. The first parts of these couplets are 'living in virtue' of the second. Man lives his present in anticipation of his future, his life is, in a way, moved by its fulfilment. This presupposition implies that God's self-communication through Christ does not encroach upon man from outside history; it comes, rather, in and through history, the climax of which is Christ, the absolute bringer of salvation.[126] Thus, Christ

> . . . is himself a historical moment in God's saving action, . . . a moment of history . . . a part of the history of the cosmos itself.[127]

This is why not only the Judaeo-Christian revelation, but also the history of religions points to the coming of this event.[128] It also follows that by means of an all-embracing history of the cosmos as directed to a particular event, that of Christ's coming, Rahner can universalize the latter and claim that its message is valid for every man and woman. Jesus Christ in the concrete event of his coming, is the true man and as such the ultimate possibility (*letzte Wesensmöglichkeit*) of human existence challenging him to the courage of accepting him (Jesus of Nazareth) as the Saviour.[129]

Within this anthropological horizon of understanding, as

Rahner repeatedly shows, the fact of the Incarnation and the dogma of hypostatic union cease to be mythological. God becoming man, the Infinite finite – God uniting himself with the human, etc., are now conceivable as prolongations of the spiritual being of man who is ex-*statically* orientated towards God. Whereas this orientation yields the idea of Christ of a transcendental Christology, the encounter with the Jesus of the Bible in a Christology 'from below' will confirm or verify our belief that he is the Christ to come. At the mid-point of these two approaches stand the main statements of classical Christology.[130]

In *Foundations* Rahner sums up in a few concise pages[131] in what sense the statements of classical Christology fit into his anthropological scheme. In these he reassumes several previous attempts, now with the evolutionary world view at the back of his mind. This is why he insists that by Incarnation we should mean God's becoming *flesh*, something material. Incarnation does not mean the saving of what is spiritual in this world from the hindrance of matter. We, in our 'more materialistic' times, can better reject this tempting view than our predecessors at the time of Chalcedon, because we know that this material universe is in dynamic evolution, the climax of which is the accomplished self-transcendence of the world as a whole borne by the Word of God. In the Incarnation the Logos of God establishes a material part of the world as his own reality precisely at that point where matter turns to spirit, that is, in man. In this sense has God become man: in everything which being human entails.

If now this dynamism of a developing world is seen from the viewpoint of God's self-communication, then we can assume in a limit-idea (*Grenzidee*) an irreversible fulfilment of the same. There must be a point where the world's development towards its divine goal is not only aimed at, but is already achieved. This limit-idea is that of the absolute Saviour in which the accomplished union of God and man is a fact. The self-transcendence of man under the event of God's gracious self-communication implies the notion of hypostatic union through which the dogma of the Incarnation was understood.

All this sounds rather abstract and speculative. It can, however, be tested, if we translate the relationship between man's transcendence and the self-communication of God as an offer of grace for the whole of mankind. This offer of grace, as we have seen elsewhere, means man's destination to the vision of God, to the immediacy of his presence to him, or simply, the union of God and man. Now, the precise question is whether the Incarnation in Christ means a union which is on a higher level than the vision as offered to every individual or 'is it a singular and unique moment in the universal bestowal of grace'? Is the grace present in the humanity of Jesus the Christ the same as is offered to every other creature?

Rahner's answer is affirmative:

> . . . the intrinsic effect of the hypostatic union for the assumed humanity of the Logos consists precisely and in a real sense *only* in the very thing which is ascribed to all men as their goal and their fulfilment, namely, the immediate vision of God which the created, human soul of Christ enjoys.[132]

In other words, the hypostatic union in the Incarnate is an intrinsic moment within the whole process by which grace is bestowed on this world. Yet the Incarnation, though a moment within the process of God's self-communication, is a *unique, unsurpassable and irreversible* event. It is unique, because in Christ it is, unlike in us, not only a promise, but a reality. It is unsurpassable, because in him God's self-communication to all men has reached its fullness and is historically tangible. It is irreversible, because in Christ God's universal offer of grace and glory has reached the stage of definitive acceptance on behalf of the whole of mankind. Grace offered to Christ as man, and grace offered to us all is the same in both instances. The difference is that for us the offer of grace and glory is Jesus himself. We are only at the receiving end of God's self-communication, since the promise of the immediacy of God (vision of God) is mediated to us by him in whom God's offer was accepted. In this sense the hypostatic union in Jesus is not only established by God, but is God himself.[133]

In this way, therefore, the statements of classical Christology are implied in the world's transcendence through man and in God's self-communication which is the offer of grace to everyone, including Jesus. They stand, as we saw, at the mid-point between a transcendental Christology and man's existential access or categorial verification of his belief that Jesus of Nazareth is the one in whom God was in a hypostatical union with a sample of our material world.[134] Now the question remains what is the existential access of man to this belief. In a way the whole of transcendental Christology, which Rahner in *Foundations* sums up is an access to this belief. But beyond this, Rahner at several stages of his writings points to possible ways of approaching the same Mystery from an existential or personalistic point of view. These are briefly summed up in the *Foundations* under the title of 'New Approaches of Orthodox Christology'. One of these was termed 'Inquiring or Searching Christology'.

4.4.3 Inquiring Christology

To illustrate what Rahner means by an inquiring Christology I recall the message of the Incarnation: the full acceptance of one's human being. Now, if transcendental Christology analyses the questions arising from being human and leads up to an idea of Christ, a further inquiry seems to be needed to prepare the human subject for a responsible leap into faith entailing an explicit acceptance that the universal bringer of salvation *is* Jesus of Nazareth. In short, the question posited by a transcendental approach has to be transposed into an existential experience. This experience leaves the realm of theory: as Rahner says in *SM*:

> For man does not affirm abstract ideas and norms as the ground of his nature, but a reality which is already or which will be, present in his own, historical experience.[135]

The transcendental quest inevitably yields to an existential search for Jesus who is the Christ.

The question, however, as to where this inquiring, existential Christology systematically belongs is in itself immaterial. Whereas in *SM*, Rahner introduces it by giving three arguments from man's existential experience preparatory to the encounter with Jesus in faith, in *Foundations* he puts it after the 'biblical evidence' about Jesus of Nazareth. The reason seems to be that the arguments of such an inquiring Christology are the witness of believers before anonymous Christians who 'can be presumed to be [persons] of morally good will and hence to be existing in the interior grace of God and in Christ' and whom one *presupposes* to have 'already uttered an interior and unreflexive "yes" to

Christ'.[136] Or, in the similar words of *SM*: the proposed arguments appeal to man 'who resolutely accepts his own human existence and in fact acts upon what may be called "an inquiring Christology".'[137]

Thus, this Christology is, as it were, a *demonstration Christiana ad extra*, as pronounced by those who want to give an account of their faith in Christ, whilst the theological reflection on the Jesus of the Bible is an *apologia ad intra* which confirms the faith of the believers themselves. Yet, whichever way we take this branch of Christology, it is an existential analysis based not on words but on human *praxis*. It has to show one possibility among many others, which is not only abstract and theoretical but is a unique and liberating experience, the basis of one's life 'which includes everything within a hidden and unfathomable meaning' for those 'who are waiting upon someone who is to come'.[138] A searching Christology affirms at least a hope for the future and 'asks whether Jesus and the faith of his community does not justify an act of faith that what is in any case being sought is found in *him*'.[139] Such a Christology strives to confront the waverer with the absolute claim of Jesus to whom faith, not reflection, responds with an absolute 'yes'.[140] In one sentence: transcendental and inquiring Christologies will have to create a bridge between an abstract understanding of the doctrine of Christ (as exemplified in Rahner's theory of symbolism) and their concrete reception by man's faith.

As his early analysis of man yielded a transcendental ontology of *obediential potency*, so the transcendental approach to Christ requires an equivalent counterpart. When, with the next step in the same analysis, he arrives at the *supernatural existential* as a historical *a priori* (open to human experience) he finds a parallel in this inquiring Christology. Thus,

man as obediential potency=transcendental Christology

man as possessed by the supernatural=inquiring Christology

Of course, the systematic balance of these remains fluid and subject to atmospheric changes in emphasis. Thus, a more historically orientated context and a growing interest in a personalistic and communitarian approach to his anthropological analysis may have caused Rahner to change the parameters of these terms slightly. Yet the progress of his implicit system has remained basically the same. Its aim is the communication of faith in Christ, in a word: witness.

Now, in both 'History' and *Foundations*, Rahner assigns three main topics to an inquiring Christology:
(a)   absolute love of neighbour;
(b)   readiness for death; and
(c)   hope in the (absolute) future.

The topic (a), especially as based on the experience of personal encounter, was already worked out in Rahner's beautifully written theological meditation, published in 1968, 'I Believe'.[141] Here, Rahner dwells mainly upon man's venture of unrestricted love of his neighbour. At the same time, it introduces the reader to the basic elements of Rahner's Christological thought. To quote its main thesis:

> Whenever someone with full justification trusts himself to another without reserve [i.e. absolutely] and this other *of himself* is able to accept this trust being enabled by God alone to do so, then this other man is in such a singular union with God that this union in its depth can only be understood in the sense of an assent to the Jesus of orthodox Christian faith.[142]

The above text should not be misunderstood. Rahner wants to achieve here more than a transcendental disclosure of God in and through the analysis of an encounter where mutual trust comes about. His emphasis is on the 'of himself' (*von sich her*) of the person encountered, that is, the trust of one person terminates not in what transcends the other, but in the person himself. It is supposed, however, that this other person is empowered by God alone (*von Gott her ermächtigt*) to reciprocate the trust of the other. The thus engendered mutual trust and radical love between two human persons can only be grounded on an implicit assent to him whose trustworthiness is beyond doubt, Jesus the Christ.

Now, this love is something existential for every man and woman. For, as Rahner says: 'Man is the being who can only exist if he attempts to trust himself totally to the other, if he by giving himself up totally commits himself.'[143] This act of total commitment is self-transcending. Thus, such a love 'as far as it really occurs, leads to an experience of God as the very ground of this love': God is transcendentally 'given' in the love of the neighbour.[144] Yet, at the same time, the lovers are aware of the futility of their enterprise: whether trusting or distrusting one's fellows, one is exposed to 'forlornness' (*Verlorenheit*), unless, of course, this love is 'saved' by God, who in a certain sense takes upon himself the radicality of this *human* love, to his own transcendent 'otherness'.[145] From the part of man it means that he not only tends to this radical love of the other, but rather he postulates someone, a real human being, 'who is justified to take upon himself this radically trusting love of the other.[146] In other words, the experience of love which Rahner attempts to describe is directed to a human person in whom God's acceptance of human love is manifest. He alone can justify the lovers' mutual trust without reserve. Were not this radical love directed to another *human* being, it could be regarded as a pointer to the affirmation of the transcendent God and man's relation in grace with him. It would by-pass the very human experience out of which it has arisen. In that case, the other human being would be regarded only as an *occasion* for a human effort of 'loving' God without the lovers' real venture of trusting one another unconditionally. Radically trusting love is directed instinctively not at God, but at a *human* being.

Needless to say, by the end of Rahner's meditation, this human being will be identified with Jesus the Christ. He, on the one hand, must be of the same kind as the other humans whom we trust unconditionally and, on the other hand, must in himself be different from any other man and woman. In him alone can our love transcend its particularity and open us up to the love of every man and woman. The possibility and reality of such universal love towards 'the least of our brethren',[147] contains in an anonymous way a human act already transformed by hope and love,[148] because it is initially founded on a *fides qua*, on an implicit faith in Jesus Christ. Rahner can conclude: 'In one's love of neighbour – if it is radically understood in its very roots – one encounters (not in a romantic, mystical or mythological identification, but really) Jesus whom we confess to be the Christ.'[149] It is already faith in the universal bringer of salvation, corresponding to the Christological doctrines of our explicit faith, the *fides quae*.

Rahner's procedure in *Foundations* is less elaborate. In briefly sketching the human attitudes of absolute trust in the other, of man's 'acceptance of being disposed of absolutely in the radical powerlessness . . . endured in death'[150] of his hope against hope of being in future fulfilled individually and socially despite the present self-alienation, Rahner points to the basic absurdity of these experiences which might move men and women to an existential search for the reality of a person who through the events of his life can give *the* answer. He suggests that man's self-surrender is existentially inevitable, if he sets off on the way of a human life, lived in its very depths. To apply these arguments in a fundamental theology is nothing other than to lead man not only to a search for the absolute Saviour, but to the implicit affirmation of his coming in the flesh.[151] Such an inquiring Christology is the preparation for the acceptance of Jesus of Nazareth as the Saviour of absolute claim – the Christ of the Bible.

4.5 The Biblical Verification of Christology

Rahner as witness to Christ, certainly manages to scatter the seeds out of which faith in Christ can grow. Yet he knows that none of his pointers suffice for the last and essential leap – the acceptance of Christ in Jesus of Nazareth.

Man may accept, Rahner says, in fully conscious freedom what one indeed unwittingly knows and existentially loves: the idea of an absolute Saviour and the postulated need of this Saviour's reality. Yet, 'the more difficult question is how and where and when one may give an earthly name to him who is such a being.'[152]

To say, 'this is the being' is, in any case, a most difficult matter of identification. It has to be left to an act of faith. Those who already believe his name to be Jesus of Nazareth, the man one reads about in the Bible, have attained the goal of their existential search, but must nevertheless give an account of their faith in *him*. This account unavoidably refers the believer first to the history of the life and death of Jesus of Nazareth[153] and inevitably leads to the theology of the death and resurrection of Jesus the Christ.[154]

To read these sections of *Foundations*, along with 'Easter', 'History', and 'New Christology', is likely to be disappointing for those interested in New Testament exegesis. Rahner is never at his best when dealing with the Bible and biblical theology. He uses Scripture exclusively as a theologian and apologist. In his essay 'Exegesis' he reflects, in my opinion, his own embarrassment when he presents the 'biblical evidence' of faith as a conflict between exegesis and theology proper.

What, then, is the correct procedure in dealing with the Jesus of the Bible? The exegete has to build on scientifically based evidence, whereas the theologian's conviction, according to Rahner, is an existential one. Whereas the exegete must not assume any dogmatic truth about Jesus, the theologian is in a more awkward position. On the one hand, it would be an error (and a heresy to boot) if he thought that faith in Christ is altogether independent of the Jesus of history; and, on the other hand, it would be equally erroneous to think that his faith in Christ is certain only if it is built on the historical evidence of the exegete.[155] Since the procedures of both exegete and theologian are equally valid in their different fields, a conflict between exegesis and theology is inevitable. To be precise, this conflict is not about the historical existence of a person called Jesus of Nazareth, but rather about what Jesus claimed to be and what, in fact, happened to him. Is it an objectively ascertainable truth for exegesis and theology that Jesus was conscious of himself as being the Messiah and the Son of God? Is it an objective truth that he has risen from the dead? Modern exegesis and theology may answer these questions in entirely different ways, and their conflict may lead to an irreconcilable divergence between the Jesus of history and the Christ of faith.

Now, Rahner assumes this conflict – and in so doing hopes to find a common denominator on which exegesis and theology can find a minimal basic agreement. From this basic agreement each can go its own way: the exegete can go on analysing the human history described by the Gospels; and the theologian can propose his own teachings. This common ground is worked out in a scheme for a new Christology in the interdisciplinary lectures which Rahner gave with W. Thusing at Munster in 1970/1. The upshot of these lectures is the central part of *Foundations*, to which I have already referred in this chapter.

In what follows, I shall disregard a possible line of development in Rahner's writings from the early essays up to this present work. It will be enough to point out the exegetical grounds on which his Christology stands, to outline the theological extension of the same and discuss the systematic position of his foray into the, to him alien, field of exegesis.

4.5.1 The 'Agreement' of Exegesis and Theology

In spite of the conflict between exegesis and theology, Rahner asserts a certain agreement, on the basis of which their dialogue should not be suspended. He is concerned with two historical facts, namely the self-awareness of Jesus before Easter and the experience of his resurrection at Easter as conveyed to his disciples. Of the first, Rahner boldly affirms:

> According to the findings of the contemporary exegesis it can be said even today that the pre-Easter Jesus understood himself as the absolute eschatological event of salvation and the eschatological bringer of salvation.[156]

And for this thesis Rahner happily claims the authority of R. Bultmann.[157] He is, however, in a less happy position as regards the second.

In the same article Rahner finds it necessary to introduce this basic agreement with long-winded anthropological considerations. Yet, he finally comes down to brass tacks by assigning the factual content of the Resurrection to the resurrection experience of Christ's followers:

> If we say with the exegetes of our own time, that the Resurrection is not an event that took place in historical fact but that the historical fact consists rather simply in the faith and the conviction of the apostles and disciples about the Resurrection,

. . . the theologian can safely agree, provided that he in no sense excludes 'the fact that this experience involves some reality' not identical with his subjective conviction.[158] There is, therefore, an agreement on the content of Jesus' self-understanding *before* and of his followers' *after* Easter awareness. These two points will be the minimum required for fundamental theology.[159]

Now, Rahner's job as a theologian is to suggest that, in the ensuing dialogue, the exegete may follow the theologian's, this time 'biblical', reasoning. The suggested first step is nothing else than forming an image of the man as presented to us in the Bible. It is about the concrete and empirical structure of the life of Jesus, about his message and mission, of which he was undoubtedly aware.[160] Only at the end of the emerging picture of this man's life can we ask: was he aware of himself as the One who is to come, that is, the absolute Saviour?

Obviously, the pre-Resurrection Jesus did not speak of himself as the absolute bringer of salvation, nor did he preach a ready-made Christology. Yet, it is clear that he *behaved* in a way that was conspicuous to his contemporaries. He was, then, if not a revolutionary, certainly a radical religious reformer in his own environment. In this function he broke 'the lordship of the law which in fact put itself in God's place';[161] he fought against the overwhelming legalism of his contemporaries and regarded himself as being in radical solidarity with those social and religious outcasts of his world. His *message*, however, was basically in accordance with the religion customary in his environment. He regarded the spreading of this message as his own *mission*, hoping for its success in spite of a possible conflict with the Jewish establishment, and he held out in the face of his own death. He certainly gathered followers, who joined him by consenting to what he preached. Surely the contents of this message demanded from the disciple the same social engagement that they saw in their master.

At this stage the question can be left open as to how far Jesus identified himself with this message and how far his followers were committed to him *personally* and not to his cause, which was also social and even political. These are the only ascertainable facts. Yet, if the exegete and the theologian discover in this behaviour a growing awareness and in the message an unfolding self-understanding of Jesus they can go a step further. Rahner's trump card will be the content of Jesus' message and the quality of the mission upholding it.

Exegesis is perhaps able to agree that Jesus' relationship to God was unique and unprecedented: he called God his *own* Father and preached of him as such to his followers. This qualifies his message which can be summarized as the proclamation of the Kingdom of God.

At first sight it is clear that Jesus spoke of the Kingdom and not of his own person. He spoke of it as something imminent, as something that would occur within his own lifetime, or, at least, before the demise of his followers. He was conscious of the arrival of the Kingdom *now*,[162] and he identified himself with this conviction to the point of self-forgetfulness. This is why, as a rule, he does not speak of himself, save insofar as he himself is involved in the imminence of the Kingdom. Furthermore, the manner in which he tells his disciples of the arrival of the Kingdom is again characteristic. The Kingdom is proposed as a new situation of choice (*neue Entscheidungssituation*) for everybody. This new situation, however, does not refer only to the historical occurrence of the end,[163] nor does it simply introduce a permanent challenge for his listeners in a *spiritual metanoia*. It refers, rather, to his own experienced relationship to the Father *as valid for all*, and appeals for belief that it is somehow realized.[164] Jesus in this sense (perhaps blasphemously for a man) claims faith in himself, and this is what will lead him to his death.

These, then, according to Rahner, should be the immediately arguable *data* for exegesis. With the help of the theologian, the exegete is bound to ask further questions of a theological nature. Is it not very likely that the proclamation of the imminent Kingdom was felt by Jesus to have been brought about definitively by his life and preaching? Neither is it probable that the Father-Son relationship was understood by him to be the fulfilment of man and his history – valid for all?[165] Does he not seem to identify himself with the last in the line of prophets and as the ultimate word in God's salvific self-revelation? Was not his message, commonplace at first sight, proclaimed as an absolute novelty, both as regards the relationship preached and its salvific value? Do not these all point to the *consciousness* of Jesus according to which the radical nature of this relationship is no longer represented by anyone other than *himself*?[166]

If these questions can be answered in a positive way, not only the theologian but also the exegete will be able to see the idea of Christ as absolute bringer of salvation emerging in Jesus' self-understanding. Rahner, indeed, concludes in this positive sense:

> Jesus experienced a relationship to God which he experienced as new and unique in comparison with other men, but which he nev-

ertheless considered to be exemplary for other men in relationship to God.[167]

So what Rahner is affirming is the idea of the transcendental Christ in Jesus' human self-consciousness together with the awareness that this idea is realized in himself (Jesus was the first to be engaged in transcendental Christology!).

This realization becomes manifest not so much in the deeds of power Jesus exercised by his own miracles[168] as by his freedom in undergoing his destiny on the cross. He could die freely *and* still uphold his message about the Kingdom and about the new relationship of God to man. His death had meaning not only for him, but also for what he announced. He hoped that in the face of death his salvific message would not be annulled. It is absolute precisely in its concrete and individual occurrence.[169] At this stage in his dialogue with the exegete, Rahner can turn to the second point of their alleged agreement: the resurrection experience of Jesus' followers. How far the exegete can follow him on this point is another question. For it is here that he must leave exegesis to its own proper method and become a theologian; he extends the already over-stretched agreement and proposes his own view about the *meaning* of Jesus' death and Resurrection.

4.5.2 'Jesus who was dead has risen into the Faith of his followers'

It is remarkable that in Rahner's latest attempt to outline a Christology, the Resurrection plays an all-important role.[170] The pre-Easter consciousness of Jesus implies that the cross he was freely to undergo must have a *meaning*. But what that meaning is can only be ascertained by examining the experience of his followers after the event, called the Resurrection. It is unlikely that Jesus gathered his disciples by preaching the resurrection of the flesh. (Rahner holds that even Jesus' predictions about his own death and resurrection may be taken as later embellishments of the post-Easter community!) His disciples followed him, rather, for what he preached, and gave him their unconditional trust.[171] But how could Jesus demand and accept such a trust from them unless, deep down in his consciousness, he understood himself as someone in whom the believer could objectively find his own salvation, in spite of death?[172] How could his followers trust him, unless they, too, felt in themselves what or who he was? Rahner envisages the answer to these questions along the following lines.

Although his disciples were downcast and disbanded after the crucifixion, the curious happenings on the third day were not altogether unexpected. They may have expected the return of Jesus with a new lease of life in circumstances of temporal existence, but what in fact they had to learn was the *meaning* of Jesus' death and Resurrection. For his disciples his death meant an event that suppressed death itself and raised it at the same time (*aufgehoben!*) into the Resurrection. This was believed to be, on the one hand, the definitive and permanent salvation of Jesus' human existence (*endgültige Gerettetheit*) and the victoriousness (*Sieghaftigkeit*) of a person; and on the other hand, the irrevocable success of his cause. In other words, the Resurrection of Jesus was not taken strictly as the empirical perception of an objective fact. Those who believed at once interpreted it according to its meaning and significance. Their faith told them that, in spite of the cross, in and through the Resurrection God himself had ratified Jesus' self-understanding. And, what is more, the Resurrection was, on the one hand, the victory of the absolute Saviour himself and, on the other hand, the securing of man's salvation. On this ground alone can man hope for his own resurrection, body and soul, for only within the horizon of this expectation could the disciples believe in the Resurrection of Jesus. Jesus is risen, as Rahner asserts, 'into the faith of his disciples'.[173] This faith will then announce itself in the kerygma of Pentecost.[174]

It is here, I believe, that Rahner's foray into exegesis rebounds in full circle on his own transcendental Christology. For what he implies in the above argument is yet another Idea of Christ moving man to seek out its realized categorial counterpart. He also assumes a transcendental hope in man, on account of which the Resurrection becomes, as it were, the other side of the event of the cross.[175] The meaning of the cross is the consummation of Jesus' life, yet its full significance is only attained in the Resurrection, in which God irrevocably ratifies the life of the absolute Saviour. This is why, when the first community announces the Resurrection as an event of history, we find that it corresponds to their hopes and expectations. If Jesus is indeed risen, then this hope of the apostles and of ourselves is shown to be valid, for their and our experience is sure if, and only if, it was given from outside man's subjective consciousness. If I thought that the coming-to-life-again of a person was only an invention of blind faith, I could not take it as the definite validation of my hope. The historical fact is the truth-condition of our belief, but what we actually believe is the fulfilment of our transcendental hope concerning the Christ.[176]

In *Foundations*, Rahner only needs to collect and systematically arrange these hints dispersed in his former writings. By now the guiding principle is the coordination of death and resurrection in the life of Jesus; they are two events in which the one involves the other. The Resurrection is 'the permanent, redeemed final and definitive validity of the single and unique life of Jesus . . . precisely through his death in freedom and obedience.'[177] This leads to a tautological statement of what the Resurrection in general means: it 'is the validity of the person himself in its abiding validity'.[178]

This means that the 'validity' refers not only to the 'cause' but rather to the person himself. It is *not* enough to believe in the victory of what he preached – this would mean just the survival of an idea. Nor is it enough to believe in the permanence of an individual (Jesus) – this would mean only the acknowledgement of an historical fact. But when the Resurrection of Jesus means both, then the permanent validity and truth itself (as *fides quae* and *fides qua*) is part of the event: 'Jesus is risen into the faith of his disciples.'[179]

This latter is the proposition of faith in the Resurrection which theology tries to make acceptable. The means is the transcendental hope in one's own resurrection as the anthropological horizon of understanding the resurrection of Jesus. Within this horizon man, as Rahner says, is on the 'look out' for a concrete person to whom such an event has already been granted.[180] To this perspective belong the elements of Rahner's theology of death and the possibility of human immortality which in the situation of grace need to go beyond the status of an ideal possibility to a transcendental expectation as experienced in the individual's hope of his own resurrection; the

> transcendental experience of the expectation of one's own resurrection, an experience man can reach by his very essence is the horizon of understanding within which, and within which alone,

something like a resurrection of Jesus can be expected and experienced at all.[181]

This experience and the faith in the Resurrection of Jesus are self-involving realities: the one conditions the other. This faith, of course, is understood as referring to something concrete and unique – in a word, *categorial*.

In reaching out for the categorial object of faith in *the* Resurrection, the man of today is helped by the witness of the apostles in the Bible. Surely, 'it can be said that by "historical" means we would not reach the resurrection of Jesus, but only the conviction of his disciples that he is alive.'[182] Yet, it is precisely the task of theology, relying on the Bible, to show that we are *now* not altogether outside the experience of the apostles *in their time*, because we too, like them, are empowered by the same transcendental experience in expecting our own resurrection. This hope is understood by Rahner as an *a priori* yet historical gift of grace which belongs to the very essence of man. Jesus the risen man is the witness thereof and, it seems, woe to us if we do not accept his testimony. Though it is a 'question of decision which is directed to every individual who hears the message', yet

> . . .if this message is rejected in such a way that this also denies in unacknowledged despair the transcendental hope in resurrection . . . then this rejection of a contingent event [that is, the Resurrection of Jesus] . . . becomes a rejection which is an act against one's very own existence . . . [183]

Thus, a theology which envisages not only the possibility of Resurrection but the concrete reality of *a* resurrection opens the way to free acceptance of the life of a man who was irrevocably accepted by God. The whole of Christology can be built up on showing the possibility of believing in the Resurrection of Jesus.[184] This is the achievement of Rahner's foray into biblical theology. At this point, I must ask explicitly what is the status, in Rahner's mind, of these considerations about the biblical word.

4.5.3 The Status of the Biblical Story of Jesus in Rahner's System

To enquire *in general* into the status of the Bible in this apparently unbiblical theology would take us too far afield.[185] It is, however, clear that in Rahner's view the 'biblical evidence' belongs not to dogmatics but to *fundamental* theology. Dogmatic theology and systematics are a kind of superstructure which try to create a verbal synthesis *of speaking* about the faith. Yet, the infrastructure of this systematic effort is fundamental theology which either confirms the believer in his faith (*demonstratio fidei ad intra*) or introduces the unbeliever to a possible acceptance of it (*demonstratio fidei ad extra*). Any actual dealing with the biblical story, however, finds a place only in the first way (apology *ad intra*), and even here it is restricted to a question the answer to which we can obtain from the historical message of Jesus before his Resurrection.[186] For the post-Easter Jesus cannot be considered without human faith corresponding to the meaning of death and resurrection. But this meaning is gained from Rahner's own man-centred fundamental theology. Not this, but the former (about the pre-Resurrection Jesus) is the tiny section where the Bible is allowed to speak. At this point the reader might ask to what extent it is important for Rahner to address himself at all to the story of Jesus as narrated in the Bible. *Foundations*, having solemnly concluded to the message of the Incarnation, gives a typically Rahnerian answer:

> Anyone who accepts his humanity fully . . . has accepted the Son of man'.[187]

Could it be that Rahner is embarrassed at having to deal with such a contingent event as the life of Jesus in the Gospels? Moreover, if this statement is what our Christological faith boils down to, can it be warranted by the scriptural story of Jesus? Or does the concrete life of the man Jesus remain for ever a surd, an unsystematizable fact? This, of course, would not be Rahner's conclusion, for an anthropological interpretation of the Christ event, even if it relies on man's transcendentality, cannot ultimately be convincing.

Rahner states:

> However one might interpret transcendentality and existentiality more exactly, and make them a real ground of his faith, we cannot in principle possess them without a reference to real history . . .

there is no one who could actualize his transcendentality without its being mediated by history.[188]

It is, however, not stated what Rahner means by real history. For real history can mean:

(a)   any existential fact of human experience in which we feel the mysterious presence of God in our lives; or

(b)   it can refer to another human person, to Jesus the Christ, with his own experience as shown by the detailed and surprising story of the Gospels.

In the first case, (a), the Bible might be, but is not necessarily, a *verification* of our human commitment to Jesus. It is, however, the verification of this faith, if, in facing the story of the biblical Jesus, our own previous experience fades away to give room to that of, (b), the Other Person, Jesus the Christ. Then we know in *whom* we believe.

I am not going to try to decide here to which alternative Rahner's answer points – I shall leave that problem to the comments and questions about Rahner's whole Christology in the next chapter.

Chapter 5

Comments and Questions: Who is Jesus the Christ?

Hans Geisser sums up the possible sources which might have influenced Rahner's Christology.[1] Without dwelling upon the obvious deficiences of the biblical foundations, Geisser speaks of Rahner's kinship with the main insight of Greek soteriology (the Incarnation as the central salvific fact); of his borrowing of Antiochene motives in his insistence on Christ's human autonomy; of Origen's *mundus intelligibilis* in his cosmo-Christology; and of the necessity of the Incarnation-event in a hypothetical absence of the fall, as coming from Duns Scotus.

As a Protestant, Geisser cannot help discovering in Rahner's consciousness Christology parallel traits with Schleiermacher,[2] Schelling and especially Hegel. In the kenotic allusions of Rahner's Christology, Geisser connects him with the views of G. Thomasius, F. R. R. Frank, and especially J. M. Dorner.[3] In Rahner's approach to the Incarnation through creation one can almost hear Barth speaking,[4] and, in Rahner's interpretation of the God-world relationship in an existential and anthropological dimension, R. Bultmann is mediated to Roman Catholic thought.[5]

Geisser's list of possible influences on Rahner could be extended indefinitely. To assign such a possible source of influence, even if only with vague association, as sometimes seems to be the case in Geisser's essay, can, it is true, help us to see the position of an author's Christology among his peers. However, what determines an author's view is not the various sources he has drawn upon, but his own central insights. Therefore, much more important to me in my own presentation of Rahner's thought, however complex it may be, was that the reader should be inspired by his insights to come to terms with someone who is believed to be God as well as man, Jesus the Christ.

This is why in my own reflections I shall be selective in referring to the manifold criticisms which have been raised against

Rahner's Christology and shall also avoid mentioning those small points of detail which may have caused perplexity in my long presentation of his ideas.

For, indeed, there are many statements in Rahner's work to which a critical correction could be appended. Yet to mention all these would increase the confusion in which my preceding volumes may have left the reader. It is, therefore, better to go straight to the real bone of contention, namely the enticing yet dangerous parallelism between creation and incarnation, which arises out of an already criticized concept of God, and results in an image of the God-man, Jesus the Christ.

I am aware, nonetheless, that in the face of the whole of Rahner's Christology, there is no little weight on the merit side of the scale, namely the anthropological and existential bias of his doctrine; Rahner as a fundamental theologian is witness to the one faith in Christ, the common object of our loving commitment. All who believe in *him* are engaged in an inquiring and witnessing Christology as they encounter their contemporaries in dialogue. So, my attempt to understand Rahner is also a venture in understanding more deeply *him* whose name, or rather title, we Christians all bear.

5.1 Creation and Incarnation

One must not complain if systematic theology can see a striking parallel between the creation of the world, and, within it, the 'creation' of *a* human nature, namely that of Jesus who was called the Christ. Applied, however, in all its detail the chances are that one either reduces the mystery of Christ to the pattern of creation or, the other way around, lets creation be absorbed by the mystery of the Incarnation. The danger of the first has been lurking there ever since the so-called rationalism of Arius: Christ is pre-eminent of all that is, yet a creature of God. The second alternative, that is, creation being absorbed by the Incarnation, is tempting to explain the former as the minor case of the latter. To make it understandable one will apply the language of metaphysical schemes. The pitfall in both cases will be that, perhaps unwittingly, we imagine ourselves to be at home in God's world and to know by unaided reason what it means to be created.

It is my view, as already stated,[6] that creation is a matter of faith and by no means of a rational conclusion. The parallelism between creation and Incarnation is only valid, if one cautiously applies Barth's *analogia fidei* in which creation is a preliminary event, the external ground of the covenant sealed by Christ's coming in the flesh. The use of the *analogia entis* is only secondary as regards creation: after we have consented to faith we can theorize about the relationship of the Creator to his world, and *vice versa*. It is here that the concept of creation can be paralleled with that of the Incarnation, or even of the procession of the Logos from his divine source. For this viewpoint the use of metaphysical language is inevitable.

Now, if I have correctly understood Rahner, this is precisely what he is doing in his theory of *symbolism* as the organizing basis of Christology. It is obvious that his symbolism cannot be taken for a merely metaphysical thesis. Were it such, one could justifiably ask, how can the plurality implied in the notion of symbolism be attributed to the being of God who is the primordial unity? By a merely metaphysical reasoning of a Thomistic type one can conclude to the absolute oneness of God, the remote principle of all that is. To state that his being, like that of the creature, is symbolic, that it has to express itself in the 'other', would be to argue along the lines of *analogia entis*. If this 'other' in God is infinite, can philosophy speak without contradiction of the reduplication of the divine? If, on the other hand, it is finite, then God's creative freedom is prejudiced: God *must* create in order to find himself. To argue by philosophical means that this plurality in God is, unlike in the creature, a positive perfection as, I am afraid, Rahner does,[7] is unwarranted. Thus, we can safely presuppose that his symbolism-essay is based on something theological. The God of whom he speaks is not just the ultimate and absolute Being, but the Trinity of our faith. Rahner's symbolism is basically the best example of an argument *ex analogia fidei*.

The language he uses for it is eclectic, yet quite a few of his critics remark that it is borrowed from Hegel. He assumes that in all being there is a plurality which is overcome by the oneness of its elements. From this rule God is no exception. God has to 'express' himself in the 'other' and this other, by taking part in the being of the former becomes its *Realsymbol*. T. Pearl, in a rather desultory article comparing this procedure with Hegel's dialectical method by quoting and paralleling the two, states:

> So, both Hegel and Rahner seem to begin with the exigency of a Being to move from itself (thesis) to 'otherness' (antithesis) as a moment in its self-realization (synthesis).[8]

Pearl then verifies this initial comparison of the two methodologies by references to Rahner's philosophical and theological statements culminating in his Christology. There, as we have seen, the Logos is the 'other' symbolizing its source, the Father; Christ's humanity is the symbol of the incarnate Logos; human nature the symbol of the Incarnate; the body the symbol of the spirit and, in a way, the whole created world the symbol of man's bodily constitution. Similar Hegelian traits are pointed out by Pearl in Rahner's *Hominisation* and 'Evolutionary View' and also in his doctrine of uncreated grace.

In all of these, Pearl points to the same divine immanence which, in a dialectical way, is regarded as the driving force of a world process coming from its Creator and striving towards its completion in God. God is the source (*woher*) and the whither (*wohin*) of this world and the promise of its safe arrival at its goal, which is granted in the hypostatic union. 'Thus God,' Pearl writes, 'not only creates the world, he also gives himself to it as ground and ultimate goal, the historical manifestation of which is the Christ.'[9] Of course, this statement does not directly derive from Hegel; a more likely source is Scotus, as Pearl quoting Shepherd correctly remarks.[10]

Nonetheless, the Hegelian connotation cannot be overlooked. In spite of his protest of being a Hegelian,[11] Rahner seems to speak the language of German Idealism. Hence, Pearl can state 'that Rahner's theology of symbol not only possesses a dialectical character, but that this . . . could be described as Hegelian in nature.'[12] It is this kind of language which may imply a Hegelian image of God and grounds the parallelism between Incarnation and creation. Now in Hegel's metaphysics God, at the beginning is not present to self (*Beisichsein*): he is not a conscious Spirit in the full sense of the word. God becomes conscious in meeting the 'non-ego' (Fichte) or entering into a dialectical oneness with created nature (Hegel). Both imply that creation itself is needed in order that God, by returning to himself may become the Absolute Spirit (*absoluter Geist* of Hegel). Or, as Pearl rightly summarizes Hegel's God as the movement of the Spirit:

> Thus Spirit at its highest level of manifestation as 'Absolute' Spirit becomes conscious of itself as the one and only reality whose incarnations are nature and finite spirit.[13]

This is *not* the image of God which Rahner would have made his own. One could argue in defence of Rahner with K. P. Fischer that his God, with or without creation, is already a perfect Spirit: he created because he is free and conscious. The application of an apparently Hegelian terminology *after* this assumption is merely a linguistic feature.[14] Or, as Barth would say, God, in his self-revelation, is the one Subject, the one Thou whom man faces. Nonetheless, this one subject being, apparently, under the rule of symbolism, *has* to express himself in the otherness of the Logos and return to himself in the unity of the Spirit. With this it is highlighted that God is the supreme consciousness, the superlative being present-to-self (*Beisichsein*). It will be this self-sufficient personal God who freely wants to be the creator and the one who in his word reveals himself.

Still, the use of Hegelian language can be misleading. To put it briefly: if Rahner wanted to have a Hegelian God, it would have been justifiable for him to speak Hegelese in his subsequent theology.

But Rahner obviously does not want to have this concept of God and therefore he would be well advised not to speak of a genesis and a 'history' of God, that is, of these characteristically Hegelian ideas.[15] For, if God is, with or without creation, a 'movement', then it is hard to draw the line between the procession of the Logos and the creation of the Incarnate's humanity, between the threefold oneness of God in his own life and the process of the world from his creativity. The one, the self-communication *ad intra*, is a necessity in order that God may be God with his own self-knowledge and self-consciousness. The other, God's self donation *ad extra* realized in the Incarnation and creation, is free. And if we add Rahner's Trinitarian principle according to which the 'two' Trinities are one and the same, then we can ask with Pearl:

How can this be if, roughly, for Rahner, God *ad extra* is supposed to be God *ad intra* in space and time?[16]

One wonders whether the two phrases, *ad intra* and *ad extra* (self-bestowal and self-alienation in the 'movement' of God), can separate the two realms in which the first happens by necessity and the other out of the ineffable freedom of the Divine. If the 'history' of God within is continued without, that is, in the realm of creation, in an isomorphous way, if creation obtains its meaning in the Incarnation of the Logos, then the relationship of God to the world can be characterized by the relationship of Jesus of Nazareth to God the Father. His relation to God is the world's relation, his grace is my grace and everyone's who is part and parcel of this world-process. And when we read in Rahner's *Hominisation* and 'Evolutionary View' that the inner moving force of this process is God himself, then we are near to the Hegelian dialectics of the Spirit developing in its incarnations in nature and ending as the 'Absolute' Notion which is God.

The parallelism, therefore, between creation and incarnation on which Rahner approaches his Christology and the semi-Hegelian language which he employs can lead to a threefold mistaken conclusion. The *first* I have already mentioned as an explicitly not admitted yet implicitly assumed image of God which is akin to that of Hegel. With this is coupled the relationship of God and the world which may remind us, as Pearl asserts, of Hegel's *panentheism*.[17]

Connected with this there is a *second* danger which makes this starting pattern suspicious. Rahner's favourite sentence, 'God the unchangeable can become' as applied both to creation and Incarnation can be misread and lead to a conclusion which is contrary to that which Rahner himself explicitly proclaims. We remember him saying:

> This is precisely an attribute of his divinity as such and his intrinsic creativity: to be able . . . to constitute something in being which by the very fact of its being radically dependent . . . also acquires autonomy . . . Radical dependence on him [God] increases in direct, and not in inverse, proportion.[18]

This apparently dialectical sentence is contrary to my everyday experience which tells me *the more one depends, the less free and autonomous one is*. It seems to me that this sentence of Rahner can work havoc in its consequences. The unchangeability of God, upheld by him, makes God's Trinitarian constitution a necessity and can impair the autonomy of the 'other' in which God, all the same, 'becomes'. This impaired autonomy affects, first of all that of the Incarnate and, second, the freedom of the created world. To the first point I shall have to return, but the second spells out for me a certain determinism. When Rahner repeatedly projects from the world process the idea of Christ and his hypostatic union, when he insists that only the Logos could have become man, and when God's 'becoming' necessarily terminates in human nature, then the conclusion is almost at hand: every man and woman is potentially that which Christ is, namely, the God-man. In other words: the danger of patterning the Mystery of Christ on creation (or *vice versa* for that matter) can lead to the view that we humans are all potentially God and man, like the Incarnate was. I could call this view *pan-Christism*. In it is there a difference *of kind* between the Incarnate and the coming-to-be of man? Or is Rahner speaking merely of a difference *in degree*?

The reader who at this point refers back to the preliminary pages of this book will share my dilemma. Concerning the relationship between human transcendence and the hypostatic union, Rahner himself puts the same question:

> Is the hypostatic union an absolutely higher level on which the bestowal of grace on a spiritual creature is surpassed [that is a difference *in kind*] or is it a singular and unique moment in the universal bestowal of grace [that is a difference *in degree*]?[19]

Now, in view of the fact that 'Christian revelation says that this self-transcendence is offered to everyone' and that it is a real potentiality of their existence[20] Rahner concludes:

> Although the hypostatic union is a unique event in its own essence, and viewed in itself it is the highest conceivable event, it is nevertheless an intrinsic moment within the whole process by which grace is bestowed upon all spiritual creatures.[21]

Therefore:

> When God brings about man's self-transcendence into God
> through his absolute self-communication to all men in such a way
> that both elements [that is, self-transcendence and self-communi-
> cation] constitute a promise to all men which is irrevocable and
> which has already reached fulfilment in one man, then we have
> precisely what is signified by hypostatic union.[22]

One might justifiably ask: why did God not allow this event to
take place in *me*? After all I, with the whole of mankind have the
possibility, if not the potentiality, to become what Christ the Lord
has been.

To this question about the difference between God's creation
and the Incarnation of the Logos I can find no clear-cut answer
from Rahner. And from this follows the *third* conclusion. Sure,
the Incarnation in this man Jesus is an *unique* event, yet an event
which, though in different form, could be repeated several times
in the course of history. Could, for example, Buddha or
Mohammed, etc., not be regarded as having in their lives and
teaching, fulfilled the task of Jesus? Were they not manifestations
of God's salvific and loving relationship to our world and
mankind? And what is more, does not the concrete history of this
man Jesus, his birth, his teaching, his suffering and death leading
to a risen life, become a parable of an abstract Idea which comes
to itself in its development? If so, we are back to Hegel, of whom
J. N. Findlay states:

> In the Christian story of the Incarnation, passion and resurrection
> of Christ, Hegel comes to see a *pictorial expression* of his central
> thesis: that what is absolute and spiritual can emerge only in
> painful triumph over what seems alien and resistant.[23]

Mutatis mutandis is not this question applicable to Rahner's
overall theory underpinning the traditional idea of the hypostatic union?

5.2 God's Becoming Incarnate

Having pointed out the dangers in Rahner's basic pattern in
approaching the Mystery of Christ and feeling uncomfortable in
Hegelian shoes, we can now move on to appreciating his first
steps in Christology.

'Movement', 'history', in God himself, with which Rahner reckons in order to explain the Incarnation, although in his own dialectical way, is an idea which I earlier advocated in Chapter 3. He, too, with qualification, speaks of a 'changing' God, which twice aroused the severe criticism of I. Trethowan:

> If anyone thinks that the theological statements need not be in any way meaningful, or that the idea of changing God is meaningful, there is nothing one can do about it, except to state one's own conviction. For me, that God is unchanging is a statement which is as fundamental to a true approach to religion as a statement can be ... The changelessness of God, I want to say, is a datum of the religious consciousness.[24]

Trethowan's protest is an echo of the traditional viewpoint which can be regarded as a dogma of the ancient Church. Of course, he argues from religious consciousness and on this level one can oppose the contrary conviction: the God of the Bible acting in history must be *in some* sense a changing God.

Now, just as I did in Chapter 3, so R. E. Doud[25] applies the panacea of a Whiteheadian critique to improve Rahner's Christology. The nerve point at which Doud tackles Rahner is his theory of *Realsymbol* and uncreated grace by means of *quasi-formal causality*. It can be presupposed that Rahner was not acquainted with Whitehead's, and the process theologians', metaphysics, nor can we discover traces in his writings of their odd terminology. Nonetheless, the Hegelian traits of his Christology, as argued by Pearl, as well as his protest against being a Hegelian, suggest the vicinity of his thought to the class of theologians who consciously adopt the language of Whitehead's process philosophy. For who more than this class of philosophers would applaud when they hear that in God himself there is a process of self-uttering (that is, the Logos) homogenously continued on self-alienation (that is, Incarnation and creation), and that this genesis of God is mainly grounded on the divine 'becoming'.

From Chapter 3 it will be remembered that I by no means accepted wholesale this kind of metaphysics. Yet I did appreciate Rahner's attempts to solve the unsolvable problem of a God who changes by remaining unchanging. In this, however, I am neither

Hegelian nor process theologian, but find myself in the company of a fair number of Catholic theologians.[26] For the Incarnation means in some sense the becoming of God. In stating this Rahner is right and I, in turn, have suggested a further step. Instead of remaining with Rahner's dialectical statement ('while remaining unchangeable he becomes'), I have preferred to say: God as he is in himself does change and become – *in his personal reality*, while he posits his own 'nature or essence' irrevocably. His unchangeability is his personal fidelity to himself and to his creation. With this, the original approach to God by the Whiteheadians has been converted, yet their insight in explaining the world process under the guidance of God is not altogether abandoned.

To be able to maintain this position, which is meant to be an amendment of Rahner's view, I have to point out its implications. The first corrective of this view concerns the image of God himself. As we remember, Rahner in his defence against the charge of Hegelianism strictly distinguishes two levels in the alleged 'movement' of God. The one, *ad intra*, occurs by necessity, whereas the one *ad extra* by which the Godhead alienates itself in the non-divine emanates from the abundant freedom of God. Creation is his *free* self-communication. God the Absolute *does not have to* but *can* communicate himself in his sovereign freedom.

This view presupposes in God two kinds of freedom. The first is a free necessity in obeying the symbolic nature of the Trinitarian God: God must express himself in the Logos. The processions within the blessed Trinity are of necessity. The second concept of freedom is something we, too, can experience: it is a choice of possibilities. God who *can* create, but *does* not *have* to, faces at least this alternative: to create or not to create. Or, as Rahner puts it

> . . . the Absolute, or more correctly, he who is the Absolute, has, in the pure freedom of his infinite and abiding unrelatedness, the *possibility* of himself becoming that other thing, the finite; God, in and by the fact that he empties himself gives away himself, poses the other [namely, the creature's] as his own reality.[27]

What does freedom of the Absolute who is utterly unrelated

mean, contrasted with freedom in facing real alternatives? Whereas of the first we have no experience, the second 'freedom' means something to us: in the choice of our possibilities we become aware of our freedom. For God, Rahner wants to maintain both.

Contrary to this view, I should assert that a Being which is absolute and unrelated *cannot be free*. To be free is to be related to the alternatives of one's choice. This is why in Chapter 3 I have preferred to speak of God not as of a Being, but as a possibility.[28] God's Being is possible not because the searching creature may or may not assert it, but because God, if he exists, is of an infinite range of possibilities, including his own self. He can define himself and posit his own nature. Now, if we have, through the revelation in Jesus Christ, an inkling of his triunity, we are bound to say that the so-called processions in his triune nature are free positions of his personal reality. Abstractedly speaking, God could have been otherwise than the God of Christian revelation.

From this it would follow that if God chooses to create, he is not bound to do it according to his Trinitarian nature. Abstractedly speaking, the created world does not have to follow the pattern of the Logos. To say, like Rahner does, that only the Logos could have become human can, in principle, be questioned. However, these are only highly speculative consequences of our alternative view, for we cannot deny that *de facto* the Logos took flesh. Consequently, to know something about the nature of God in himself, about his Trinitarian oneness, can only be *on the grounds of man's faith in Jesus the Christ*. In him and in his Spirit the God-world relationship in its factuality is manifest.

There is another implication in my position which from the point of view of customary dogmatics is of significance. If God's freedom is based on his relationship to his infinite possibilities, then the *ex nihilo* tag of the dogma of creation gains another perspective. If God creates, it is not out of absolute nothingness, but out of the possibilities to which he in himself is related.[29] And when the world *is*, it will be a possibility for God's immanent 'action' within his creation.

If we assume, therefore, that God is free both in defining his inner life and acting in the realm of his creation, then the insight of the process theologians (and not that of Hegel) might be useful for explaining both the general God-world relationship and the hypostatic union. Even the last sentence of our Rahner quotation,

> God, in and by the fact that he empties himself gives away himself, poses the other as his own reality.'[30]

will become more understandable. According to process view, creation does not mean the detailed definition of the nature of created things. 'Their own reality' which is different from that of God is the sum total of those possibilities which the creature is about to freely actuate. In its freedom the creature is, like God, as regards his inner life, *autonomous*, even if its real possibilities are limited. *What* the creature in itself is or will be is not determined by God. Yet process theology insists that the Creator by allowing his creatures a set of possibilities assigns each of them a certain direction, a not circumscribed 'subjective aim' (Whitehead) of their free becoming.[31] Furthermore, process theology regards every single created 'entity' as a kind of subject capable of 'prehending' their way of progress. They are free to realize, to actuate themselves, though in the context of their God-given possibilities and under the 'subjective aim' or guidance received by God's creativity in original and continuous 'creation'.

The significance of this insight, as we shall see, will pay its dividends in Christology. To anticipate: in a Christology which wants to be along the directives of Chalcedon, the human nature of Christ as a creature of God will have to be regarded as an autonomous self, as a subject capable of his own human 'prehensions' of his own human decisions. His erroneous views (such as the conviction about the imminence of the end), his wavering decisions (often felt in the account of the gospels) until he finds his God-given purpose are due to his autonomous human subjectivity. That this human subject, Jesus of Nazareth, was different in kind from us human beings is due to his union with the Logos who was made flesh. As we shall see, it is the process theologians who will again help us to see a corrective understanding of the *hypostatic union*.

5.3 Hypostatic and/or Personal Union

In presenting Rahner's criticism concerning the formula of

Chalcedon it is difficult to abstain from critical questions as regards the emerging image of the incarnate Logos. In fact, my main questions arise in dealing with his later consciousness Christology[32] – whether the person we encounter in Jesus the Christ is the merely human I-centre or the personal Logos of God. Or, in dealing with his symbolism: is the one whom the believer is allowed to meet in Jesus *God's being*, or is it rather the personal Logos of the Father? In short, in presenting Rahner's Christology, I have sensed a certain lack of the genuinely 'personal' in the hypostatic union of the God-man. One has the impression that the question *who* Jesus the Christ is, is not adequately expressed.

A similar point is reflected in an article extremely hostile to Rahner's Christological thought. In fact, Alberto Galli[33] tries to prove, through the quotation of innumerable texts from Rahner's philosophical and theological writings, that Rahner misunderstood the hypostatic union of Christ and, in spite of his claim to correctly interpret the traditional teaching of the *Magisterium*, evacuates the conviction according to which Jesus as the incarnate Logos was in possession of the beatific vision. For what Professor Galli reproaches Rahner's thinking with is his everywhere recurrent fight against the danger of mythical monophysitism or monothelitism.[34] This is why, affirms Galli, Rahner

> . . . must energetically affirm the human autonomy of Christ from two points of view; on the one hand, by attributing to the manhood of Christ a perfect autonomy on the entitative level, on the other, by excluding the essential influence of the Logos on his human nature. One could paradoxically say that as regards Rahner's image of Christ, the Chalcedonian formula is turned upside down [*risulta capovolta*]: there would be two persons in one and the same nature.[35]

In other words, Rahner is accused of crypto-Nestorianism in which two persons, the one divine and the other human, are paradoxically united in one and the same nature which is then the highest achievement of humanity. I do not need to summarize Galli's argumentation in support of his charge against Rahner. It is mainly built up on the already discussed coherence of creation and incarnation,[36] on the Hegelian substructure of Rahner's Christology.[37] From this, and from Rahner's philosophical premisses follows that he has no time and much less sympathy for the possession of beatific vision in Christ.[38]

Furthermore, if Galli's criticism is correct, then the person we meet in Jesus is his autonomous *human* self as manoeuvred by God's becoming in and through the Logos. In Jesus we may encounter God's being as we might do in any of the prophets. As regards his human consciousness, says Galli, all he said and did could be reduced to more or less successful human attempts to interpret his own being.[39] His own 'divinity' is manifest to us in the grace with which he is endowed in the depth of his being. It is infinitely more than that which we have, yet of the same ilk.

From the point of view of a rigid Thomistic Christology where the created humanity of Jesus as the *instrumentum conjunctum divinitatis* is different from ours, Galli's criticism of Rahner is correct. Indeed, in order to avoid the danger of a mythical monophysitism, Rahner over-emphasises Christ's autonomous human freedom and regards his humanity as one of God's creatures. From this point of view he sides with Nestorius. But this is only one side of his theory. By the dialectical assertion that the creature's autonomy is dependent on the act of creation, 'the more dependent, the more free', he limits this autonomy of the created nature of the God-man. In explaining the tag in the case of Christ, *ipsa assumptione creatur*, by means of quasi-formal causality or by the self-communication of God's Logos to Jesus he cannot and does not want to make his humanity different from ours: we, too, are created not only by God's efficient, but by his quasi-formal causality. In creating this world God communicates himself to it. If Christ's human nature is essentially similar to ours, then his autonomy, like ours, is limited. Thus Galli can assert that the human nature of Christ in Rahner's view is *quasi* an 'emanation' of the Logos. If it is so, we may read a residue of monophysitism into Rahner's Christology.[40] In a sentence, Rahner fails to avoid either the Scylla or the Charybdis of Nestorianism and monophysitism: he manages to hit them both.

Strangely enough, Robert E. Doud, the Whiteheadian critic of Rahner's Christology, comes to a similar conclusion. In analysing Rahner's metaphysics of symbolism, Doud concludes:

> Rahner only develops the Logos as, *Realsymbol*, eternally ready to become man. For this reason Rahner's Christology of

> *Realsymbol* fails to convey his larger Christological intention of asserting the full manhood of Jesus. [This] one-sidedness . . . causes him to jeopardize the humanity of Christ and to relapse into monophysitism.[41]

We know now that this is exactly what Rahner wanted to avoid at all costs. Therefore, in working out, by means of quasi-formal causality, the autonomy of Christ's human self he should come to the assertion that in Christ there are two subjects each provided with their own freedom. Since for Rahner freedom as *Beisichsein* highlights the person, there are two persons in the Incarnate. With this we are back at Nestorius. Whereas Galli was utterly hostile to this crypto-Nestorianism, Doud accepts it as a starting point of his Whiteheadian counterposition:

> In order to avoid Nestorianism, Rahner needs a metaphysics of internal relations, . . . in which the subjects are internally related, without compromise to the autonomy of either subjects . . . Thomistic metaphysics cannot offer such a doctrine, but the process philosophy of Alfred North Whitehead does supply exactly this kind of metaphysics.[42]

What then does this Whiteheadian internal relation mean?

In my former reference to process thought I mentioned that the atomic 'entities' are regarded as 'occasions' or subjects capable of 'prehending' their possibilities.[43] Now the other side of the Whiteheadian 'prehension' is the fact that these 'entities' are *internally related* to one another. As Doud renders Whitehead's so-called 'categories of explanation':[44]

> The prehensions actually render one entity internal to another . . . The immanent entity offers essential definition to the host entity . . . So Whitehead's entire metaphysics is concerned with how one subject is internally related to another subject.[45]

In other words, whereas the God-given possibilities for each creature are externally related to the subject, the ones actuated by the creativity of the subject will enter into their internal constitution. (Whitehead calls it 'nexus' or 'concrescence'.) Thus entity X, by remaining itself, is internally related to, that is, it is constituted by entity Y.[46]

Whitehead, of course, has never produced a Christology, but process theologians, like John B. Cobb, jnr.,[47] in revising their master's concept of God, apply his categories to the theandric constitution of Christ. Their starting point, too, is anthropological. Whitehead's 'living person' is constituted by a series of innumerable influences from its environment. In his own odd terminology the human self is a 'society' of various subjects or occasions each of which retains its own characteristic yet becomes part and parcel of that new organism in which it is incorporated. The new organism with its different 'personal order' is internally related to them: it 'prehends' its past in order to gain its present identitiy as an enduring self. It is this living self which in freedom faces its own God-given possibilities. One, and a most important, of these is that *subjective aim* by means of which, according to Whitehead, God provides for each of his creatures. Applying this to the constitution of Jesus' human self Doud can state

> . . . Jesus prehends God as he prehends his own past. Since prehending his own past gives man his identity, prehending God gives Jesus his identity.[48]

This cryptic sentence, of course, needs to be explained further. If we with Rahner assume two subjects in the God-man, and if we assume with the process theologians that these two subjects are constituted by a series of past occasions,[49] then it will be possible that in one man, Jesus, the divine subject, as prehended by the human, will be constitutive of the human subject. Though he has a double identity as God and man, he is one owing to the constitutive inner relationship of God's self-utterance in this human subject. The dominance of the Logos in this theandric union by no means absorbs the human or diminshes its autonomy, since *per definitionem* 'concrescent' – as Whitehead says – entities retain their own characteristics. Furthermore, it is to be noted that by speaking of 'subjects' Whitehead does not mean 'substance' or 'nature', but an ever-developing process. The latter is, of course, also applied to the divine subject.[50]

Jesus' human history, as with any other human being, is ruled by that God-given subjective aim which he freely ratifies. But in differing from mere humans, 'God's decision is to radically communicate himself as God to Jesus'.[51] From this follows that his free obedience to this God-given aim is, unlike that of any other humans, more than a merely moral one; 'it is an act of self-appropriation and self-integration that is a matter of the identity of Jesus'.[52]

With this rather tortuous argumentation, based on Whitehead's inner relationships, Doud could indeed have corrected Rahner's suspected Nestorianism. Though, like Rahner, Doud assumes two subjects in Christ, but he does not affirm that these two are *persons* whose union would only be a moral togetherness. They are ontologically one.

Furthermore, like Rahner, Doud insists that the divine subject in Jesus owing to God's radical self-communication, gradually defines the human. Here his Whiteheadian inner relations stop him from a crypto-monophysitism: the divine subject does not absorb the human. Whether Rahner – who does not work with this Whiteheadian insight, as Galli and Doud suggest – would lead to a kind of monophysitism, remains an open question.

Now, I am prepared to agree with Doud's underlying Whiteheadian anthropology[53], *provided* I can insist upon a distinction which I do not find in elaborated process theology. One's past experiences (Whitehead: occasions) prehended as inner constituents in a new constellation of possibilities define the identity of man's *self* and not his *person*. Although both are constitutive relations, self and person are different. Self-identity can be perceived from my inner relationship to all those events which have formed my history. I do incorporate them freely in what I am now and what I want to be in the future. This enduring as well as developing self-identity corresponds to what in Jesus was traditionally termed as his human nature. However, I become a living person, if I am constituted by my inner correlation to other persons. The self is present to itself, a *Beisichsein*, the person is present to other persons, a *Mitsein*, to use Rahner's terminology. If we now assume in the case of Christ that his self, apart from being constituted in his self-identity by his own human history, is at the same time a 'living person' constituted by his inner correlationship to the person of the Logos, then *mutatis mutandis* we have reached the formula of Chalcedon.

My suggestion, in groping for a view, corrective to Rahner's interpretation of Chalcedon, is a possible distinction between the two terms consecrated by the same Council. I differentiate between the two words *hypostasis* (subsistence) and *prosôpon*. True enough, the two terms were meant to be equivalent and, as we have seen, were used as the one logical subject of Jesus the Christ to whom two sets of properties, human and divine, were to be attributed. The Fathers at Chalcedon were about to solve the question of *communicatio idiomatum* and thereby reasserted the hypostatic union of the Council of Ephesus. The philosophical or theological contents of the two words were not asked for. Yet both of them have their own connotations.

Hypostatic, that which *sub-sistit*, 'stands under', denotes the perduring self internally related to its past history, and *prosôpon* is that personal reality which sets the self in communion with other persons. This understanding of the person and 'personal' is more in the sense of Whitehead's 'living person'[54], rather than Rahner's view who, as a rule, regards the person as a conscious I-centre of free activity. As we remember, it was for this reason that he has refused to use 'person' in the Triunity of God and in this sense he speaks in one of his contributions on Jesus Christ to *SM*.[55] There he states:

> Objectively the affirmation of the one divine person in Jesus Christ can with certainty only mean that the (in the modern sense) personal, human reality of Jesus Christ has entered into such a unique God-given union with God that it became God's real self-utterance and radical gift of God to us.[56]

We should not overlook in this quotation that Rahner apparently abandons the Chalcedonian two *physeis*, and speaks of a *personal-human* reality in Jesus Christ who is at the same time, because of God's self-utterance and radical gift to us, *the* 'divine person'. With this are we not back to Nestorius? Or, if the divine person, now taken for God's self-utterance and self gift, overwhelms the already personal human subject then are not his human consciousness and freedom only instruments in God's hand? We are now close, at least, to a kind of monothelitism.

The same quotation, however, can be taken in the sense of

process thought. The divine person in Jesus Christ can be understood as the personal Logos of God in *correlationship* with Jesus' human self, and in what the Chalcedonian 'divine nature' stands for is the same relationship inasmuch *constitutive* for Christ's whole being, including his self. The God-given union is asserted not first of all betwen Jesus' human self and his constitutive relationship to the Logos (it is *per definitionem* given), but between the same self and the personal Logos of God who 'posits', defines or delimits the role of Christ as regards the Father and the Spirit, on the one hand, and as regards our human society of persons, on the other.

Here, 'person' does not mean a human I-centre of free action, but rather an organizing factor within the purality of the self. This indeed is Whitehead's metaphor of the 'living person': it is the unifying factor within a pluralistic society. I repeat: personal reality is neither a substance nor a substantial power. It is with this that I have characterized the bipolar God, and now I apply the same to Jesus Christ. Nor is personal reality the *direct* logical subject of predicates about him. The person rather *owns* that plural self which it assumes in union. In this way it can be the *secondary* subject of our affirmations. In the case of Jesus, human attributes are borne by his self and divine ones (if any) by the self as *related to the Logos* – an expression in which I later point to its free responsibility. Furthermore, the person is bearer of dignity: for dignity is not a solipsistic attribute, but one that accrues to someone *in relation to his fellows*. For the time being: so much for the Chalcedonian union which is first and foremost *personal*.

I shall have to revise in this case the other Chalcedonian term, namely, the human *nature* of Christ. If I assume that personal reality is through and through relational, then I can regard what was called 'human nature' in Christ as the enduring position of the personal. Relying on what I have said on the 'persons' in the Trinity,[57] Jesus Christ is so constituted that in his bipolar being, unlike us humans, the personal posits the enduring human self. Just as in God the personal prevails over the permanent and 'substantial', so it is, *mutatis mutandis*, in the basic constitution of Jesus the Christ. Therefore, it is by no means the human in him which incorporates the divine, but the other way round: the divine posits what is permanently human in him. Thus, the first Christological insight in the history of dogma, that of Nicea, is reaffirmed: the divinity of Jesus the Christ.

The just proposed view entails the already mentioned *anhypostasia* or *enhypostasia* of Leonce of Bizance,[58] however not in the sense that Jesus' nature being a-personal is nothing but a lifeless instrument. In a constitutive correlationship, as I noted above, that which is incorporated in another retains its own characteristic, its own freedom, and its own way of progress. Thus subsistence/*hypostasis* can be taken as the ultimate and enduring determination of what is human in Christ, that is, his self. It is free in our created human way. Then it is false to reserve freedom only for human consciousness or for the so-called 'personal' in its modern sense. On the contrary, in accordance with process thought, I am convinced that all that is, from simple physical entities up to human self can be characterized by freedom. This is why Whitehead's organistic philosophy regards all actual entities as subjects capable of prehending, capable of choice and decision, however odd this might seem at first sight.

If this is true, then we should cease to speak of a static human nature in Christ, but rejoin Rahner in speaking of an autonomous and free I-centre which is, in all but one aspect, similar to ours. It has its own history, its own present and future. It is free and autonomous with the only difference that its ultimate identity is based on its origin – coming from the Logos, and its future ruled by the possibility of arriving at him. For the Whiteheadian 'subjective aim' of this human self is the ultimate identification (of the man Jesus the Christ) with God's merciful utterance to the whole world. God in his Logos has posited or defined himself as man in Jesus the Christ. And with this he opened for us a possibility of a different way of being human.

This last statement is borrowed from W. Kasper's *Jesus the Christ* who is with Galli another severe critic of Rahner's, as he calls it, 'accommodation-Christology'.[59] Leaving aside his detailed criticism, he approaches the mystery of Christ from the dimension of the 'personal'. The Christ whom Kasper aims to explain in accordance with, yet going beyond, Chalcedon, is the one in whom 'we are faced with a new possibility . . . of being human, that of living a human life for God and others'.[60] The newness which is for us only a possibility is a reality at least in the origin and in the fulfilled destination of Jesus of Nazareth. We, men and women, have to *become* personal not by gaining a new quality or arriving at the highest pitch of our subjectivity, but in encounter and communion, in correlationship and solidarity with other persons. What we believe of Christ is that the dawn of his life and its ending are rooted in the Trinitarian 'history' of God.[61]

This, indeed, is the trend of Kasper's Christology. When we speak in the above explained sense of the 'personal union' over and above the 'hypostatic union' of Chalcedon, it is not only the personal Logos which enables by entering into a constitutive relationship with the human I-centre of the man Jesus, but the Blessed Trinity. If the Logos is the person who is also united with the Father in the bond of the Spirit of inner-Trinitarian communion, then the personality of Jesus the Christ is not straightaway constituted by the Logos, but ultimately by the communion of the Trinitarian Father and Son – by the Holy Spirit. In faith's encounter with Jesus the Christ, we meet through the man Jesus not only the Logos, but also that personal 'We' of the Blessed Trinity, in whom H. Mühlen discerns the Holy Spirit.[62] We encounter in him the personified Love of God.

I am not here going to argue this apparently abstract and speculative scheme in all its ramifications. It should be enough to show that my position is defensible against the charge of Nestorianism on the one hand, and monophysitism or monothelitism on the other. Since I have assumed and argued above that the ultimate reality as regards the divine is the personal, it cannot be held against me that a 'merely' personal union between the two Chalcedonian natures in Christ is tantamount to Nestorian 'moral' unity and nothing else.[63] On the other hand, by stating the a-personality of the human in Christ I do not diminish his manhood, since I can safely ascribe full individuality, freedom and selfhood to what is human in him. With Rahner, or even with Deodat de Basly[64] I can speak of an autonomous I-centre in Christ which *de se* could exist and develop outside the union: it is complete in all

its refinements. What is human in Christ can safely be sub-
jected to the analysis of psychology and sociology, and Jesus
himself can be listened to as man of his age. There is, however, a proviso: with this, in itself necessary, analysis one
could not encounter *the person who Jesus of Nazareth was*.
Rahner's ontological consciousness Christology certainly
does not lead to this recognition. As Galli correctly remarks at
the end of his hypercritical article, Rahner confronts us with a
man who in all his life was in search of who he in fact was.[65]
Who the man Jesus of Nazareth was can only be believed in
the encounter of faith. But this encounter in faith has a better
chance if we follow the here outlined Christological scheme,
to meet God's personal Logos in his Trintarian role. His
human self is, no doubt, of interest for our human striving, but
it is his divine presence gradually transforming the human self
where we are challenged to lead a new life. It is there that the
'personal' in him is revealed to us.

Still, the question remains, what difference does it make
when I prefer to speak of a *personal*, and not of the traditional
hypostatic, union? To illustrate this, let us take the classical
view of Christ's *sinlessness*, according to which the God-man
was not capable of sin: *peccare non potuit*.

To quote Trethowan:

> A human person is exposed to sin . . . The human nature of
> Christ is not that sort of created reality . . . [that is, in Jesus
> Christ], *there was no human centre of moral responsibility*, but
> the divine person acted upon the human will, acted in that will
> without hindrance and without the possibility of hindrance.[66]

I guess Rahner would, with some right, have regarded this
argumentation as basically monothelistic. Especially had he
read Trethowan's other article where he repeats the rule of
thumb of orthodox Christology: the acts of Jesus were the acts
of the Word made flesh.[67]

Yet in one aspect Trethowan is right: it is to the person that
moral responsibility belongs and not to one's natural self. He
is, however, wrong in saying that the person 'acts' through or
in his natural self. No, to act is something which belongs to
the natural self with its human history. To be fully responsible

for, or even taking responsibility for one's own or someone else's actions presupposes the person. Thus I should say in correcting Trethowan that the Word *owns*, so to speak, all the actions of the man Jesus: not the free self, but the person is responsible. Therefore, in the case of Christ we cannot speak of an *essential* impeccability of his human self. His so-called nature is not essentially sinless, but he is personally not capable of sin. For sin in its depth is not a natural failure, not an act, but an event in the texture of society, within the community of persons. Only the person whose guilt it proves to be, the person who is made to, or is ready to take reponsibility for an act can be blamed for sin.[68] In allowing this, we shall be better prepared for the doctrine of atonement, the treatment of which belongs elsewhere.

Thus personal rather than hypostatic union of Jesus the Christ means that we can safely attribute genuinely human actions, including error and uncertainty, fatigue and weakness to the human self of Jesus. We can equally attribute actions which apparently break through our human possibilities (for instance, miracles) or, much more, a world view, a rapport with God, an attitude which transcends our normal human capabilities, to what was divine in Jesus the Christ. But all of these are owned by the one person who was made, or made himself, responsible for it. When it was said a divine person died on the cross, it does not mean that the act of dying is attributed to God. Yet the saying is true, if the divine Person is ready to make it his own, be responsible for the death of the man Jesus of Nazareth. And as we shall see in the doctrine of atonement the death and resurrection of Jesus, by the very fact that it is owned by the Logos, becomes an event in the 'history' of God, one and three.

I am aware that my argument is theoretical and abstract. It cannot be otherwise, for so were the Christological discussions at the time of Chalcedon. Anyone who tries to follow and understand their meaning has to make an effort to reach the level of an abstract discourse which, in any case, is not the sort of language in which to confront our contemporary world. Yet, as we hope, if we are able to convince our fellow Christians, and eventually those who are searching for the ultimate sense of life, that our speculation proffers an answer to the question still alive in the hearts of many: *who was Jesus the Christ?* For this is the question that the Chalcedonian Fathers attempted to answer more than 1,500 years ago. And it is the question which guided Rahner in the best part of his Christology.

5.4 Christology and Anthropology

From among the many facets of Rahner's Christological thought the most attractive, I believe, is and will continue to be, his *anthropological* approach to the Mystery of Christ. It is this aspect which I have left to the very end of this section. My guess is that it will not be Rahner the theologian of the doctrine of Christ, but rather Rahner the apologist of faith in Jesus the Christ who will occupy a memorable place in the history of Christology.

This statement, however, immediately needs to be qualified. I am referring to those elements of Rahner's many-faceted Christology in which he tries to explain Christian faith *ad extra* to persuade the waverer of the truth of Jesus the Christ. Amongst these one should include, what I have termed, witnessing and inquiring Christology.

When I speak of Rahner's anthropological approach to Christ I shall mainly have these facets in mind and not what is mostly associated with his name, his transcendental Christology. If it proves that his reinterpretation of Chalcedon, his all-embracing theory of symbolism as applied to the Mystery of Christ, is ruled by the *Idea of Christ* and by his so-called transcendental Christology, I shall have to part company.

This disagreement arises on the grounds of what, following W. Kasper, I have stated above: 'The God-man Jesus the Christ opened for us a possibility of a *different way* of being human.'[69] If this is true, then the whole edifice of Rahner's transcendental Christology would be put to the test. For from whatever angle I consider his Christological efforts, Rahner's message for us entailed in the Incarnation of Christ is the imperative of our being fully human. It is written in our human existence, in its transcendental openness, in our existential situation that we are with God's grace enabled to expand our human potentialities and thereby follow the one in whom humanity has reached its highest peak, Jesus the Christ. This, according to Rahner can be made understandable from the relationship between creation and incarnation, from the becoming of God in his 'symbol' the Logos, from the role of man and Christ in an evolutionary world view, etc. So where is the absolute newness which the coming of Christ bestows upon us? According to this view we could not speak of a *different way* of being human. A similar suspicion made me ask, in discussing the status of the biblical story in Rahner's system, what is the factual element in man's belief in Christ – that we are all in the situation of grace and hence can see in this man Jesus the universal bringer of salvation, or that, out of our concrete encounter with the historical event of Jesus and moved by his message of his Kingdom, we can come to the grace of faith? To put it more concretely: does the actual acquaintance with the story of the New Testament *generate* faith in Jesus the Christ, or is it rather that the faith that we, perhaps implicitly, already have verifies the man Jesus with whom we are confronted in the Bible? I am, then, left with these questions as the problem of this concluding section.

The ambiguity of Rahner's answer has already been hinted at in the previous sections of this chapter. There, I had to point out that transcendental Christology as a whole conflates two kinds of experience: an experience inbuilt in man's transcendental subjectivity producing the Idea of Christ, the absolute Saviour, *and* an experience which already has something to do both with the concrete Christian community's belief in Christ (for example, the dogma of Chalcedon) and with the concrete historical figure of Jesus of Nazareth. I understood Rahner as saying that transcendental Christology was not only the former (that is, the finding of the Christ-idea), but somehow also this latter concrete experience which some have. Thus, in Rahner's mind, transcendental Christology was hovering delicately between the *a priori* and *a posteriori*, the strictly transcendental and the categorial, yes, between a mentally disclosed idea and an encounter with something concrete. The one is universal, the other particular. Perforce to hold these two together by means of a transcendental Christology (whose 'epochal', that is, contemporary necessity, Rahner argues in *Foundations*) is to envisage the Mystery of Christ under the question which launched the eighteenth- and nineteenth-century *Aufklärung* and the movement of German Idealism: how can a concrete and particular event be of universal significance?[70]

Now, both the pronouncement of the dogma and man's encounter with the Jesus of the Bible are particular events, whereas the Christ-idea is spoken of as something universally possible, nay, unavoidable. If, therefore, this question rules Rahner's anthropological approach to the doctrine of Christ, then I can only leave him to his own devices and continue my search in other quarters.

Yet, it is Rahner himself who repeatedly admits that our Christological faith implies a moment of 'synthesis, which ultimately cannot be made completely reflexive' (that is, it cannot be disclosed by transcendental reflection).[71] The question is, what is this moment of synthesis which is ultimately not systematizable? I find it hard to give a clear-cut answer on Rahner's behalf. Again, it is the later Rahner of the *Foundations* who, in arguing against the critics of transcendental Christology, concedes the following three points:

(a) the decisions of practical reason and the relationship to a concrete person in his historical concreteness can never be deduced completely in a transcendental way . . .

(b) although a transcendental Christology *per se* is *a priori* to a concrete, historical relationship to Jesus Christ and to the Christology which reflects upon this relationship . . . nevertheless it is temporally and historically *subsequent* to the usual [that is, traditional] Christology' . . .

(c) the incarnation of the divine Logos in our history is an absolute miracle which encounters us and cannot be deduced . . . [nor] be reached surreptitiously by speculation.[72]

If Rahner stands by these premises (proffered by him as objections to transcendental Christology), and even if he tries in his reply to maintain their 'epochal' necessity,[73] I still do not see their usefulness. For, as he himself says, faith is a decision of practical reason, and as such, is bound to an encounter with a concrete person. This encounter is, *pace*

Rahner, unforeseeable. Once it occurs it may, but most likely will *not*, correspond to that idea of absolute saviour which one has *a priori* worked out. If, however, as Rahner concedes, this idea is projected *after* the encounter, it is by no means sure that it will be acceptable for faith or for theological discourse. Hence Rahner's last sentence (c) is all that we can say of the above-mentioned unsystematizable moment of our belief in Jesus who is the Christ. My conviction is that the Christian today has to abide with the limited particularity of the Christ-event in which some men and women in one way or another encounter the historical man, Jesus of Nazareth, and become convinced that he is *witness* to truth beyond the reach of man and that *his* message is able to give meaning to the absurdity of human existence.

Nonetheless, apart from his dubious transcendental Christology, Rahner's anthropological approach to the Mystery of Christ is today of great significance. I have tried to indicate my own position by presenting his transcendental Idea of Christ as sandwiched between the concepts of *witness* and *inquiring Christology*.[74] The first was a more concrete version of his ontological theory of symbolism[75] and the second (that is, 'inquiring Christology') an approach to Christ based on the analysis of concrete human existence. At least on the one side, *witness* presupposes faith in that unsystematizable element of one's encounter with Christ, whereas the analysis of concrete human *existence* can point, as Rahner shows,[76] to the absurdity of human living. Starting with witnessing in awareness of the absurdity of the *'condition humaine'* we are on the level of human inter-subjectivity manifest in the *human* encounter of person to person. It is a matter of hope that in this human encounter the *demonstratio christiana ad intra* and *ad extra,* a reflexive theological grasp of Christ's Mystery or a Christological mystagogy, can come about. So much for Rahner, and the common basis on which we can both talk of an anthropological Christology. This partial agreement with Rahner's approach is our shared starting point.

Of course, this initially common basis with Rahner can be developed with varying emphases. Our starting points being practically the same, the goal of both anthropologically orientated Christologies might be similar. Both views aim at a universal validity for faith in Jesus the Christ. For Rahner, it will, no doubt, be a universality of an *a priori* kind, whereas I shall be satisfied with the universality that was Jesus' own claim and his practical message: to convince those who have ears to listen and eyes to see that we are God the Father's children and that it is our mission to spread the Kingdom of God on earth until it grows up into the communion of mankind in peace with the 'community' of God. Jesus' claim and message reached few. Together with every Christian it is my task now to extend it in the same history which he consecrated with his presence. Briefly, the universality is only in this sense an *a priori* one, which I cannot but anticipate in hope.

Rahner is correct in starting his analysis of witnessing with an interpersonal encounter. The question is, what happens in this witnessing encounter? As I have summed up Rahner's answer:

> When these individuals encounter one another as free persons their communication becomes an intercommunion in which not only their respective ego is witnessed to, but also that grace which is the impetus of their 'radicalized' transcendence towards God.[77]

This answer, I believe, is not only abstract, but it presupposes the whole of Rahner's transcendental anthropology. Why could not we simply state that witnessing Christ consists in a *narrative* which relates the story of Jesus in such a way that it corresponds to the concrete situation of persons in encounter.[78] Thus a theology of witness would lead straight to the historical Jesus, however, with the question in the background whether his life and teaching could be relevant for our present situation.

Rahner is right in saying that a communication in an encounter must become an intercommunion in order that it may function as a witness. But we know that such an intercommunion is never complete: it is always in the making; it is always exposed to difficulties and common problems. An encounter between persons is at the same time a communion in search of shared happiness despite all the obstacles which threaten it. And when in this common search the partners hear about the story and teaching of Jesus, they might grasp the significance of their own fellowship. He was the man whose double relationship to and intercommunion with the Father and with his fellows defined his life. This communal search is, I believe, the *Sitz im Leben* of all witnessing.[79]

In this communal search we may initially discover neither the eternal Son nor his Father, but as a human intercommunion quickened by the common spirit, we may be enabled to believe in the Holy Spirit in whom and through whom Jesus is united with the Father and with his fellows. To have faith in the Spirit of God is not an experience of some supernatural driving force in each individual, but rather the experience of being able to be together, reconciled in purposeful peace: a community becoming a true fellowship. Only then, in reflecting on our own human fellowship, can we surmise that this man Jesus is, and always was, living in *koinonia* with that Person of whom he says: 'I and the Father are one', that is, in their union of love. In this love the Spirit can be recognized.

Yet, this side of our Christological build-up is only a possibility which, however, Christian *praxis* proves to be inevitable. And this Christian *praxis* is, precisely, growing up into that absolute trust in our fellows, in our future, despite inevitable death, as motivated by nothing else than our acquaintance with this man, Jesus of Nazareth. In this trust, which can take the form of love of neighbour, hope in tomorrow and faith beyond the grave, we do not, as Rahner maintains, discover the absolute saviour as an idea of a person to whom vicariously our commitment is given. It is rather a commitment to the other person in whose company the narrative about Jesus was first heard, and together with whom we sought the mystery of this man, Jesus. In the Christian *praxis* it takes the shape of living according to his message, of discovering his Kingdom gradually forming itself in our communion, of spreading the message about this Kingdom for others in search of their own happiness, not, as we shall see, in the transcendent *beyond*, but here and now. The intimation of this common happiness with our fellows in search of a faith in Jesus the Son of God is the best witness to him who, for our sake, became man and lived in fellowship with us until his death on the cross. As Paul says, 'no one can say "Jesus is the Lord" except by the Holy Spirit (1 Cor 12:3b). But this Spirit which will be 'poured into our hearts' (Rom 5:50) will be ours if in our human witnessing we discover the true and eternal Witness, Jesus the Christ.

Is the above plan an alternative position to Rahner's witnessing and inquiring Christology? That is something which the reader must decide. In any case, my conviction is that in assuming Rahner's anthropological bases (excepting his transcendental Christology), and by developing a parallel approach to Christ, we should ultimately reach the same goal. This goal is, as Rahner himself constantly emphasized, to believe in and to see the salvation of mankind in Jesus of Nazareth. Since the ultimate value of his Christology depends upon soteriology, our attempt to understand him must now look toward this doctrine of salvation.

Epilogue

It will have been in many ways a *tour de force* for the reader to have grasped what Rahner intended in reconsidering the doctrine of God, the Trinity and of Jesus the Christ. Yet it has perhaps been even more difficult to follow my critical reflections and alternative positions. I by no means pretend that these latter will offer a ready-made doctrinal synthesis. My suggestions are not meant to be a kind of counter-systematics opposed to Rahner's whole theological thought. I hope, nevertheless, that in struggling with his various ideas the theologically interested reader may have been moved to develop his own thought. For, in entering the field of Christian doctrines, no longer proposed *ad usum delphini* (that is, the first level of theological reflection), I am free not to abide with traditional formulations alone, but to proceed to further insights. A dogma, as Rahner says, when it is clearly defined by the Church or held by her major theologians, is never an end, but a beginning. To these major theologians, I believe, Karl Rahner also belongs.

But even so, what he says is not the last word. Theology is advanced by trial and error and never by reducing its tenets to what is immediately within the reach of our experience. Yet, to speak of experience within theology is inevitable. In doctrinal theology this experience is of a complex kind: it implies, among other things, the attempt to understand our partner in dialogue as well as to find holes in his reasoning. To fill up these holes is the task of an advancing systematic theology. It is such an experience which I sought to convey throughout these pages.

If my own understanding of dogma and Christian doctrines, my repeated insistence on the belief in (and not knowledge of) creation, my concept of a bipolar God who, on the level of his personal reality, can change and, finally, that theandric unity which is constantly defined and posited by the personal Logos of God can be regarded as viable, then we have moved closer to a theology built on objective faith and its content. This theology is about the revelation of God who in Jesus the Christ gives us the opportunity to encounter his divine Majesty not only as a personal reality, but as the loving communion of the Father, the Son, and the Holy Spirit. To grasp that in faith allows us to reinterpret man and his world and to lay the bases for our own future. For, ultimately, having seen ourselves mirrored in God, theology is, and should be, about man and his world. The mirror is Jesus the Christ and his salvation offered for our free acceptance.

In my next volume I shall concentrate on this reflection which enlightens us when looking into the mirror. What we shall see can be summed up in one word: salvation.

Bibliography

Aquinas, St Thomas (1950) *Summa Theologiae*, Turin.

Bantle, F. X. (1979) 'Person und Personbegriff in der Trinitätslehre Karl Rahners', *Münchener Theologische Zeitschrift* 30, pp. 11–24.

Barth, K. (1963) *Church Dogmatics*, Vol. I, Edinburgh.

Bent, C. N. (1969) *Interpreting the Doctrine of God*, New York, NY, Amsterdam, London.

Bracken, J. A. (1974) 'The Holy Trinity as a Community of Divine Persons', *Heythrop Journal* 15, pp. 166–80 and 257–70.

—— (1975) 'Toward an Ecumenical Consensus on the Trinity', *Theologische Zeitschrift* (Basel) 31, pp. 337–50.

Casper, B. (1967) *Das dialogische Denken. Eine Untersuchung der religionsphilosophische Bedeutung Franz Rosenzweigs, Ferdinand Ebners und Martin Bubers*, Freiburg-im-Breisgau.

Cobb, J. B. jnr., and Griffin, D. R. (1967) *Process Theology: An Introductory Exposition*, Brescia.

Donceel, J. (1971) 'Second Thoughts on the Nature of God', *Thought* 46, pp. 346–70.

Donnelly, M. J. (1947) 'The Inhabitation of the Holy Spirit: A Solution according to de la Taille', *Münchener Theologische Studien*, 8, pp. 445–70.

Doud, R. E. (1977) 'Rahner's Christology: a Whiteheadian Critique', *Journal of Religion* 57, pp. 144–55.

Eicher, P. (1970) *Die anthropologische Wende*, Freibourg (Switzerland).

Evans, D. B. (1970) *Leontius of Byzantium*, Washington, DC.

Findlay, J. N. (1958) *The Philosophy of Hegel*, New York, NY.

Fischer, K. P. (1974) *Der Mensch als Geheimnis*, Freiburg-im-Breisgau.

Galli, A. (1969) 'Perchè Karl Rahner nega la visione beatifica in Cristo. Premesse filosofiche della cristologia Rahneriana', *Divinitas* 13, pp. 414–56.

Galot, J. (1971) *La Conscience de Jésus*, Paris.

—— (1971) 'Dynamisme de l'incarnation. Au–de–la de la formule de Chalcedoine', *Nouvelle Revue Théologique* 93, pp. 225–44.

Galtier, P. (1950) *L'habitation en nous des trois personnes*, Rome.

Geiselmann, J. R. (1962) *Handbuch theologischer Grundbegriffe*, Vol I, Munich, pp. 225–41.

Geisser, H. (1968) 'Die Interpretation der kirchlichen Lehre des Gottmenschen bei Karl Rahner', *Kerygma und Dogma* 14.

Greiner, F. (1978) *Die Menschlichkeit der Offenbarung*, Munich.

Grillmeier, A. W. (1965) *Christ in Christian Tradition: From the Apostolic Age to Chalcedon (AD 451)*, London.

Gutwenger, E. (1968) 'Zur Trinitätslehre von "Mysterium Salutis" ', *Zeitschrift für katholische Theologie* 90, pp. 325–8.

—— (1971) *Bewusstsein und Wissen Christi. Eine dogmatische Studie*, Innsbruck (1960).

Hartshorne, C. (1962) *The Logic of Perfection*, New Haven, Conn., and London.

—— (1967) *The Divine Relativity, A Social Conception of God*, New Haven, Conn., and London.

Heijden, B. van der (1972) *Karl Rahner: Darstellung und Kritik seiner Grundpositionen*, Einsiedeln, pp. 372–85.

Hendry, G. A. and Richardson, A. (eds) (1974[3]) *A Dictionary of Christian Theology*, London, p. 58.

Hill, E. (1971) 'Karl Rahner's Remarks to the Dogmatic Treatise "De Trinitate" and "St Augustine" ', *Augustinian Studies*, 2, pp. 67–80.

Hoye, W. J. (1979) *Die Verfinsterung des absoluten Geheimnisses. Eine Kritik der Gotteslehre Karl Rahners*, Dusseldorf.

Jüngel, E. (1972) 'Die Welt als Möglichkeit und Wirklichkeit', *Unterwegs zur Sache*, Munich, pp. 106–233.

—— (1975) 'Das Verhältnis von "ökonomischer" und "immanenter" Trinität', *Zeitschrift fur Theologie und Kirche*, 72, pp. 353-64.

—— (1977) *Gottes Sein ist im Werden*, Tübingen. (ET *The Doctrine of the Trinity. God's Being is in Becoming*, Edinburgh 1976.)

—— (1977) *Gott als Geheimnis der Welt*, Tübingen.

Kaiser, P. (1968) *Die Gott-menschliche Einigung in Christus als Problem der spekultiven Theologie seit der Scholastick*, Munich.

Kasper, W. (1976) *Jesus the Christ*, London.

Kelly, A. J. (1970) 'Trinity and Process: The Relevance of the Basic

Christian Confession', *Theological Studies* 31, pp. 393–414.

Kunz, E. (1969) *Glaube-Gnade-Geschichte*, Frankfurt, pp. 47ff.

Langemeyer, B. (1963) *Der dialogische Personalismus in der evange-lischen und katholischen Theologie der Gegenwart*, Paderborn.

Link, C. (1976) *Die Welt als Geheimnis*, Münich, p. 164.

Lonergan, B. (1964) *De Deo Trino*, Vol II, Rome.

—— (1971) *Method in Theology*, London.

Macmurray, J. (1961) *Persons in Relation*, London.

Macquarrie, J. (1966) *Principles of Christian Theology*, London.

Malmberg, F. (1960) 'Über den Gottmenschen', *Quaestiones Disputatae* 9, Freiburg-im-Breisgau.

Marinelli, F. (1969) 'Dimensione trintaria del' incarnazione', *Divinitas* 13, pp. 272–343.

Metz, J. B. (1973) 'Kleine Apologie des Erzählens', *Concilium* 9, pp. 334ff.

Mühlen, H. (1963) *Der heilige Geist als Person*, Münster.

—— (1965) 'Person und Appropriation: Zum Verständnis des Axioms: Deo omnia sunt unum', *Münchener Theologische Studien*, 16, pp. 37–57.

—— (1969) *Die veränderlichkeit Gottes als Horizont einer zukünfti-gen Christologie*, Münster.

Neufeld, K. H. (1974) 'Fortschritt durch Umkehr: Zu Karl Rahners bussgeschichtlichen Arbeiten', *Stimmen der Zeit*, 192, pp. 274–81.

O'Collins, G. (1977) 'What are they saying about Jesus?', New York, NY., and Toronto, Ont.

O'Donnell, J. J. (1983) *Trinity and Temporality: The Christian Doctrine of God in the Light of Process Theology and the Theology of Hope*, Oxford.

Ogden, S. (1967) *The Reality of God*, London.

Pannenberg, W. (1970) *Jesus God and Man*, London.

Pearl, T. (1975) 'Dialectical Panentheism: on the Hegelian Character of K. Rahner's Key Christological Writings', *Irish Theological Quarterly*, 42, pp. 119–37.

Pittenger, N. (1968) 'Process Theology', in *A Dictionary of Christian Theology*, (ed.) A. Richardson, London, pp. 275ff.

Rad, G. von (1957) *Theologie des Alten Testaments*, Vol I: 'Die Theologie der geschichtlichen Überlieferung Israels', Munich, p.182.

—— (1965) 'Das theologische Problem des alttestamentlichen

Schöpfungsglaubens', *Gesammelte Schriften*, Munich, pp. 136–47.

Renton, H. M. (1917) *A Study in Christology: The Problem of the Two Natures of Christ*, London.

Robertson, J. C. (1970) 'Rahner and Ogden: "Man's Knowledge of God" ', *Harvard Theological Review* 63, pp. 377–407.

Rousselot, P. (1910) 'Les yeux de la foi', *Recherche Science en Religieuse*, 1, pp. 241–59 and 444–75.

Sanna, I. (1970) *La cristologia antropologica de P. Karl Rahner*, Rome.

Scheffzyk, L. (1977) 'Trinität: Das Specificum Christianum', *Schwerpunkte des Glaubens*, Einsiedeln.

———— (1977) 'Christentum als Unmittelbarkeit zu Gott. Erwagungen zu K. Rahners Grundkurs des Glaubens', *Communio* 6, pp. 442–50.

Schell, H. (1889) *Katholische Dogmatik*, Vol I, pp. 23f and Vol II, pp. 20f.

Schilson A. and Kasper, W. (1974) 'Christologie im Präsens', in *Kritische Sichtung neuerer Entwürfe*, Freiburg–im–Breisgau.

Schleiermacher, F. *(1968) Christian Faith*, Edinburgh.

Schmaus, M. (1960) *Katholische Dogmatik*, Vol 1, Münich, pp. 494ff.

Schmidt, W. H. (1977) *Biblische Kommentare*, Vol. II: 'Exodus', Neukirchen-Vluyn, pp. 102 and 175ff.

Schoonenberg, P. (1984) 'Zur Trinitätslehre Karl Rahners' in E. Klinger and K. Wittstadt (eds), *Glaube im Prozess, Christentum nach dem II Vatikanum, Für Karl Rahner*, Freiburg–im–Breisgau, pp. 471–91.

Schulte, R. (1975) 'Die Gottesoffenbarung des AT als vorläufige Trinitätsoffenbarung', *MS* II, pp. 55–73.

Schupp, F. (1974) 'Auf dem Weg zu einer kritischen Theologie' in *Quaestiones Disputatae*, 64, Freiburg–im–Breisgau.

Sellers, R. V. (1953) *The Council of Chalcedon*, London, pp. 210f.

Shepherd, W. (1969) *Man's Condition, God and the World Process*, New York, NY., p. 199.

Tillich, P. (1960) *Systematic Theology*, Vol I, London and Chicago, Ill.

Torrance, T. (1975) 'Toward an Ecumenical Consensus on the Trinity', *Theologische Zeitschrift* (Basel) 31, pp. 337–50.

Trethowan, I. (1966) 'A Changing God', *Downside Review* 84, pp. 247–61.

———— (1977) 'Christology Again', *Downside Review* 95, pp. 1–10.

Vogel, H.-J. (1978) 'Personen oder Weisen? Zur Trinitätslehre Karl Rahners', *Rheinischer Merkur*, 33 (18 August).

Wainwright, A. W. (1962) *The Trinity in the New Testament*, London.

Walgrave, J. (1972) *Unfolding Revelation, Theological Resources*, London and Westminster, Pa.

Whitehead, A. N. (1978) *Process and Reality*, (eds) D. R. Griffin and D. W. Shelbourne, New York, NY., and London.

Wiederker, D. (1973) 'Konfrontationen und Integrationen der Christologie', *Theologische Berichte*, Vol. II, Einsiedeln, pp. 11-120.

———— (1978) 'Christologie im Kontext', *Theologische Berichte*, Vol. VII, Einsiedeln, pp. 11–62.

Notes

Chapter 1: Objective Faith

1. See 'Scheme' and 'Heresy'. See also 'Zur Reform des Theologiestudiums', in St Thomas Aquinas, *Quaestiones Disputatae*, 41, Freiburg-im-Breisgau (1968), pp. 48ff. (An ET of this edition is not yet available.)
2. By *Fachidiotie* Rahner means a specialist in a narrow field of doctrine, or doctrinal history. This specialization would not be appropriate to teaching (that is, introducing students to theology on the first level of reflection, as defined in his *Foundations*).
3. See *Investigations* XV which contains studies published around 1950. The subject of these studies is the penitential doctrine of Hermas, Tertullian, Cyprian, the Didascalia and, above all, of Origen. See also, K. H. Neufeld, 'Fortschritt durch Umkehr: Zu Karl Rahners bussgeschichtlichen Arbeiten', *Stimmen der Zeit*, 192 (1974), pp. 274–81.
4. It is mainly from private conversations and occasional television and radio interviews, that Rahner's modesty, approaching almost an inferiority complex, concerning his genuine scholarly achievement (his *Wissenschaftlichkeit*) can be perceived. See, for example, the introductory letter in P. Eicher, *Die anthropologische Wende: K. Rahners philosophischer Weg vom Wesen des Menschen zur personalen Existenz*, Freiburg-im-Breisgau (1970) where Rahner remarks: 'Apart from a few essays on the history of penance (which belong to the history of dogma) nothing I have written can be called theological scholarship, let alone (professional) philosophy.' See also, 'Some Clarifying Remarks about my Own Work', *Investigations* XVII, pp. 243ff (=*Schriften* XII, pp. 599ff).
5. It is to be noted that early, and also later, systematic studies on penance can be regarded as fruits of Rahner's historical research. See, for example: 'Forgotten Truths concerning the Sacrament of Penance', *Investigations* II, pp. 135–74 (=*Schriften* II, pp. 143–83); 'The Meaning of Frequent Confession of Devotion', *Investigations* III, pp. 177–89 (=*Schriften* III, pp. 211–25); 'Problems concerning Confession', *Investigations* III, pp. 190–206 (=*Schriften* III, pp.

227–45); 'Guilt-Responsibility-Punishment within the View of Catholic Theology', *Investigations* VI, pp. 197–217 (=*Schriften* VI, pp. 238–61); 'Penance as an Additional Act of Reconciliation with the Church', *Investigations* X, pp. 125–49 (=*Schriften* VIII, pp. 447–87).

6. Cf. 'Man and his World as a Nature with a Supernatural Finality', *Investigations* I, p. 24 (=*Schriften* I, p. 34).

7. See 'Zur Reform des Theologiestudiums', in St Thomas Aquinas, *Quaestiones Disputatae*, 41, Freiburg-im-Breisgau (1968), p. 49.

8. Cf. Volume 2, especially section 5.2.2.

9. See F. Schupp, 'Auf dem Weg zu einer kritischen Theologie' in *Quaestiones Disputatae*, 64, Freiburg-im-Breisgau (1974), especially pp. 43–81 and pp. 124–58. Schupp is not altogether beside the point when he, in extension of and in confrontation with Rahner's ideas, projects the programme of a critical theology as eminently suitable for this second level of theological reflection.

10. For a short appraisal of the same, see K. H. Neufeld, 'Fortschritt durch Umkehr: Zu Karl Rahners bussgeschichtlichen Arbeiten', *Stimmen der Zeit*, 192 (1974), pp. 274–81. Also, M. Mugge, 'Entwicklung und theologischer Kontext der Busstheologie Karl Rahners' in H. Vorgrimler (ed.), *Wagnis Theologie, Erfahrungen mit der Theologie Karl Rahners*, Freiburg-im-Breisgau (1979), pp. 435–50.

11. Cf. B. Lonergan, *Method in Theology,* London (1971). Lonergan describes the so-called 'functional specialities' and distinguishes between 'foundations' and 'communications'. The former is the moment of choice for faith, to be expanded by 'doctrines' and 'systematics' which in their turn find their way to 'communications'. This differentiation, of course, is hardly reflected by Rahner.

12. For a general and most reliable commentary on the Roman Catholic concept of dogma, see J. R. Geiselmann, *Handbuch theologischer Grundbegriffe*, Munich (1963) Vol I, pp. 225–41. See also the early study on Rahner by C. N. Bent, *Interpreting the Doctrine of God*, New York, NY., Amsterdam, Turin and London (1969), especially pp. 140–224.

13. Cf. Geiselmann, *Handbuch*, pp. 225–30.

14. See 'Dogmatic', p. 43 (= p. 55) and p. 46 (= p. 59). Compare this to 'Dogma', p. 95: 'The absolute character of claim and obligation of dogma is addressed precisely to man's freedom . . . Dogma and freedom are . . . actually complementary terms.'

15. 'Dogmatic', p. 46 (= p. 59).

16. 'Dogma', p. 96.

17. Ibid.: 'Consequently, dogma now exists in the full sense of the

absolute and supreme claim by which ultimate salvation or perdition is decided.'
18. 'Dogmatic', p. 48 (= p. 61).
19. Ibid., p. 50 (= pp. 63f).
20. Ibid., p. 47 (=p. 60).
21. See Volume 2, section 5.3.
22. 'Dogmatic', p. 46 (=p. 59).
23. Ibid., pp. 48f (= p. 62).
24. Ibid., p. 51 (= p. 64).
25. Ibid., p. 60 (= p. 74).
26. See the third thesis of 'Dogmatic' and point 3 of 'Dogma'.
27. 'Dogmatic', p. 52 (= p. 65).
28. 'Dogma', p. 96.
29. 'Dogmatic', p. 60 (= p. 75).
30. Ibid., p. 53 (= p. 67).
31. Ibid.
32. Ibid.
33. 'Dogma', p. 96.
34. 'Dogmatic', p. 55 (= p. 68).
35. Ibid., p. 58 (= p. 72).
36. Cf. 'Heresy', pp. 28ff. See also: 'What is Heresy?', *Investigations* V, pp. 468–512 (= *Schriften* V, pp. 527–76); 'Heresies in the Church Today', *Investigations* XII, pp. 117–41 (= *Schriften* IX, pp. 453–78); 'Schism in the Catholic Church?', *Investigations* XII, pp. 98–115 (=*Schriften* IX, pp. 432–52); 'Concerning our Assent to the Church as She Exists in the Concrete', *Investigations* XII, pp. 142–60 (= *Schriften* IX, pp. 479–97). Note, however, that in these essays one can hardly see the difference between heresy and schism.
37. As I am not going into detail regarding Rahner's contributions to the problem of development, readers are referred here to J. Walgrave, *Unfolding Revelation,* Theological Resources, London and Philadelphia, Pa. (1972). See also, C. N. Bent, *Interpreting the Doctrine of God*, New York, NY., Amsterdam, Turin and London (1969), especially pp. 140–224.
38. For Rahner, the historicity of Christian truth is a constantly recurring theme. See, for example: 'The Historicity of Theology', *Investigations* X, pp. 64–82 (= *Schriften* VIII, pp. 88–110); 'The Future of Theology', *Investigations* XI, pp. 137–46 (=*Schriften* IX, pp. 148–57).
39. 'History', p. 10 (= p. 19).
40. Ibid., p. 33 (= p. 45).
41. See Volume 2, especially sections 1.1 and 1.3.

42. See J. R. Geiselmann, *Handbuch* in Vol 1, p. 226. And compare with the understanding of dogma as an 'opinion' in P. Tillich, *Systematic Theology*, Vol I, London and Chicago, Ill. (1960), pp. 36f.

Chapter 2: **God Revisited: The Doctrine of the Trinity**

1. See Volume 1, sections 4.2 and 5.2.
2. Volume 1, section 7.1. See also Volume 2, Introduction.
3. That is, the implicit knowledge of God and of salvation; the explicit knowledge of God and creation; free decision for God and the possibility of guilt in 'original sin'.
4. *Foundations*, p. 133 (= *Grundkurs*, p. 139).
5. Remember that the *ST* was written for beginners; see St Thomas's Prologue: '. . . *non solum provectos instruere, sed incipientes erudire* . . .'
6. For the significance of 'Theos', compare 'The Mystery of the Trinity', which is an introductory letter by Rahner to a work published in Portuguese. And compare, too, with *Investigations* XVI, pp. 255–9 (= *Schriften* XII, pp. 320–5).
7. Cf. Rahner's references in *Revelation* (corresponding chapters), especially to DS 3004 and the corresponding canon DS 3025 (see Tanner, pp. 806 and 810). The statement about the possibility of knowing God by natural reason was extended by Pius X in the redoubtable oath against Modernism. This alone features the words *'per demonstrationem'*, that is, by unaided natural reason (cf. DS 3538).
8. Note, at the beginning of 'Theos', pp. 82ff (= pp. 93ff), Rahner does not refer to the definition as advocated by Vatican I. He rather presupposes a primordial or natural revelation as given with the fact of creation. This is why he finds in the New Testament, that 'the . . . unquestioning assurance of God's existence does not arise from any properly metaphysical considerations . . . proofs for the existence of God are never produced', p. 95 (= p. 109). Thus, the formula 'for New Testament monotheism does not run, there exists one God . . . but on the contrary, he who has actively manifested himself in Christ and in the pneumatic reality of salvation . . . that is the unique God', p. 102 (= p. 117).
9. See 'Theos', p. 112 (= p. 128): 'A person does not strictly have attributes with respect to another person: he has freely and personally adopted attitudes.' See, too, a similar approach in J.

Macquarrie, *Principles of Christian Theology*, London (1966), especially pp. 186–93.

10. 'Theos', pp. 104–12 (= pp. 119–28).
11. See *LTK* IV, p. 1093. Also the very revealing article, 'Being Open to God as Ever Greater', *Investigations* VII, pp. 25–46 (= *Schriften* VII, pp. 32–53).
12. 'Observations', p. 127 (= p. 165).
13. Ibid., p. 128 (= p. 166).
14. Ibid. This rather obscure and tortuous text in the German of the *Schriften* seems to mean simply that natural reasoning about God is necessarily implied in the relationship of faith accepting God.
15. Ibid., p. 131 (= p. 169).
16. Ibid., p. 132 (= p. 170). See also, p. 136 (= p. 176) and p. 140 (= p. 180).
17. Ibid., p. 133 (= p. 172).
18. Ibid., p. 134 (= p. 173).
19. Ibid. And see K. Barth, *Church Dogmatics, Vol* III, Edinburgh (1963), p. 41, especially first paragraph.
20. Cf. 'Observations', p. 136 (= p. 176).
21. Ibid., see p. 138 (= pp. 178f): 'The man who has not the courage to pursue metaphysics (which is not the same as a closed system), a metaphysics which can be contradicted, cannot be a good theologian. Even when one is conscious of possessing a constantly inadequate metaphysics, it is still possible to rely on it, *to use it in addressing the true God and in directing man towards the experience which he always has already from God.*' (My italics.) And see also 'Science as a Confession', *Investigations* III, pp. 385–400 (= *Schriften* III, pp. 455–72); 'The Man of Today and Religion', *Investigations* VI, pp. 3–20 (= *Schriften* VI, pp. 13–33); 'Being Open to God as Ever Greater', *Investigations* VII, pp. 25–46 (= *Schriften* VII, pp. 32–53).
22. 'Observations', pp. 143f (= p. 185).
23. Ibid., p. 143 (= p. 184).
24. The basis of this extended contribution to *MS* II is Rahner's article from 1960: 'Remarks on the Dogmatic Treatise "De Trinitate" ', *Investigations* IV, pp. 77–102 (= *Schriften* IV, pp. 103–33). Furthermore, in his article on 'The Concept of Mystery in Catholic Theology', *Investigations* IV, pp. 36–73 (= *Schriften* IV, pp. 51–103), the doctrine of the Trinity exemplified the *mysteria stricte dicta* of Vatican I. Thus, the anthropological conversion was exemplified by the doctrine of the Trinity, in his article on 'Theology and Anthropology', *Investigations* IX, pp. 28–45 (= *Schriften* VIII, pp. 43–65), especially pp. 31f (= pp. 47ff).

25. Cf. K. Barth, *Church Dogmatics, Vol I/I*, Edinburgh (1963), p. 1. For instance: 'God the Revealer is identical with his act in revelation, identical also with its effect', (ibid., p. 340); 'It is also and precisely in the That and How of this revelation that he shows himself as this God. In fact, this God will and can show himself in no other way than in the That and How of his revelation. Moreover in this That and How he is completely himself', (ibid, p. 342). Hence, 'the statement that "God reveals himself as the Lord. . . " can be called the "root of the doctrine of the Trinity",' (ibid., p. 353).
26. *Trinity*, p. 21.
27. 'Divine', p. 298.
28. See Volume 2, section 4.1.
29. It should be recalled that there are two ways of stating anything of the divine Persons: by way of *appropriation* one predicates an attribute of the divine essence as adopted to one of the Persons; the *proper* way of speaking of one Person does not contain any reference either to the common essence or to the other Persons (for example, 'The Father is Creator' can only be said *via* appropriation, whereas 'fatherhood' as predicate concerns the Father alone).
30. Cf. discussion in Volume 2, section 3.
31. *Trinity*, p. 23. (My italics.)
32. See Tanner, pp. 570f: 'These three persons are one God not three gods, because there is one substance of the three, one essence, one nature, one Godhead, one immensity, one eternity, and everything is one where the difference of a relation does not prevent it.' See also, a historical account of this principle in M. Schmaus, *Katholische Dogmatik*, Vol 1, Munich (1960[6]), pp. 494ff. Also, H. Mühlen, 'Person und Appropriation: Zum Verständnis des Axioms: Deo omnia sunt unum', *Münchener Theologischer Studien*, 16 (1965), pp. 37–57.
33. *Trinity*, pp. 25 and 27.
34. In fact this was a bone of contention in the debates concerning the *appropriated* or *proper* inhabitation of the divine Persons in engraced man. See the opposing views of P. Galtier, *L'habitation en nous des trois personnes*, Rome (1950[2]); and that of M. J. Donnelly, 'The Inhabitation of the Holy Spirit: A Solution according to de la Taille', *Münchener Theologischer Studien*, 8 (1947), pp. 445–70. Rahner's mind moves here on this second line of thought, even extending in a way the proper action of the Trinitarian God towards the creation of man and his world.
35. See Rahner's technical treatment in *Trinity*, pp. 68–73.
36. *Trinity*, pp. 26f.
37. Ibid., p. 28.

38. In *Trinity*, p. 29, and the corresponding article in *Investigations* IV, p. 84 (= *Schriften* IV, p. 112). As for Rahner's comparing Augustinian and Greek doctrines of the Trinity, see E. Hill, 'Karl Rahner's Remarks to the Dogmatic Treatise "De Trinitate" and St Augustine' in *Augustinian Studies* 2 (1971), pp. 67–80.
39. *Trinity*, p. 29.
40. Ibid., p. 28.
41. *Trinity*, pp. 32f.
42. Ibid.
43. In this reasoning Rahner's theory of symbolism is presupposed. For him, the whole of theology is incomprehensible if it is not essentially a theology of symbol. The first and foremost of these symbols is, of course, the Trinity; cf. 'The Theology of the Symbol', *Investigations* IV, pp. 221–52 (= *Schriften* IV, pp. 275–312).
44. *Trinity*, p. 36.
45. See Volume 2, section 4.1.
46. Cf. *Trinity*, p. 40.
47. Ibid.
48. *Trinity*, p. 47.
49. Ibid., p. 52.
50. Rahner here contrasts two ways of explanation of dogmatic tenets: whereas a *logical* explanation clarifies the statement independently of anything else by making it more precise, an *ontic* explanation considers the context out of which the wording of the dogma has arisen: it 'takes into account another state of affairs in such a way that this helps us to understand what is to be explained', *Trinity*, pp. 53f. Thus, a strictly dogmatic development restricts itself to a logical explanation, whereas the theologian should extend it to an ontic one.
51. *Trinity*, pp. 50f.
52. Ibid., pp. 63–8.
53. Ibid., p. 108.
54. The reader will recall that by a Sabellian modalism one understands the one and the same Godhead according to its various ways of 'appearing' to those to whom revelation is addressed: there are no distinctions in God and the so-called Persons are the 'modes' of God's appearance.
55. *Trinity*, p. 106.
56. Ibid., p. 47.
57. See Rahner's comments in *Trinity*, p. 74, n 27 and pp. 110ff, where he explains his preference to speak of *Subsistenzweisen* instead of Barth's *Seinsweisen*. Cf. K. Barth, *Church Dogmatics*, I/1, Edinburgh (1963), pp. 382, 401ff, 411f and *passim*.

58. *Trinity*, p. 107.
59. Ibid., p. 106.
60. Ibid., p. 192.
61. Ibid., pp. 11ff.
62. Ibid., p. 93.
63. Ibid., p. 94.
64. See Rahner's arguments supporting this analogy by comparing it to Augustine's psychological analogy of the Blessed Trinity (cf. *Trinity*, p. 116).
65. 'Divine', p. 300.
66. *Trinity*, pp. 97f.
67. K. Barth, *Church Dogmatics*, Edinburgh (1963), see paragraph 9 *passim*.

Chapter 3: **Comments and Questions: God in Process?**

1. I have translated freely from 'Person oder Weisen?: Zur Trinitätslehre Karl Rahners', *Rheinischer Merkur* 33, 18 August 1978.
2. Cf. this chapter, see 3.2.
3. Ibid., 3.3.
4. Ibid., 3.4.
5. Ibid., 3.1.
6. See the following criticisms: F. X. Bantle, 'Person und Personbegriff in der Trinitätslehre Karl Rahners', *Münchener Theologische Zeitschrift* 30 (1979), pp. 11–24; L. Scheffzyk, 'Trinität: Das Specificum Christianum', *Schwerpunkte des Glaubens*, Einsiedeln (1977), pp. 156–74, especially pp. 165f. See also, 'Christentum als Unmittelbarkeit zu Gott. Erwägungen zu K. Rahners *Grundkurs* des Glaubens', *Communio* 6 (1977), pp. 442–50, especially pp. 449f.
7. Cf. F. X. Bantle, 'Person und Personbegriff in der Trinitätslehre Karl Rahners', *Münchener Theologische Zeitschrift* 30 (1979), pp. 18ff. Bantle criticizes Rahner's patristic views and unmasks his false quote from St Thomas Aquinas, presumably copied from B. Lonergan, *De Deo Trino*, Vol. II, Rome (1964). See also the thoroughgoing analysis of F. Marinelli, 'Dimensione trintaria del' incarnazione', *Divinitas* 13 (1969), pp. 272–343, which is entirely from the point of view of Thomistic doctrine. For a passionate defence of Augustine's principle, to whom Rahner ascribes the view of the Father's and the Spirit's incarnability, see E. Hill, 'Karl

Rahner's Remarks to the Dogmatic Treatise "De Trinitate" and St Augustine', *Augustinian Studies*, 2 (1971), pp. 67–80.

8. T. Torrance, 'Toward an Ecumenical Consensus on the Trinity', *Münchener Theologische Zeitschrift* 31 (1975), pp. 337–50. E. Jüngel, 'Das Verhältnis von "ökonomischer" und "immanenter" Trinität', *Zeitschrift für Theologie und Kirche* 72 (1975), pp. 353–64.

9. J. A. Bracken, 'The Holy Trinity as a Community of Divine Persons', *Heythrop Journal* 15 (1974), pp. 166–80 and 257–70. A. J. Kelly, 'Trinity and Process: The Relevance of the Basic Christian Confession', *Theological Studies* 31 (1970), pp. 393–414. To both of these authors I am indebted for what follows in the rest of this chapter.

10. Cf. DS. 3016 and in Tanner, p. 808.

11. The process theology movement is by no means extinct: beyond the confines of the United States it is making its way to Europe. For a short introduction see N. Pittenger's contribution in A. Richardson (ed.), *A Dictionary of Christian Theology* , London (1968), pp. 275ff. See also, J. J. O'Donnell, *Trinity and Temporality: The Christian Doctrine of God in the Light of Process Theology and the Theology of Hope*, Oxford (1983), especially pp. 55–61 (Ogden) and 72–86 (Hartshorne).

12. Cf. J. C. Robertson, 'Rahner and Ogden: Man's Knowledge of God', *Harvard Theological Review* 63 (1970), pp. 377–407.

13. A. J. Kelly, 'Trinity and Process: The Relevance of the Basic Christian Confession', *Theological Studies* 31 (1970), pp. 393–414.

14. J. Donceel, 'Second Thoughts on the Nature of God', *Thought* 46 (1971), pp. 346–70.

15. I. Trethowan, 'A Changing God', *Downside Review* 84 (1966), pp. 247–61. See also Trethowan's, 'Christology Again', *Downside Review* 95 (1977), pp. 1–10.

16. For example, T. Pearl, 'Dialectical Panentheism: on the Hegelian Character of K. Rahner's Key Christological Writings', *Irish Theological Quarterly* 42 (1975), pp. 119–37.

17. *Trinity*, p. 23.

18. J. C. Robertson, 'Rahner and Ogden: Man's Knowledge of God', *Harvard Theological Review* 63 (1970), pp. 377–407. And see, too, S. Ogden, *The Reality of God*, London (1967), pp. 222f. Ogden, in summing up the basic tenets of process thought, explains that 'to be effected by all' is just as much a divine perfection as 'to effect all things'.

19. In discussing the concept of creation in process thought, see J. J.

O'Donnell, *Trinity and Temporality: The Christian Doctrine of God in the Light of Process Theology and the Theology of Hope*, Oxford (1983), especially pp. 89f and pp. 92f.

20. 'Observations', p. 143 (= p.184).

21. My quarrel here is not with metaphysics as such, but rather with *a* certain type of metaphysical thinking which not only Rahner, but also the process theologians, claim for their respective approaches to the concept of God.

22. It is a fact which I repeatedly pointed out in Volume 1, especially Chapter 4, *passim*. For Rahner, God at the edge of man's transcendental horizon is an instance of being.

23. See the argument of C. Hartshorne, *The Divine Relativity, A Social Conception of God*, New Haven, Conn., and London (1967), especially pp. 70ff. See, too, Hartshorne's earlier work, *The Logic of Perfection*, New Haven, Conn., and London (1962).

24. Compare Rahner's definition of the God-World relationship with that of the panentheism of Hartshorne. See, C. Hartshorne, *The Divine Relativity, A Social Conception of God*, New Haven, Conn., and London (1967), p. 89. Hartshorne's 'panentheism' is ' . . . an appropriate term for the view that deity is in some real aspect distinguishable from and independent of any and all relative items, and yet, taken as an actual whole, includes all relative items.' In *Foundations*, p. 62, Rahner writes: 'The difference between God and the world is of such a nature that God establishes and is the difference of the world from himself, and for this reason he establishes the closest unity precisely in the differentiation.' There is hardly any difference between these two descriptions.

25. There is no need to recap here what I have previously said about Rahner's philosophical doctrine of God. See Volume 1, Chapter 4, pp. 47–64.

26. W. J. Hoye, *Die Verfinsterung des absoluten Geheimnisses. Eine Kritik der Gotteslehre Karl Rahners*, Düsseldorf (1979).

27. Ibid., pp. 47, 62ff and 65.

28. As corrected in the second edition of *Hearers*. Cf. Volume 2, 2.7.1.

29. My discussion of the analogy of 'having-being' appears in Volume 1, sections 4.2.1 and 4.3a. See also, W. J. Hoye, *Die Verfinsterung des absoluten Geheimnisses. Eine Kritik der Gotteslehre Karl Rahners*, Dusseldorf (1979), especially p. 56.

30. Cf. the main definitions on creation at Lateran IV, 1215 AD, and at Florence, 1442 AD. The same (however, in different circumstances) was repeated at Vatican I, 1870 AD. See also Tanner, pp. 805f.

31. This suggestion is borne out by G. von Rad's account discussing the origin and development of Judaeo-Christian belief in creation. It

presupposes first a vague and prayerful acknowledgement of God as guiding the history of the elected people by remarkable events (Exodus). This was then extended to the origins of the whole world (Deutero-Isaiah), as narrated by Gen 1, and lastly focused on Christ the Pantocrator (Deutero-Pauline letters). See G. von Rad, 'Das theologische Problem des AT-lichen Schöpfungsglauben', *Gesammelte Studien* (1965), pp. 136–47.

32. The permanent objection against this dogmatic formula was the philosophical principle: *ex nihilo nihil fit* – a problem even in Thomas's treatment of creation in *ST* I., q.45 and q.46.

33. See M. Polanyi, *Personal Knowledge: Towards a Post-Critical Philosophy*, London (1973), especially Part III, pp. 249ff.

34. Though I am aware of the dubious nature of any argument from etymology, a glance at *The Shorter Oxford English Dictionary on Historical Principles*, Oxford (1953^3), may be used as a pointer. It seems indeed that 'might' (p. 1248) is used mainly for impersonal agents and 'mighty' (p. 1249) of things, actions, events. The usage of 'power' (p. 1559) is predominantly for personal agents. However, 'almighty' and 'all–powerful' seem to be interchangeable in English usage.

35. Cf. C. Stead, *Divine Substance*, Oxford (1977), p. 273. In a learned discussion of the logical and patristic use of the word 'substance' Stead writes: 'It's principal function . . . is to claim that God is not limited or prescribed by our experience of him, but exists in his own right . . . ' And: 'To characterize God as substance is to stake a claim as dependent on the human experience which he is invoked to explain.'

36. It is, I believe, a mistaken claim of Tillich against Barth to take 'power' in an ontological rather than in a personal sense. Cf. P. Tillich, *Biblical Religion and the Search for Ultimate Reality* , Chicago, Ill. (1955).

37. Cf. Gen 2:4ff and the subsequent Jahwist tradition.

38. Cf. Gen 1:1 and priestly tradition.

39. Cf. the late Sapiential literature.

40. Cf. G. von Rad, *Theologie des Alten Testamentes*, Vol. I: 'Die Theologie der geschichtlichen Überlieferungen Israels', Munich (1957), p. 182. See also, W. H. Schmidt, *Biblische Kommentare*, Vol. II: 'Exodus', Neukirchen-Vluyn (1977), especially pp. 175ff.

41. E. Jüngel, 'Die Welt als Möglichkeit und Wirklichkeit', *Unterwegs zur Sache* (1972), pp. 106–233, especially pp. 221ff.

42. 'Observations', p. 143 (= p. 184).

43. In speaking of a self-definition, or self-positing of God, there is the danger of confusion with the term *causa sui*. Whereas, *causa sui* is

of Plotinian origin, my use of self-definition refers to freedom by means of which the agent realizes itself in one or in a combination of its possibilities. Cf. H. Schell, *Katholische Dogmatik*, Vol. I, pp. 23f and Vol. II, pp. 20f, where an almost similar use of these terms can be found.

44. In this, and what follows to the end of this chapter, I am indebted to Jüngel's paraphrasis of Barth's doctrine of God. Cf. E. Jüngel, *Gottes Sein ist im Werden*, Tübingen (1967). Also to his later, and more comprehensive, *Gott als Geheimnis der Welt*, Tübingen (1977), especially pp. 270–306. This does not mean that I follow unquestioningly either Barth's or Jüngel's concept of God.

45. Cf. T. Torrance, 'Toward an Ecumenical Consensus on the Trinity', *Münchener Theologische Zeitschrift* 31 (1975), p. 338.

46. Ibid.

47. Ibid.

48. E. Jüngel, 'Das Verhältnis von "ökonomischer" und "immanenter" Trinität', *Zeitschrift für Theologie und Kirche* 72 (1975), pp. 353–64.

49. Ibid., pp. 470–505, especially p. 479. See also, E. Jüngel, *Gott als Geheimnis der Welt*, Tübingen (1977). Jüngel's thesis was already prefigured in his article about Rahner's Trinitarian doctrine.

50. F. Marinelli, 'Dimensione trintaria del' incarnazione', *Divinitas* 13 (1969), pp. 282, 284, 286.

51. Ibid., p. 342.

52. F. X. Bantle, 'Person und Personbegriff in der Trinitätslehre Karl Rahners', *Münchener Theologische Zeitschrift* 30 (1979), pp. 15 and 18.

53. W. J. Hoye, *Die Verfinsterung des absoluten Geheimnisses. Eine Kritik der Gotteslehre Karl Rahners*, Dusseldorf (1979), p. 61. See also his earlier article, 'Gotteserkenntnis *per essentiam* im 13. Jahrhundert', *Miscellanea Mediaevalia*, Vol. X (1976), pp. 269–84.

54. A. J. Kelly, 'Trinity and Process: The Relevance of the Basic Christian Confession', *Theological Studies* 31 (1970), p. 408.

55. *Trinity*, p. 28.

56. See Volume 1, especially sections 5.2.3 and 5.3, for the discussion of man's knowing of God's personhood. See also P. Schoonenberg, 'Zur Trinitatslehre Karl Rahners' in E. Klinger and K. Wittstadt (eds), *Glaube im Prozess, Christentum nach dem II Vatikanum, Für Karl Rahner* (1984), Freiburg-im-Breisgau, pp. 471–91. Schoonenberg seems to argue that, precisely in the revelation of the economic Trinity, God, in an analogous sense, 'becomes' personal.

57. Even Jüngel admits a *distinctio rationis*. Cf. E. Jüngel, 'Das

Verhältnis von "ökonomischer" und "immanenter" Trinität', *Zeitschrift für Theologie und Kirche* 72 (1975), p. 364.

58. K. Barth, *Church Dogmatics*, Vol. I/1, Edinburgh (1963), pp. 383–99.

59. Cf. C. Link, *Die Welt als Geheimnis*, Munich (1976), p. 164.

60. It is this divine relationality I shall basically identify with God's personal reality. Cf. E. Gutwenger, 'Zur Trinitätslehre von "Mysterium Salutis" ', *ZKT* 90 (1968), pp. 325–8, especially p. 327.

61. I shall have to come back to this argument later; see Chapter 5.

62. Cf. A. W. Wainwright, *The Trinity in the New Testament*, London (1962), especially pp. 15–40. See also, R. Schulte, 'Die Gottesoffenbarung des AT als vorläufige Trinitätsoffenbarung', *MS* 11, pp. 55–73.

63. Torrance, surprisingly enough, admits a kind of *theosis* and participation in God's being. Cf. T. Torrance, 'Toward an Ecumenical Consensus on the Trinity', *Münchener Theologische Zeitschrift* 31 (1975), p. 342.

64. Ibid.

65. I have already indicated the elements of the concept of human personhood in this section of the chapter. See also, Volume 2, Chapter II, where I dealt with it at length from an anthropological point of view.

66. For an introduction to the thought of personalism see B. Langemeyer, *Der dialogische Personalismus in der evangelischen und katholischen Theologie der Gegenwart*, Paderborn (1963). See also, B. Casper, *Das dialogische Denken. Eine Untersuchung der religionsphilosophische Bedeutung Franz Rosenzweigs, Ferdinand Ebners und Martin Bubers*, Freiburg-im-Breisgau (1967). For further discussion, see, J. Macmurray, *Persons in Relation*, London (1961). And, for a brief comparison of personalism with process theology, cf. J. B. Cobb, jnr., and D. R. Griffin, *Process Theology: An Introductory Exposition*, Brescia (1967), especially chapter 6.

67. See Volume 2, pp. 44f.

68. Cf. E. Gutwenger, 'Zur Trinitätslehre von "Mysterium Salutis" ', *ZKT* 90 (1968), p. 328.

69. Bantle tried to show that the notion of 'person' in its patristic usage, first was not employed for economic relations of God and, secondly (contrary to Rahner), when employed, it was used univocally. Cf. F. X. Bantle, 'Person und Personbegriff in der Trinitatslehre Karl Rahners', *Münchener Theologische Zeitschrift* 30 (1979), pp. 18ff.

70. T. Torrance, 'Toward an Ecumenical Consensus on the Trinity', *Münchener Theologische Zeitschrift* 31 (1975), p. 346.
71. Ibid.
72. Cf. J. A. Bracken, 'The Holy Trinity as a Community of Divine Persons', *Heythrop Journal* 15 (1974), p. 259f. Here, I agree with Bracken where he observes that Rahner is ready ' . . . to redefine the ontological meaning of the term "person" within the Trinity . . . He is not however quite so open to the possibility of revising the other key term, "nature" . . . ' Torrance has made a similar suggestion. See, T. Torrance, 'Toward an Ecumenical Consensus on the Trinity', *Münchener Theologische Zeitschrift* 31 (1975), pp. 344f.
73. For discussion on this rather speculative problem, see H. Mühlen, *Der heilige Geist als Person*, Münster (1963), pp. 26, 32, 168. Mühlen insists, on the one hand, that the concept of 'person' cannot be used univocally as one of the 'universalia' and, on the other hand, in relying on personalistic categories, he shows that the personality of the Spirit is the common act of the Father and the Son. The relationship of the Father and of the Son, of the 'I' and the 'Thou' is in the 'We' of them both.
74. My view here is nearest to Bracken's description of God as a 'unity of community'. Cf. J. A. Bracken, 'The Holy Trinity as a Community of Divine Persons', *Heythrop Journal* 15 (1974), p. 179.

Chapter 4: **God Incarnate: The Doctrine of Jesus the Christ**

1. See, for example, 'Gnade als Mitte Menschlicher Existenz', *Herder Korrespondenz*, 28 (1974), pp. 77–92.
2. See the Bibliography, especially Christological writings, and also the Table of Abbreviations where 'Basic Types', 'Christology', 'Consciousness', 'Evolutionary View', 'Exegesis', 'I Believe', 'Incarnation', and 'On the Eternal Significance' are all relevant. See, too: 'The Quest for Approaches Leading to an Understanding of the Mystery of the God–Man Jesus', *Investigations* XIII, pp. 195–200 (= *Schriften* X, pp. 209–14); and 'Remarks on the Importance of the History of Jesus for Catholic Dogmatics', *Investigations* XIII, pp. 201–11 (= *Schriften* X, pp. 215–26). From Rahner's older essays, see:'The Eternal Significance of the Humanity of Jesus for our Relationship to God', *Investigations* III, pp. 35–46 (= *Schriften* III, pp. 47–60); 'Mysteries of the Life of Jesus', *Investigations* VII, pp. 121–204 (= *Schriften* VII, pp.

123–96); 'I Believe in Jesus Christ: Interpreting an Article of Faith', *Investigations* IX, pp. 165–69 (= *Schriften* VIII, pp. 213–17); and 'Jesus Christ', *SM* III (part IV), pp. 192–203.

3. *Foundations*, pp. 176–312 (= pp. 180–311).

4. Apart from doctoral dissertations (which I do not propose listing), I can refer here summarily to I. Sanna, *La cristologia antropologica de P. Karl Rahner*, Rome (1970), and to J. H. P. Wong, *Logos–Symbol in the the Christology of Karl Rahner*, Rome (1984).

5. Here I refer mainly to German literature. Cf. R. Lachenschmid, 'Christologie und Soteriologie' in H. Vorgrimler and R. Van der Gucht (eds), *Bilanz der Theologie im 20 Jahrhundert*, Vol. III, Freiburg-im-Breisgau (1970), pp. 82–120, especially pp. 98ff and pp. 107ff. And two works by D. Wiederkehr: 'Konfrontationen und Integrationen der Christologie', *Theologische Berichte*, Vol. II, Einsiedeln (1973), pp. 11–120, especially pp. 76–81; and 'Christologie im Kontext', *Theologische Berichte*, Vol. VII, Einsiedeln (1978), pp. 11–62, especially pp. 48–56. See also, A. Schilson and W. Kasper, *Christologie im Präsens, Kritische Sichtung neuerer Entwürfe*, Freiburg-im-Breisgau (1974), especially pp. 80–90. For an introduction, see the informative pamphlet by G. O'Collins, 'What are they saying about Jesus?', New York, NY., and Toronto, Ont. (1977).

6. Cf. W. Kasper, *Jesus the Christ*, London (1976), which I have used throughout this chapter, being the ET of the fifth edition of the original German, *Jesus der Christus*, Mainz (1976).

7. My references here are to the English study edition, W. Pannenberg, *Jesus God and Man*, London (1970^2). This being the ET of the original German, *Gründzuge der Christologie*, Gutersloh (1964).

8. See the apt remark by W. Kern in his article, 'Karl Rahner's *Grundkurs*, Kleine Einfuhrung in eine grosse Einführung', *Stimmen der Zeit* 195 (1977), pp. 326–36, especially pp. 332f.

9. See W. Kasper, *Jesus the Christ*, London (1976).

10. Ibid., p. 17.

11. *Foundations*, pp. 193–5 (= pp. 194f), where the two notions find a definitive form. See also, 'Christology' pp. 185ff (= pp. 206ff) where these are already hinted at.

12. W. Kasper, *Jesus the Christ*, London (1976), p. 49.

13. Ibid.

14. As discussed earlier. See Volume 2, pp. 7–15.

15. See W. Pannenberg, *Jesus God and Man*, London (1970^2).

16. 'Basic Types', pp. 220f (= p. 235).

17. Ibid.
18. *Foundations*, p. 176 (= p. 178) and also pp. 311–21 (= pp. 303–12).
19. Ibid., p. 177 (= p. 179).
20. *Foundations*, p. 203 (= p. 203).
21. Ibid.
22. Ibid., p. 206 (= p. 205).
23. Rahner wrote: 'In this relationship to Jesus Christ a person grasps the absolute saviour in Jesus and makes him the mediation of his immediacy to God in his own self, and when it is actualized and understood adequately it contains in itself its own validation before the tribunal of man's existence, his conscience and his intellectual honesty. Consequently, as a *concrete absolute*, which it has to be in order really to be itself, it cannot by definition be produced and constructed "from outside".' (My italics.) See *Foundations*, p. 206 (= p.205).
24. Cf. R. V. Sellers, *The Council of Chalcedon,* London (1953), pp. 210f. I quote here its definition in full: 'One and the same Christ, Son, Lord, Only-Begotten, made known in two *natures* [= *physesin*] which exist without confusion [= *asynchytos*], without change [= *atreptos*], without division [= *adiairetos*], without separation [= *achoristos*]; the difference of the natures having been in no wise taken away by reason of the union, but rather the properties of each being preserved and [both] concurring into one Person [= *prosopon*] and one hypostasis – not parted or divided into two persons [= *prosopa*] but one and the same Son and Only-Begotten, the divine Logos, the Lord Jesus Christ; even as the prophets from of old have spoken concerning him, and as the Lord Jesus Christ himself has taught us, and as the Symbol of the Fathers has delivered to us.'
25. Cf. A. W. Grillmeier, *Christ in Christian Tradition: From the Apostolic Age to Chalcedon (AD 451)*, London (1965), as published originally in English. I shall refer to this edition instead of the extended edition (now available in ET), *Mit Ihm und in Ihm: Christologische Forschungen und Perspektiven*, Freiburg-im-Breisgau (1975).
26. Cf. 'Christology', pp. 150f (= pp. 170f).
27. Ibid., p. 156, n. 1 (= p. 176, n. 3).
28. Ibid., p. 158 (= p. 179).
29. Cf. *Foundations*, p. 291 (= p. 285). And here, as in many other places, Rahner specifies this danger 'of a monophysitic and hence a mythological misunderstanding'. Cf. *Foundations*, p. 290 (= p. 284).
30. Ibid., pp. 288f (= p. 282).

31. Ibid., pp. 287f (= p. 281).
32. Cf. ibid., p. 289 (= p. 283).
33. It is to be recalled that the Antiochene school, and with it Nestorius, tended to understand the theandric union in Christ as being between two complete, even individualized items (divine and human). However, the present state of scholarship excuses Nestorius himself from such an erroneous view, often characterized as a mere 'moral' union between the divine and the human in Christ.
34. Cf. Hendry's short account in G. S. Hendry and A. Richardson (eds) *A Dictionary of Christian Theology*, London (1974³), p. 58.
35. Cf. 'Christology', p. 182 (= p. 202): ' . . . we have a unity which (a) cannot as uniting unity [*einende Einheit*] be confused with (b) the united unity [*geeinte Einheit*].'
36. See Grillmeier's account of the reception of the Ephesine definition regarding the *anathemata* of Cyril, which influenced the terminology as it was to be used up to Chalcedon. A. W. Grillmeier, *Christ in Christian Tradition: From the Apostolic Age to Chalcedon (AD 451)*, London (1965), pp. 419ff.
37. Cf. *Foundations*, p. 287 (= p. 281).
38. Ibid., pp. 419ff.
39. 'Christology', p. 176, n. 1 (= p. 196, n. 1): 'In fact the whole of Christology could be seen as the unique and most radical realization of this basic relationship of God to what is other than himself, measured by which all else in creation would be only a deficient mode, fading away into indistinctness.'
40. P. Kaiser, *Die Gott–menschliche Einigung in Christus als Problem der spekultiven Theologie seit der Scholastik*, Munich (1968), especially pp. 266ff. I am indebted to this scholarly work throughout what follows in this chapter.
41. 'Christology', pp. 163f (= p. 184).
42. Ibid., p. 164.
43. Ibid., pp. 162f (= p. 183).
44. Ibid.
45. Ibid., p. 173 (= p. 194).
46. Ibid., p. 179 (= p. 200).
47. Ibid., p. 181 (= p. 202).
48. Ibid., p. 181, n. 3 (= p. 202, n. 3).
49. Here I have avoided Rahner speaking for himself. However, we must try to understand the following: 'The only way in which Christ's concrete humanity may be conceived of in itself as diverse from the Logos is by thinking of it *in so far* as it is united to the Logos . . . In this way, the diverse term as such is the united [*geeinte*] reality of him who as prior unity (which can thus only be

God) is the ground of the diverse term, and therefore, while remaining 'immutable' 'in himself', truly comes to be *in* what he constitutes *as* something united [*geeinte*] with him *and* diverse from him.' 'Christology', p. 181 (= p. 202).

50. Cf. *SM*, Vol III, p. 196.

51. *Foundations*, pp. 290f (= pp. 284f). See, too, the similar explanation in 'Christology', p. 179 (= p. 200), concerning this last part of the Chalcedonian formula.

52. The problem is already stated in 'Christology' where Rahner says: 'God the Word of the Father, so we are told, "changes" in no way when he assumes the human nature as his own. The change, the novelty is entirely on the side of human nature', p. 175 (= p. 196). In a corresponding footnote, p. 175, n. 1 (= p. 196, n. 176), he admits the validity of this metaphysical statement. However, he asks whether this metaphysics should not be re–thought, for indeed, there must be a change in God also. To this he remarks, p. 181, n. 3 (= p. 202, n. 1): 'One may, and indeed must, say this, without for that reason being a Hegelian. For it is true, come what may, and a dogma that the Logos himself has become man: thus he himself has become something that he has not always been; and therefore what has so become is, as just itself and of itself, God's reality.' [Thus] ' . . . ontology must allow itself to be guided by it . . . [it] must seek enlightenment from it and grant that while God remains immutable "in himself" he can come to be "in the other . . . ", etc.'

53. *Foundations*, pp. 212–24 (= pp. 211–22).

54. See the long explanatory note in 'Incarnation', pp. 113f, n. 3 (= p. 147, n. 3). And the sentence itself appears in *Foundations*, pp. 221f (= pp. 218f), with the emphasis that the 'Incarnation must be in God himself, and precisely in the fact that, although he is immutable in and of himself, he *himself* can become something in another.'

55. It is remarkable that Rahner in his Christological writings hardly ever directly quotes the Bible. In the long section on Christology in the *Foundations* there are altogether two direct quotes from the Pauline epistles. This, of course, does not mean that Rahner's Christology is a-biblical: the well–known Christological texts are paraphrased in his writings.

56. 'Incarnation', p. 114 (= p. 148).

57. Ibid., p. 115 (= p. 148).

58. Ibid.

59. A very similar question has been raised by Pannenberg. Cf. W. Pannenberg, *Jesus God and Man*, London (1970[2]), p. 318 and n.

92. See, too, I. Sanna, *La cristologia antropologica de P. Karl Rahner*, Rome (1970), p. 204, n. 11.

60. Cf. W. Pannenberg, *Jesus God and Man*, London (1970²), p. 319.

61. 'Incarnation', p. 116 (= p. 150).

62. Ibid.

63. P. Kaiser, *Die Gott–menschliche Einigung in Christus als Problem der spekulativen Theologie seit der Scholastik*, Munich (1968), especially pp. 282ff, 285, 288f, 325ff.

64. Cf. 'Incarnation', p. 115 (= p. 149).

65. Ibid., pp. 116f (= pp. 150f).

66. Ibid.

67. 'On the Eternal Significance', p. 44 (= p. 58).

68. *Foundations*, p. 287 (= p. 281).

69. 'Christology', p. 157 (= p. 178).

70. Ibid., p. 159 (= p. 180).

71. Ibid., p. 158 (= p. 179).

72. Ibid., pp. 156f, n. 2 (= p. 177, n. 1). See the corresponding discussion of Cyril's post-Ephesine approach to the humanity of Christ in A. Grillmeier, *Christ in Christian Tradition: From the Apostolic Age to Chalcedon (AD 451)*, London (1965), pp. 402f.

73. This statement is proposed by the acts of the ordinary *Magisterium*. Cf. the encyclical, *Corpus Christi Mysticum* (1943), especially DS 3812. See, also, an answer of the Holy Office (1918), especially DS 3646 and DS 3647, denying the admissibility of the following: 'It is not certain that there was in the soul of Christ during his life among men that knowledge which the saints or those enjoying the Beatific Vision have.'

74. 'Christology', p. 160 (= p. 180).

75. *Foundations*, p. 292 (= p. 286).

76. Ibid., pp. 302ff (= pp. 295f). Rahner gave this later draft the title 'Possibility of an Orthodox "Consciousness" Christology'.

77. In order to see the complexity of the problem, see the literature referred to at the beginning of 'Consciousness'. See also a good introduction to the same by Galot who deals with Rahner's position. Cf. J. Galot, *La Conscience de Jesus*, Paris (1971), especially pp. 169–72.

78. Schleiermacher could be named as the father of consciousness Christology. To be human means to be capable of God-consciousness. When human God-consciousness reaches its superlative degree it has to be identified with the Divinity. Thus, Christ was human (that is, capable of God-consciousness) yet divine, since his was absolutely powerful, unbroken God-consciousness at every moment of his life. Cf. A. Schleiermacher, *Christian Faith*,

Edinburgh (1968). In the judgement of his critics Schleiermacher's Christ is the one who in every moment of his life is being *adopted* as divine by the Godhead. In view of the similarity between him and Rahner one could raise a similar objection against Rahner's consciousness Christology.

79. Note that for Rahner the vision of Christ is not an empirically ascertainable fact; as he says, 'it is not at all necessary to find a proper and direct proof for this in the tradition of all ages'. Cf. 'Consciousness', p. 205 (= p. 233).

80. Ibid., pp. 200f (p. 229). Rahner explains this in his statement, '. . . there is among the [various] forms of knowledge an *a priori*, unobjectified knowledge about oneself, and this is a basic condition of the spiritual being [*als eine Grundbefindlichkeit des geistigen Subjekts*] in which it is present to itself and in which it has at the same time its transcendental orientation to the totality of possible objects of knowledge and free choice.'

81. The argument deducing the presence of the vision in Jesus can be thus summed up: hypostatic union is the self-communication of the absolute Being of God. This, in the case of Jesus, happens to reach its highest and unsurpassable degree by means of the ontic givenness of this unity. But if communication of being reaches its highest form, it cannot be without the corresponding degree of self-consciousness, even if it is not objectifiable. Therefore, in this way the vision can be postulated in Jesus' *Grundbefindlichkeit*. Thus, 'the *visio beata* is an intrinsic element of the hypostatic union'. Cf. 'Consciousness', p. 206 (= p. 235).

82. Cf. 'Consciousness', pp. 210f (= pp. 239f). Rahner argues: 'After all, this basic condition [*Grundbefindlichkeit*] is itself of such a nature as to demand a fixed form and conceptual objectification which in itself is not yet, though leaves room for it in the *a posteriori*, objective consciousness of Christ.' In other words, it is here that history and development can take place. This consists in learning 'to express to himself what he is and what he indeed has always already been in the self-consciousness of his basic condition.' Thus, 'Christ's consciousnes of divine sonship . . . realized itself only gradually during his spiritual history.'

83. 'Consciousness', pp. 202f (= pp. 232f).

84. Cf. 'Christology', p. 158 (p. 178).

85. *Foundations*, pp. 302f (= p. 295).

86. Cf. B. Lonergan, *Method in Theology* , London (1971), pp. 335ff.

87. This specified form of the principle is stated in a variety of Rahner's writings. Here, I quote only from 'Incarnation': 'In the Incarnation, the Logos creates by taking on, and takes on by emp-

tying himself [*indem er sich selbst entäussert*]. Hence we can verify here, in the most radical and specifically unique way the axiom of all relationships between God and the creature, namely that the closeness and the distance, the submissiveness [*Verfügtheit*] and the independence of the creature do not grow in inverse but in like proportion.' Cf. 'Incarnation', p. 117 (= p. 151).

88. 'Symbol', p. 235 (= p. 291).
89. For example, P. Tillich, *Systematic Theology*, Vol I, London and Chicago, Ill. (1960), pp. 264–79 *passim*.
90. 'Symbol', pp. 224–78: 'Our first statement which we put forward as the basic principle of an ontology of symbolism, is as follows: all beings are by nature symbolic, because they necessarily "express" themselves in order to attain their own nature.'
91. 'Symbol', p. 227 (= p. 281).
92. Ibid., p. 234 (= p. 290).
93. Ibid., p. 221, n. 1 (= p. 275, n. 1). Also relevant here are the following items from Rahner's mainly spiritual writings. 'Behold this Heart: Preliminaries to a Theology of the Devotion of the Sacred Heart', *Investigations* III, pp. 321–30 (= *Schriften* III, pp. 379–90); 'Some Theses for a Theology of the Devotion to the Sacred Heart', *Investigations* III, pp. 331–52 (= *Schriften* III, pp. 391–415); 'The Word and the Eucharist', *Investigations* IV, pp. 253–86 (= *Schriften* IV, pp. 315–55); 'Poetry and the Christian', *Investigations* III, pp. 357–67 (= *Schriften* III, pp. 441–54); 'The Theological Meaning of the Veneration of the Sacred Heart', *Investigations* VIII, pp. 217–28 (= *Schriften* VII, pp. 481–91).
94. 'Symbol', p. 229, n. 9 (= pp. 284f, n. 3) and also p. 235 (= p. 291).
95. Ibid., p. 228 (= p. 282).
96. Cf. 'Symbol', p. 235 (= p. 292).
97. Ibid., p. 236 (= pp. 293f).
98. Ibid.
99. 'Incarnation', p. 116 (= p. 150).
100. Col 1:17.
101. 'Incarnation', p. 119 (= p. 154). (My italics.) And note also that in his last sentence Rahner's 'in our nearest and dearest' refers to the Incarnate, and not to anyone near and dear to us.
102. Instead of discussing Rahner's various writings which refer to Christ, I shall take another look at the complex structure of the sixth chapter of *Foundations*. In forming his argument, Rahner incorporates here rehashed versions of previously published essays. Cf. 'Christology within an Evolutionary View of the World', *Investigations* V, pp. 157–92 (= *Schriften* V, pp. 183–221) and 'The Order of Redemption within the Order of Creation' in *The*

Christian Commitment, London and Sydney (1970), pp. 51–81. Rahner's entry into Christology *via* an evolutionary view of the world, *Foundations*, p. 178 (= p. 203), which itself is a rehashed version of previously published essays is meant to introduce his readers to the transcendental idea of Christ. His transcendental Christology, the epochal necessity of which is vehemently argued, and its outline duly sketched, is meant to indicate those nerve-points where Christ can be 'experienced' – transcendentally of course. The unusually long section on the history of the life and death of Jesus, *Foundations*, p. 228 (= p. 264), as I will presently show, should not mislead the reader into thinking it is the essential core; it leads to a *theology* of death and resurrection, *Foundations*, p. 264 (= p. 285), at the end of which Rahner feels himself to be in a better position to draw the limits of classical Christology, *Foundations*, p. 285 (= p. 293). This extended central part will be embraced by the concluding three sections as a counterpart to his introduction to a Christology based on the *a priori* idea of Christ. It is here that Rahner, again, emphasizes the necessity of a funda-mental-theologian's approach, outlines the possible contents of a 'searching Christology', *Foundations*, p. 293 (= p. 298), and hints at the tasks of a Christology from below, at the framework of a con-sciousness Christology and at an existential Christology, *Foundations*, p. 298 (= p. 311).

103. Cf. 'Witness', pp. 154f (= pp. 165f).

104. Ibid., p. 154 (= p. 165).

105. Ibid., p. 157 (= p. 169): 'Witness is *de facto* a grace-given event, or it is not really witness at all.' That is to say, 'the imparting of one-self in witness to one's fellow constitute, if it is really achieved (that is, if it consists in an act of unreserved self–acceptance in the transcendence which is *de facto* elevated by grace to a higher plane) . . . a witness of God himself.'

106. Ibid., p. 158 (= pp. 170f): 'Witness is directed towards someone else. The one bearing witness seeks to communicate himself to him.' Thus, as Rahner adds, p. 159 (= p. 171): 'When an individual commits himself to his fellow absolutely, though in himself, in view of the finitude of his human nature and the threats to which he is subject from forces within himself, he cannot guarantee the absolute character of his commitment, then, whether he recognizes it consciously or not, he is *ipso facto* appealing in hope to the one sustaining and reconciling basis of all free and unique acts.'

107. Cf. ibid., p. 156 (= p. 168).

108. For example, Geisser, who does not even take the trouble to con-sider the whole context of Rahner's approach to Christ. Cf. H.

Geisser, 'Die Interpretation der kirchlichen Lehre des Gottmenschen bei Karl Rahner', *Kerygma und Dogma* 14 (1968), pp. 307–30.

109. *Foundations*, p. 193 (= p. 194).

110. W. V. Dych is the translator of *Foundations*.

111. *Foundations*, p. 193 (= p. 193).

112. Ibid.

113. Ibid., p. 194 (= p. 195).

114. Ibid.

115. Cf. F. Greiner, *Die Menschlichkeit der Offenbarung*, Munich (1978), pp. 257–94.

116. I cannot entirely agree with Greiner's contention according to which, at least in the first edition of *Hearers*, the historical Christ only touches, as it were tangentially man's subjectivity and does not meet him in and through history.

117. 'Christology', pp. 186f (= p. 207).

118. Ibid., pp. 170f, n. 3 (= p. 191, n. 1).

119. To be fair, it is an idea by no means new for Rahner, who in his early writings had seriously studied the mysticism of St Bonaventure. Cf. K. Rahner, 'Der Begriff der Extasis bei Bonaventura', *Zeitschrift fur Aszese und Mystik* 9 (1934), pp. 1–19. The same idea is insinuated in 'Christology', pp. 170f, n. 3 (= p. 191, n. 1) about man's *Wesen* as a *Sich-Enthoben-Werden* (that is, to become self-suspended upon the absolute God). This is something which belongs to man's basic constitution. See also, K. P. Fischer, *Der Mensch als Geheimnis*, Freiburg-im-Breisgau (1974), especially pp. 189–93 and 302–10.

120. 'Incarnation', p. 111 (= p. 143).

121. Ibid.

122. See *Hominisation*, p. 57 (= p. 52): 'From what itself is material, there is no independent leap immanent in the nature of the material into the "noosphere". But the removal of the limits from what is limited (and is called material) can and does happen in mind, spirit, etc.' See also *Hominisation*, p. 92 (= p. 92): 'If matter and spirit are not simply disparate in nature, but matter is in a certain way "solid-ified" spirit, etc.' Cf. *Foundations*, p. 193 (= p. 193), where here Rahner is repeating the same position but puts it into the context of a communitarian history of free persons.

123. 'Evolutionary View', p. 191 (= p. 221).

124. Cf. 'Christology in the Setting of Modern Man's Understanding of Himself and His World', *Investigations* XI, pp. 215–29 (= *Schriften* IX, pp. 227–41).

125. Cf. 'Evolutionary View', pp. 174f (= p. 202).

126.Ibid., p. 175 (= pp. 202f).

127.Ibid., p. 176 (= pp. 203f).

128.Cf. 'Christianity and the non-Christian Religions', *Investigations* V, pp. 115–34 (= *Schriften* V, pp. 136–58). Great chunks of this article are borrowed for inclusion in *Foundations*, p. 311 (= p. 321). I am indebted to Greiner for this aspect of Rahner's gradual assimilation of history to his transcendental view by assuming into this the process of world religions. Cf. F. Greiner, *Die Menschlichkeit der Offenbarung*, Munich (1978), p. 265.

129.Cf. 'I Believe in Jesus Christ. Interpreting an Article of Faith', *Investigations* IX, p. 167 (= *Schriften* VIII, p. 216).

130.To be more precise: 'Classical Christology . . . of the one divine person and the two natures, of the Incarnation and the hypostatic union, is a sort of mid–point between a transcendental Christology (i.e. of transcendental ordination of man in history towards the absolute saviour) and categorial Christology "from below".' Cf. *SM* III, p. 197.

131.Cf. *Foundations*, pp. 195–203 (= pp. 196–202). These pages integrate many previous statements. See, for example, *SM* III, pp. 115ff and 'I Believe in Jesus Christ. Interpreting an Article of Faith', *Investigations* IX, p. 167 (= *Schriften* VIII, p. 216) for a similar and concise presentation of the same thought.

132.*Foundations*, p. 200 (= p. 200).

133.Ibid., p. 202 (= p. 202).

134.Ibid., pp. 293–305 (= pp. 287–298)

135.*SM* III, p. 195.

136.*Foundations*, p. 294 (= p. 287). The topic of anonymous Christianity will be addressed elsewhere.

137.*SM* IIII, p. 194.

138.Ibid.

139.*Foundations*, p. 295 (= pp. 288f).

140.Ibid.

141.In what follows I have used my own translation.

142.'I Believe', p. 15. (My italics.)

143.Ibid., p. 16.

144.Ibid., p. 19.

145.Ibid., p. 21.

146.Ibid.

147.Mt 25:40 and Mt 25:44.

148.'I Believe', pp. 24f.

149.Ibid., p. 29.

150.*Foundations*, p. 297 (= p. 290).

151.Ibid., p. 298 (= p. 291).

152.'Incarnation', p. 111 (= p. 144).

153.Cf. *Foundations*, pp. 228–64 (= pp. 226–60).

154.Ibid., pp. 264–85 (= pp. 260–79).

155.'Exegesis', pp. 190ff (= pp. 202ff).

156.Ibid., pp. 201f (= p. 214).

157.R. Bultmann, *Glauben und Verstehen*, I, Tübingen (1952), pp. 207f. See also, R. Bultmann, *The Theology of the New Testament*, I, London (1982), pp. 42ff.

158.'Exegesis', pp. 211f (= p. 224).

159.*Foundations*, pp. 245f (= p. 243).

160.Ibid., pp. 247ff (= pp. 244ff). See also 'Exegesis', pp. 206f (= pp. 219f).

161.*Foundations*, p. 247 (= p. 245).

162.I am not going to discuss Rahner's position on the problem of imminent expectation of the Kingdom. Cf. *Foundations*, where he repeats his own solution concerning the question whether or not the pre-Resurrection Jesus erred about its imminence. His solution, *Foundations*, p. 50 (= p. 247), is in accordance with consciousness Christology in dealing wth the immediate vision of God in Jesus the man: 'In this "error" Jesus would have only shared our lot, since to "err" in this way is better for historical man . . . than to know everything in advance . . . A genuine human consciousness must have an unknown future ahead of it.'

163.For example, in the sense of Dan 1:13–14, to which Jesus refers in Mk 13:26 and Mt 10:23, and in his trial Mt 26:64.

164.Cf. Lk 4:21: 'Today this scripture has been fulfilled . . . .'

165.Cf. *Foundations*, p. 252 (= p. 249): 'The pre-Resurrection Jesus thought that this new closeness of the kingdom came to be in and through the totality of what he said and what he did.' See also, 'History', p. 208 (= p. 248).

166.Cf. *Foundations*, p. 253 (= p. 249): ' . . . the closeness of God's kingdom which Jesus proclaimed as new and as not yet present until then . . . This understanding, which would correspond to that of any prophet who always knows or would have to know at least in principle from his basic understanding of God, that he will be succeeded by another prophet . . . [now] this understanding becomes impossible just by the fact of Jesus' imminent expectation.'

167.Ibid., p. 254 (= p. 250).

168.I have here not included Rahner's apparent digression on the importance of miracles within fundamental theology. Suffice it to say that, for Rahner, miracles are in the context of witness and not because of their bare facts; cf. *Foundations*, p. 261 (= p. 257): 'A miracle takes place in the theological sense . . . when for the eyes of a spiritual person who is open to the mystery of God the concrete configuration of events is such that there participates immediately in this configuration the divine self–communication which he already experiences "instinctively" in his transcendental experience of grace . . . and in this way gives witness of its presence (i.e. of this grace).' It is a different question as to how far this theory of Rahner's differs from that of Rousselot; cf. P. Rousselot, 'Les yeux de la foi', *Recherche Science en Religieuse* 1, (1910), pp. 241–59 and 444–75. Kunz also discusses this question informatively; cf. E. Kunz, *Glaube-Gnade-Geschichte*, Frankfurt (1969), pp. 47ff.

169.Cf. *Foundations*, pp. 254f (= p. 252). Also K. Rahner and W. Thüsing, 'Christologie: systematisch und exegetisch' in *Quaestiones Disputatae* 55, Freiburg-im-Breisgau (1972), pp. 48ff. See the rather defective translation of the latter in *A New Christology*, London (1980), pp. 38ff and mark the soteriological significance of these references.

170.To be precise: Rahner, on the one hand, insists that *de se* the pre-Easter self-understanding of Jesus as the eschatological event of salvation contains the Christology of the Church and, on the other hand, he admits that the same self-understanding has a history of its own. 'And this history in itself only attained its definitive fulness in his Resurrection. Only through this event did it become credible in a definitive sense for us.' Cf. 'Exegesis', p. 206 (= p. 218).

171.Cf Jn 6:68f.

172.Cf. 'Exegesis', p. 206 (= p. 218).

173.*Foundations*, p. 268 (= p. 263).

174.Acts 2:22–36.

175.*Foundations*, p. 266 (= p. 262).

176.Cf. 'Exegesis', pp. 209f (= pp. 221f).

177.*Foundations*, p. 266 (= p. 262).

178.Ibid., p. 267 (= p. 263).

179.Ibid., p. 268 (= p. 263).

180.Ibid., pp. 268f (= pp. 264f).

181.Ibid., pp. 273f (= p. 269).

182.Ibid., p. 277 (= p. 272).

183.Ibid., pp. 277f (= pp. 272f).

184.Ibid., pp. 279–85 (= pp. 273–9).

185.Cf. 'Theology in the New Testament', *Investigations* V, pp. 23–41 (= *Schriften* V, pp. 33–53) where Rahner points out the theological elements involved in the Bible. See also, 'Exegesis and Dogmatic Theology', *Investigations* V, pp. 67–98 (= *Schriften* V, pp. 82–111).

186. Cf. *Foundations*, pp. 235f (= pp. 233f).
187. Ibid., p. 228 (= p. 226).
188. Ibid., pp. 237f (= p . 235).

Chapter 5: Comments and Questions: Who is Jesus the Christ?

1. H. Geisser, 'Die Interpretation der kirchlichen Lehre des Gottmenschen bei Karl Rahner', *Kerygma und Dogma* 14 (1968), pp. 307–30. Geisser is one of the few Protestant critics of Rahner's Christology.
2. Ibid., p. 325; and p. 315, n. 57, where Geisser correctly refers to F. Schleiermacher's *Christian Faith*, Edinburgh (1968), pp. 377–89, where a similarity could be construed.
3. See G. Thomasius, *Christi Person und Werk II* (1855) (of the Incarnation as alienation of the Divine and humanity as the permanent shape of the Logos). See, too, F. H. R. Frank, *System der christlichen Wahrheit* II (1880) (the hypostatic union explained through the union of a double consciousness). And J. M. Dorner, *System der christlichen Glaubenslehre* I (1879) (God's self–communication to his creatures in Christ who is the most perfect idea of humankind, and the 'centre' of the world).
4. Geisser refers to Barth's theology of creation as the precondition of the Incarnation. Cf. K. Barth, *Church Dogmatics, Vol III/I*, Edinburgh (1963), as parallel to Rahner's approach to the mystery of Christ.
5. H. Geisser, 'Die Verknüpfung von Theologie und Anthropologie lässt unvermeidlich an Bultmann denken', *Kerygma und Dogma* 14 (1968), p. 326.
6. See Chapter 3, sections 3.2.3 and 3.2.6; and Chapter 6.2, *passim*.
7. Cf. 'Incarnation', p. 114, n. 3 (= p. 147, n. 3): 'We can learn from the Incarnation that immutability . . . is not simply and uniquely a characteristic of God, but that in, and in spite of, his immutability he can truly become something. He himself, he in time. And this possibility *is not a sign of deficiency but the height of his perfection* . . . This we can and must affirm, without being Hegelian. And it would be a pity if Hegel had to teach Christians such things.' (My italics.)
8. T. Pearl, 'Dialectical Panentheism: on the Hegelian Character of Karl Rahner's *Key Christological Writings*', *Irish Theological Quarterly* 42 (1975), pp. 119–37, especially p. 119.
9. Ibid., p. 135.

10. W. Shepherd, *Man's Condition*, New York, NY. (1969), p. 199: 'Rahner has asserted that creation is for the sake of Incarnation as did Duns Scotus. Rahner has further said that Christ historically culminates and defines the convergence of spirit and matter as did a number of patristic writers, *as did Hegel for that matter*.' (My italics.)

11. Curiously enough, Rahner mentions Hegel's name only once in a footnote: 'Without being Hegelian . . . ' Cf. 'Incarnation', p. 114, n. 3 (= p. 147, n. 3).

12. Pearl here quotes Hegel. Cf. T. Pearl, 'Dialectical Panentheism: on the Hegelian Character of Karl Rahner's *Key Christological Writings*', *Irish Theological Quarterly* 42 (1975), p. 128.

13. Ibid., p. 122.

14. K. P. Fischer, *Der Mensch als Geheimnis*, Freiburg-im-Breisgau (1974), pp. 350ff. See also, C. N. Bent, *Interpreting the Doctrine of God*, New York, NY., Amsterdam, London (1969), p. 155: 'Hegelian dialectic operates on the level of concept. The transcendental dialectic [that is of Rahner] . . . is rooted in the polar opposition between actuality and concepts.'

15. Cf. W. Pannenberg, *Jesus God and Man*, London (1970). Pannenberg summarily rejects (p. 318, n. 92) Hegelian dialectic as applied to the 'movement' of God which 'can have the value of a parable that is not adequate to the mystery of the divine', however useful for explaining both creation and incarnation (though in their difference). This procedure will be questioned by Pannenberg (p. 319), with some justification: 'It does not avoid the abyss of distinction between God and the creature.'

16. T. Pearl, 'Dialectical Panentheism: on the Hegelian Character of Karl Rahner's *Key Christological Writings*', *Irish Theological Quarterly* 42 (1975), p. 129.

17. Ibid., p. 134.

18. This means that only God can posit something other than himself in such a way that this other the more dependent on God it is, the more autonomous it will be. See its first cast in 'Christology', p. 162 (= pp. 182f) as quoted here. Since the publication of 'Christology', this principle has reappeared in many of Rahner's writings. In private conversation he even avowed that this principle was one of his central insights in theology.

19. *Foundations*, p. 199 (= p. 199).

20. Ibid., p. 201 (= p. 201).

21. Ibid.

22. Ibid.

23. J. N. Findlay, *The Philosophy of Hegel*, New York, NY. (1958), p.

26. My italics, and as quoted by T. Pearl, 'Dialectical Panentheism: on the Hegelian Character of K. Rahner's Key Christological Writings', *Irish Theological Quarterly* 42 (1975), p. 137.

24. I. Trethowan, 'A Changing God', *Downside Review* 84 (1966), pp. 250f.

25. R. E. Doud, 'Rahner's Christology: a Whiteheadian Critique', *Journal of Religion* 57 (1977), pp. 144–55.

26. See E. Gutwenger, *Bewusstsein und Wissen Christi. Eine dogmatische Studie*, Innsbruck (1960), especially pp. 115–21; F. Malmberg, *Über den Gottmenschen, Quaestiones Disputatae* 9, Freiburg-im-Breisgau (1960), especially pp. 61–6; and H. Mühlen, *Die veränderlichkeit Gottes als Horizont einer zukünftigen Christologie*, Münster (1969). To some extent, too, see J. Galot, 'Dynamisme de l'incarnation. Au–de–la de la formule de Chalcedoine', *Nouvelle Revue Théologique* 93 (1971), pp. 225–44.

27. 'Incarnation', p. 114 (= p. 148). (My italics.)

28. See Chapter 3, section 3.2.6.

29. The *ex nihilo* is historically a negative statement excluding any kind of monism or dualism. It cannot have any positive contents.

30. Cf. 'Incarnation', p. 114 (= p. 148).

31. Cf. A. N. Whitehead, *Process and Reality*, New York, NY., and London (1978), the corrected edition by D. R. Griffin and D. W. Sherbourne. The pagination in square brackets is the original edition; here, 'subjective aim' is defined p. 25 [p. 37] and is explained as God's guidance or 'lure' for the creature, p. 344 [p. 522].

32. See Chapter 4.

33. A. Galli, 'Perchè Karl Rahner nega la visione beatifica in Cristo. Premesse filosofiche della cristologia Rahneriana', *Divinitas* 13 (1969), pp. 414–56.

34. A reminder: in the seventh century, Sergius, Patriarch of Constantinople had tried to reintegrate the unity of the Church divided by Nestorianism and monophysitism. The division was caused by an an intermediary view, according to which there were two natures in Christ, but only one divine action and will. This intermediary position, obviously leading to monophysitism, was condemned at the Third Council of Constantinople, AD 680/1. Cf. Tanner, p. 128.

35. A. Galli, 'Perchè Karl Rahner nega la visione beatifica in Cristo. Premesse filosofiche della cristologia Rahneriana', *Divinitas* 13 (1969), pp. 437 and 440.

36. Ibid., p. 441: ' . . . il Rahner propone un'idea dell'Incarnazione come il momento supremo della creazione e interpreta questa ultima come un movimento di Dio stesso'.

37. Cf. ibid., pp. 441f.
38. Ibid., pp. 414–56, especially Galli's conclusion on p. 453.
39. Ibid., p. 454.
40. Ibid., p. 440.
41. R. E. Doud, 'Rahner's Christology: a Whiteheadian Critique', *Journal of Religion* 57 (1977), pp. 144–55, especially p. 148.
42. Ibid., p. 150.
43. In this sense there is a similarity between Whitehead's and Rahner's being as *Beisichsein*. Whereas Rahner builds on human self-reflection, Whitehead generalizes it for everything which is real.
44. Cf. A. N. Whitehead, *Process and Reality*, New York, NY., and London (1978), the corrected edition by D. R. Griffin and D. W. Sherbourne; here p. 25, in original p. [38].
45. R. E. Doud, 'Rahner's Christology: a Whiteheadian Critique', *Journal of Religion* 57 (1977).
46. Note the similarity with Rahner's theory of symbolism!
47. Cf. J. B. Cobb, jnr., *A Christian Natural Theology*, Philadelphia, Pa. (1965). For a Whiteheadian Christology, see also D. Brown, R. E. James and G. Reeves (eds), *Process Philosophy and the Christian Thought*, New York, NY. (1971).
48. R. E. Doud, 'Rahner's Christology: a Whiteheadian Critique', *Journal of Religion* 57 (1977). Doud (p. 152) says: 'Jesus prehends God as Jesus prehends himself; that is, just as Jesus' prehensions of himself give Jesus his identity as Jesus.' And goes on (p. 153): 'By the fact that any human being is the person [or self] he is only in virtue of his constitutive prehension of several occasions of his past, it is possible that some human being can be the person [self] he is by prehending some occasion not of his own past. This is exactly the state of affairs in the metaphysical constitution of Jesus.'
49. Which according to the thought of process theology applies equally to their bipolar God.
50. This is why Doud says: 'God in every instant must so constitute himself that he can be prehended with constitutional importance by Jesus.' Cf. R. E. Doud, 'Rahner's Christology: a Whiteheadian Critique', *Journal of Religion* 57 (1977), p. 153.
51. Ibid., p. 152.
52. Ibid.
53. Which is, of course, far away from Aristotle's or Thomas's hylomorphism and would literally contradict the definition of Vienne (cf. Tanner, p. 361). See also A. N. Whitehead, *Process and Reality*, New York, NY., and London (1978), the corrected edition by D. R. Griffin and D. W. Sherbourne; p. 108 [p. 166].

54. Ibid., pp. 34f [p. 51f].
55. *SM* III, pp. 206f.
56. Ibid., p. 207.
57. See Chapter 3, section 3.4.1 and also 3.4.2.
58. See D. B. Evans, *Leontius of Byzantium*, Washington, DC. (1970) and especially pp. 146ff. Also the, still valuable, H. M. Renton, *A Study in Christology: The Problem of the Two Natures of Christ*, London (1917).
59. W. Kasper, *Jesus the Christ*, London (1981), pp. 57f. Kasper asserts in connection with Rahner's transcendental or cosmo-Christology: 'Here I must part company with Teilhard de Chardin and Karl Rahner. That kind of accommodation of Christology to an evolutionary world order is not only theologically dubious; it does not accord with the facts.'
60. Ibid., p. 245.
61. This is the reason why, in telling the story of Jesus up to his resurrection the evangelists Matthew and Luke had to extend it to the poetic narrative of his conception and birth.
62. Cf. H. Mühlen, *Der heilige Geist als Person*, Münster (1963), *passim*. The basic pattern of Mühlen's approach is personalistic. The 'I' encounters the 'Thou' and from this encounter proceeds the *we* of an ineffable *koinônia*. In his Trintarian theology the primordial 'I' is the Father, the 'Thou' the Son, and the one person in two, the 'We' is the Spirit. Therefore, what I am affirming here is that Jesus Christ in the union of his humanity and divinity is an event of this Trinitarian communion.
63. It is in any case doubtful, whether Nestorius himself, especially in his post–Ephesine *apologia* ever held this kind of unity.
64. The French Franciscan Deodat de Basly (who died in 1937) renewed the *homo-assumptus* theory of the early Middle Ages. He held that the God-man is a complex ontological whole consisting of two components, the Word and Jesus, both with its own centre of individuality. They are linked by *subjonction physique et transcendentale*. On this basis a 'duel of love' exists between these 'two' subjects. His view has been censured by the Bull *Sempiternus Rex* in 1951 (see DS 3905).
65. A. Galli, 'Perchè Karl Rahner nega la visione beatifica in Cristo. Premesse filisofiche della cristologia Rahneriana', *Divinitas* 13 (1969), p. 434.
66. I. Trethowan, 'A Changing God', *Downside Review* 84 (1966), pp. 258f. (My italics; text rearranged.)
67. Cf. ibid. See also, I. Trethowan, 'Christology Again', *Downside Review* 95 (1977), pp. 1f.

68. See Rahner's note about the sinlessness of Christ in 'Christology', pp. 160f and in n. 2 (= p. 181, n. 1). Although from this note it will be obvious that his concept of the person is different, Rahner feels his way towards a similar solution of Christ's sinlesness.
69. Cf. Chapter 5, section 5.3.
70. Rahner often repeats this question; see, for example, *Foundations*, pp. 234f (= pp. 231f).
71. Ibid., p. 231 (= p. 229), in discussing the circular structure of faith knowledge in Jesus the Christ.
72. Ibid., pp. 206f (= p. 206).
73. Ibid., ' [This transcendental Christology] cannot appear clearly and explicitly until, on the one hand, man has found this historical and *self-validating* relationship to Jesus Christ, and, on the other hand, until he has reached *the historical era of transcendental anthropology* and of transcendental reflection upon his historical nature, and may no longer forget it.' (My italics.) Can this self-validating relationship be found without a concrete encounter?
74. Cf. Chapter 4, section 4.4.2.
75. Ibid., section 4.4.1.
76. Ibid., section 4.4.3.
77. Ibid., section 4.4.1.
78. See J. B. Metz, 'Kleine Apologie des Erzahlens', *Concilium* 9 (1973), pp. 334ff.
79. Which ought to be distinguished from the kerygma: the preaching confession of one's faith before the unbeliever. The preacher, as a rule, does not enter into this intimate relationship with his addressees.